Voices of Song

Voices of Song

Kate Alexander

PIATKUS

First published in Great Britain in 1994 by
Judy Piatkus (Publishers) Ltd of
5 Windmill Street, London W1

*A catalogue record for this book is available
from the British Library*

ISBN 0 7499 0272 8

Phototypeset in 11/12pt Compugraphic Times by
Action Typesetting Limited, Gloucester
Printed and bound in Great Britain by
Biddles Ltd, Guildford & King's Lynn

Chapter One

In the summer of 1979 two girls found a diamond ring in the gutter at the top of Woodington High Street and it changed their lives.

They were on their way home from school after a particularly long, hot day. They both wore the uniform of Woodington High School – grass-green pleated skirts and short-sleeved white cotton blouses – but they had discarded their navy blue blazers and hung them over the heavy satchels they carried on their shoulders.

The taller and fairer of the two girls paused to glance in the window of a dress shop near the crossroads at the top of the hill, but her friend urged her on.

'Hurry up, Tina. It's all right for you with three buses to choose from, but we're late already and I don't want to hang around an extra half hour if I miss the country bus.'

They paused at the traffic lights and then crossed to the bus stop. Tina heaved the satchel off her shoulder with a groan.

'You'd think they would have let us off homework this weekend,' she complained. 'Especially considering all the extra practice we're putting in for the school concert.'

'Only one more week,' Rosamund said consolingly. She glanced down and added, 'Your blazer's dragging on the ground.'

'Beastly thing,' Tina said. 'I told Mum this morning that it would be too hot to wear it, but she made me put it on.'

She bent down to rescue her blazer from the dust and something in the gutter attracted her eye. She might have missed it, but the afternoon sunshine struck such a vivid

1

spark from the stones that her attention was caught. Tina pushed aside a torn potato crisp packet and straightened up, holding a ring in her hand.

'I say, look at this! Ros, do you think it's real?'

'Must be worth a fortune if it is,' Rosamund said, looking in awe at the three immense diamonds set in gold. 'What are you going to do with it?'

'Well ... if it's real ...' Tina said doubtfully. 'It's only a step down the road to the Police Station. I suppose I ought to take it in there.'

She looked up with a grin and added, 'If it's not real then I'll wear it to school on Monday.'

'Miss Hurlington will slaughter you if you do – "*No* jewellery with school uniform, girls". Oh, bother, here's my bus. Tina, I must go, but I think you're right, you'll have to take it to the Police Station.'

When Tina eventually reached home she was not surprised to see the curtain at the front room window twitch as she pushed open the gate. A wave of irritation swept over her as she realised that her mother had been watching for her safe return. By the time she had opened the front door with her latchkey Mrs Burford had gone through into the kitchen. She was a thin woman of medium height whose fifteen-year-old daughter was already as tall as she was and would soon outgrow her. Her expression was habitually anxious and although she tried to control her nervous fears she could not help worrying at any departure from normal routine, however slight.

'A bit late, aren't you, dear?' she said. 'I remembered you were staying behind for singing practice, but I saw the green bus go by and you weren't on it.'

As they were both aware, the only way Elsie Burford could have watched the green country bus route was by going upstairs and looking out of the back bedroom window.

In her exasperation, Tina spoke more brusquely than she had intended.

'I had to go to the Police Station.'

She got the reaction she expected and was immediately

2

ashamed. Her mother's hand went to her mouth and her eyes widened in alarm.

'Oh, Tina, whatever have you done?'

'Nothing, except behave like a good citizen. I found a ring and I went and handed it in.'

'All on your own? If you'd brought it home your dad would have gone with you.'

'Oh, Mum! It would have looked a bit funny if I'd picked up a diamond ring and put it in my pocket, wouldn't it? I found it right by the bus stop, outside the music shop. Rosamund was with me, but she simply had to get the bus to Locksley Green, so she went on and I nipped back to the Police Station. It only took me ten minutes and I ran for the next red bus — and here I am. Not all that late, am I?'

'I suppose you did the right thing,' her mother conceded. 'Was it a good ring?'

'Mm, beautiful. Three great diamonds set in gold.'

'If no one claims it, it'll come to you, won't it?' Mrs Burford asked, beginning to enjoy the small excitement.

'Not much hope of that. Someone must be frantic at having lost it. But I may get a reward. What's for tea?'

'I thought salad as it's so hot. I've got some nice ham and there's lettuce and tomatoes from Dad's allotment. I must do the potatoes. He'll be in shortly.'

An airmail envelope, stuck behind the clock on the mantelpiece, caught Tina's eye.

'I say, have you heard from Auntie Daphne?'

Elsie had not meant to speak about the news she had received that morning until her husband got home, but now she felt the need to unburden herself.

'She's coming home,' she said abruptly.

Tina, who had slumped down in the armchair, sat up.

'Brilliant! I'm longing to see her. I don't remember her at all.'

'Not surprising, considering she went off to America when you were five years old. Not that you saw much of her when she was in England, always dashing round the country from one theatre to the other.'

'She did the right thing when she went to the States. She's been really successful,' Tina remonstrated.

3

'Twice married and twice divorced. Not my idea of success.'

'One of the hazards of show business.'

'Much you know about it.'

'I still think it'll be terrific, getting to know her, especially now that I'm a singer myself.'

'A solo in a school concert doesn't turn you into a singer,' her mother snapped. 'Don't get any silly ideas into your head, Tina. You're going to take a good secretarial course and get a job in an office. It's not been easy for your dad and me, sending you to the High School, even though you did win a special place, and you owe it to us to get yourself a proper job.'

'Miss Hurlington would like me to go to university.'

'Very nice for them as can afford it.'

'Honestly, Mum, in the nineteen-eighties a proper qualification is going to be ...'

'You'll learn a skill that'll be useful all your life and you'll be earning while some of your friends are still taking exams. Now, stop lolling about and go and take your uniform off. Your dad'll be home in a minute and tea'll be on the table as soon as the potatoes are done.'

Tina had to wait no later than eight o'clock that evening to know that the diamond ring had been reclaimed. Will Burford was in his small front garden, spraying his roses, when a large grey car drew up outside the gate. Will straightened up and stared. A Rolls Royce! Not something to be seen in James Street every day of the week.

It was driven by a young man, not in uniform, so presumably not a chauffeur, although he did get out and open the door for the other passenger, helping her out with a solicitude that might have been explained by the ebony stick he handed her as soon as she was on the pavement. Will Burford was no judge of women's dress, but even he was struck by her elegance. Money, he thought confusedly, and something else ... authority. She looked like someone who was used to having the red carpet rolled out for her.

She was not an old woman, for all she walked with a stick, not even middle-aged, and there was no hint of grey in the

4

mass of vivid red hair she wore wound into an immaculate chignon. Her complexion, too, was dazzling, as was the smile she turned on him.

'I'm looking for Miss Valentina Burford.'

'My daughter,' Will said.

'She found my ring.' The woman held out her hand and the setting sun struck sparks from the diamonds on her finger. 'I'd like to thank her.'

'Better come inside,' Will said and led the two visitors into the house and through to the kitchen where Elsie sat watching television.

She got to her feet, her hand clutching nervously at the neck of her dress, and cast a harassed look round the kitchen. The remains of the evening meal had been cleared away, the washing up was done and everything was clean and tidy. All the same, Will should have taken visitors of this quality into the front room.

'Tina's upstairs, doing her homework,' she said when she realised why they had come, but even as she spoke Tina came clattering down the stairs, eager to know who had come to the house in a huge Rolls Royce. When she saw the red-headed woman she was suddenly still, her eyes wide in disbelief.

'You're Valentina?' her visitor asked. 'I just wanted to tell you how grateful I am to have my ring back.'

There was the faintest touch of an Australian drawl in her voice, confirming to Tina that she had not been mistaken in the identification she could hardly bring herself to accept.

'You're Annis Gilroy!' she said, so stunned that it came out almost as an accusation.

'That's right! I'm flattered to be recognised.'

'I've seen your pictures. We've g-got some of your records at school. *Don Giovanni* ...'

'That was a good recording.' She turned to her companion. 'I sang Donna Elvira and, of course, dear Bruno was Giovanni.'

'I remember.'

For a moment Annis Gilroy looked overwhelmingly sad and then she recovered her poise. 'I forgot to say, this is Oliver Leone, my manager. Tina — is that what they call you? — I nearly died when I found I'd lost my ring. My husband gave

5

it to me, you see ... my late husband ... '

She turned towards Elsie as the other woman made an inarticulate sound of sympathy.

'Yes, it means a lot to me. Your clever daughter found it and I'd like to show my gratitude. Money's a poor return for what she did for me, but it's all I can offer and I hope you'll accept it in the spirit in which it's meant. Oliver ... '

The young man took out his wallet and extracted five ten-pound notes.

'Here you are, Tina,' Annis Gilroy said. 'Buy yourself something nice to remember me by.'

'I'll get some of your records,' Tina said. With desperate courage, her face scarlet, she added, 'I sing myself.'

'Do you indeed! Soprano?'

'Yes. I'm singing Cherubino's canzona from *The Marriage of Figaro* in our school concert.'

'Well, ambitious! How are you making out?'

'Not too bad. Miss Gilroy, would you ... could you possibly come to our concert? It's next week ... the twenty-fourth.'

'Er ... I'm not sure. Oliver ...?'

Tina thought that the young man looked both bored and impatient. He was tall and thin, probably in his late twenties; his hair was thick and black and he had dark eyes. There was a white scar across his left eyebrow which twisted it and perhaps it was that which gave him an habitually sardonic expression. Again he felt in his pocket and this time he produced a diary. He looked searchingly at Annis. She looked back and gave the faintest of nods.

'You're not actually doing anything on the twenty-fourth,' he said.

'The tickets are a pound,' Tina said in a breathless rush. 'But, of course, I'll pay for them ... '

'Certainly not. Come on, Oliver, hand over another couple of pounds.'

'I'll make sure you have seats reserved in the front row,' Tina assured her. 'Miss Black − she's our music teacher − will drop *dead* when I tell her Annis Gilroy is coming to our concert.'

'Oh, I do hope not, dear − not before the performance!'

6

'You ought not to bother Miss ... Mrs Gilroy,' Elsie said.

Her embarrassment as she stumbled over the title prevented her from saying anything more.

'I'm Miss Gilroy in my professional capacity,' the singer said. 'My married name is Marcellini, but I've more or less dropped that since my husband died.'

She had a friendly ease of manner that made even Elsie relax.

'Would you ... could I get you a cup of tea?' she asked.

'I think not. We have to be on our way. I just wanted to thank Tina in person for handing in my precious ring. I'm wearing it again, but I must have it made smaller or get a guard for it. I've lost weight since ... over the last year or so, and it must have slipped off my finger after I'd been into a shop to buy some records.'

Will, who had taken no part in the conversation since he had brought the two visitors into the house, felt called upon to speak up.

'Tina did no more than was right,' he said. 'She knew it was what we'd expect of her.'

It might have been her own father speaking, Annis reflected with wry inner amusement. In fact, the whole set-up was so like her own background that she found herself identifying with this youngster who had inveigled her into attending a school concert. The parents, hard working, proud, ill at ease in an unexpected situation, and yet rock fast in their adherence to a set of values that enabled them to hold their heads up high; the small house, the struggle to keep above the poverty line, the inarticulate affection, all these were familiar to her. All that was missing was the blazing Australian sun and the miles of empty space in which she had grown up.

It was from the father that Tina got her height, while her fairness came from her mother, presumably. Fortunately, even though she had stumbled when she had spoken about her singing, she did not seem to have inherited the mother's timidity.

Annis gave Oliver a quick glance and he moved smoothly into the routine he used to extricate her from her admirers. It was not Annis who insisted she had to go − she was regretful

7

about it — but Oliver knew all her engagements, and if he said it was time to move on ... such a pity, but she would look forward to seeing them all at the school concert.

When they had settled in the car again and had waved goodbye, Oliver asked, 'Do you really mean to go to that concert?'

'Of course! It would be too cruel to let the child down. And you're coming with me.'

'It'll be dreadful.'

'Possibly. Goodness, how that girl does remind me of myself at that age.'

'I can't believe you were ever such a lump.'

'I was! Oh, indeed I was! A great, lolloping, overweight mess with a voice that could shatter glass. Tina will fine down, just as I did.' With a reminiscent smile she murmured, '*Voi che sapete* at fifteen, bless the child!'

Tina could hardly wait to get to school on Monday to tell everyone about her meeting with the great singer, especially Rosamund. Tina and Rosamund Drew had drifted into being 'best friends' over the last year, drawn together by their love of music and the fact that they both had good soprano voices. If it had not been for this interest they might have had little in common. Tina had brains, which had secured her a special place at the High School; Rosamund was no less intelligent, but she was a fee-paying pupil. Tina's father was a telephone engineer who drove around in a Post Office van, but George Drew was a bank manager and the Drews had a new car every three years. The Burfords' house was well maintained and spotlessly clean, but one of the things that kept them poor was that Will was buying it, and it was a small terraced house which Will had modernised himself, while the Drews owned a four-bedroomed villa in the village of Locksley Green. When they met at the school concert George Drew and Will Burford would have little to say to one another, Elsie Burford and Monica Drew even less. Elsie spent her days dressmaking, knitting, cooking and keeping the house clean; Monica employed a daily woman and played bridge.

When Rosamund had exclaimed sufficiently over the identity

of the owner of the diamond ring, Tina produced her trump card. 'And she's coming to the concert!'

'Tina! You actually had the nerve to ask her?'

'I sold her two tickets. Wait till I tell Miss Black.'

'She'll die,' Rosamund said with conviction.

'That's what I said and Annis Gilroy said "Not before the performance, I hope". Ros, she was so *nice*.'

'Oh, you are lucky!'

'I'll introduce you,' Tina promised generously. 'If her manager man doesn't whisk her away, that is. I didn't much take to him. I say, your mum and dad are coming to hear you sing, aren't they?'

'Well ... they've paid for a couple of tickets.' For a moment Rosamund looked despondent, then she brightened. 'If I tell Mum Annis Gilroy will be there, she's sure to come.'

Monica Drew's bridge club had met at her house that afternoon. When Rosamund got home she found a room full of smoke, half a dozen of her mother's cronies still shrilly discussing the hands they had held and a pile of untidily stacked cups and plates in the kitchen.

'Are you home already?' her mother said, looking at her in a distracted way that Rosamund recognised as meaning that she had had poor success at the bridge table. 'The afternoon has simply flown. Darling, you might be an angel and wash up.'

Rosamund nodded. She did not bother to greet any of her mother's friends, who mostly looked through her as if she were not there. She went upstairs and dumped her satchel on the floor of her bedroom. It was a pretty room, pink and white, with a row of the dolls Rosamund had outgrown arranged on a shelf, a well-filled bookcase and, in the corner, a large music centre. While she was changing out of her school uniform Rosamund put a record on the turntable, an aria she had been remembering ever since Tina had told her about meeting Annis Gilroy. As the lovely voice soared in '*Vissi d'arte*' Rosamund sank down on her bed, her promise to wash up forgotten.

She came to with a guilty start as she heard the front

door close behind the last of her mother's chattering friends. Fortunately, her mother had gone back into the lounge and did not realise that Rosamund was only just coming down the stairs. By the time she came through to the kitchen with a pile of ashtrays to be emptied into the dustbin Rosamund had stacked the dishes neatly and was running hot water into the sink.

'Really, smoking is a disgusting habit,' Mrs Drew remarked, wrinkling her nose. 'I don't know why one doesn't give it up, especially when it's become so expensive and there's all this talk about it being dangerous.'

'Did you have a good afternoon?' Rosamund asked.

'Disastrous! That Angela Western ... I swear it isn't skill ... she just has the luck of the devil.'

'Talking of luck,' Rosamund said, seizing her opportunity, 'Tina was wonderfully lucky yesterday.'

'Tina? Is she the vulgar little girl who calls you Ros?'

Suppressing the information that most of her school friends called her Ros, Rosamund went on doggedly, 'She found a diamond ring near the bus stop and you'll never in a million years guess who owned it.'

'So, I'll never guess, but you're going to tell me,' Mrs Drew said, lighting another of the cigaretttes she had no intention of giving up.

'Annis Gilroy! You know, the opera singer.'

'Of course I know. I mean, one isn't exactly into opera, but even so I've heard of Annis Gilroy. What was a celebrity like that doing in Woodington, of all places?'

'She told Tina she'd been into Vernon's, the music shop. Anyway, she went to Tina's house to thank her and she gave her fifty pounds reward and she's coming to our school concert.'

'Fifty pounds! She must have money to burn. I would have thought ten would have been ample for a scrubby little schoolgirl.'

Mrs Drew seized a tea towel and began drying plates as if she were suddenly impatient with watching her daughter's slow progress.

'Mum, you and Dad are coming to the concert, aren't you?' Rosamund asked.

10

'When is it? Next Friday? Oh, darling, I don't know. The bridge club is meeting at Angela's on Friday and you know we always stay on for drinks. It makes me so late getting home to cook dinner. And don't say I could come away early because unless someone gives me a lift I can't get home at all from Angela's.'

'I'm singing a solo,' Rosamund said, playing with the bubbles in the washing-up bowl.

'Yes, I know, but I can hear you sing any day of the week.'

'Tina said she'd introduce me to Annis Gilroy — and you, too, of course, if you're there.'

Monica Drew gave an angry little laugh. 'Thank you! I don't know that I care to be obliged to Tina Thing for an introduction to anyone.'

'I wish you'd come,' Rosamund said in a low voice.

'I'll think about it. Do please stop fiddling around with that water. I've never known anyone take so long over washing a few cups and saucers. And stop frowning in that ugly way.'

It apparently did not occur to her that Rosamund's fierce frown was a desperate attempt to hold back the tears she told herself were childish. Rosamund had already abandoned any hope that her parents would be at the concert, but she did make one more attempt to interest them when her father mentioned an item of news while they were eating the dinner Monica had thrown together for them.

'When you open a tin I know you've had a bad afternoon at the card table,' George Drew said, trying to make a joke of it.

'True enough,' Monica admitted. 'Losing money always gives me a headache.'

'Well, here's a bit of news that may cheer you up. The people who bought Rigby House have moved in at last.'

'Really?' The peevish expression on Monica's face changed and she sat up straighter, looking alert. 'A nice family?'

'I know very little except that the new owner is a Mrs Marcellini.'

'An Italian name? How strange.'

'Annis Gilroy's married name is Marcellini,' Rosamund said. 'She was married to Bruno Marcellini, the baritone.

11

He died in a car accident and she was hurt, too, and now she walks with a limp and she'll probably never sing in an opera again.'

'That fits,' Mr Drew said. 'A tall woman with red hair who walks with a stick. I only heard the vaguest details when I was having lunch at the Red Dragon, but there was something about a musical background.'

'How exciting. Rosamund, that settles it; we'll definitely be at your school concert and I shall speak to Miss Gilroy and introduce myself as a new neighbour. I must say, Rigby House should be worth seeing after all the work that's been done on it in the last few months.'

Rosamund began to attack her supper with a sharpened appetite. Everything was going to be all right. Whether or not her mother managed to meet Annis Gilroy, at least she was going to be at the concert and Rosamund would be spared the embarrassment of having to explain her parents' absence to schoolmates whose fathers and mothers would have waded through rivers to hear them sing.

Annis and Oliver arrived at the school concert barely five minutes before it was due to begin, walking in with all the assurance of people who knew that their places would be kept for them. Tina, peering anxiously round the side of the stage, drew a breath of relief.

'You see? I told you she'd come,' she said triumphantly to her disbelieving classmates. 'Doesn't she look gorgeous?'

Annis wore a dress and loose jacket of pale grey crepe-de-chine above which her red hair blazed. The quality that Will Burford had noticed in her was well in evidence. Here was a personality that could not be ignored. The headmistress, who had shared Tina's friends' scepticism, hurriedly moved forward to greet their distinguished guest.

'That's put old Hurley-Burley in a tizzy,' Tina observed with satisfaction. 'Serves her right for not believing me.'

Woodington High School, a minor member of the Public Schools Trust, had a good reputation for music. The choir was well trained and the repertoire was suited to their fresh young voices. Oliver might look faintly bored, but Annis listened with every appearance of the keenest enjoyment.

12

The instrumental solos were less appealing to a professional musician, but Annis sat up and looked alert when Rosamund began her first song. Rosamund sang like a lark, with a lovely, unforced purity of sound ... 'O mistress mine! Where are you roaming?'

'Charming,' Annis said, turning to the headmistress and clapping vigorously as Rosamund made a careful bow at the end of her song.

'Rosamund Drew is one of our most promising pupils,' Miss Hurlington said. 'A delightful girl ... quite apart from her pretty voice.'

The choir sang again and then Tina came forward. No one, seeing the easy way she stood, with her hands clasped loosely in front of her, her head raised and her eyes fixd on the school clock at the back of the hall, could have guessed that she had been shaking from head to foot with nerves only five minutes earlier. Annis had thought her too young for the aria, but as the girl sang she realised that she was just the right age to express Cherubino's adolescent longing for love. The voice did not have the silvery quality that distinguished Rosamund's, but Tina delivered every note bang on the middle, with a power and clarity that were astonishing in so young and untaught a singer. What was even more surprising was the way she conveyed Cherubino's half-understood passion. Annis wondered if the parents in the audience were sufficiently familiar with the opera to translate the words. If so, they must be feeling a trifle uncomfortable at this outpouring of immature frustration.

This time it was to Oliver that Annis turned and the comment that came into her head was not 'charming'. She raised her eyebrows in a silent query and he grimaced slightly in return.

'The child has a voice,' he admitted.

'More than that.'

'All right, I'll admit I'm surprised. If that dramatic ability could be harnessed ...'

'More and more she reminds me of myself.'

'Hold your horses, Annis. The girl probably has no intention of ever using her ability in anything beyond the local music society. Her parents won't be able to do much for her, you saw that for yourself.'

Annis subsided, but she felt convinced that Oliver was wrong. Valentina Burford was destined to sing, just as Annis Gilroy had been.

The two girls sang a duet towards the end of the concert — 'Where 'ere you walk ...'. The two voices twined together harmoniously and the girls exchanged smiles. It was almost over, they had done well, the concert had been a success. The last note died away, the applause broke out and the girls bowed, Rosamund gracefully and Tina with an abrupt bob. One more rousing chorus from the choir and the school orchestra and it was all over.

The headmistress murmured that there were refreshments at the back of the hall. Oliver looked rebellious, but Annis nipped him on the arm and he subsided.

'It's exactly like being back home,' she said in an undertone. 'Orange squash and fairy cakes — and don't turn up your nose, you snobby Pom!'

Oliver grinned, but he managed to bypass the orange squash in favour of a cup of coffee as Tina came pushing through the crowd to speak to Annis.

'Congratulations,' Oliver said.

Tina looked at him as if she had forgotten his existence.

'Oh ... thanks. Is Miss Gilroy ...' She saw Annis and went up to her. 'Was it all right?' she asked.

'A bit rough at the edges, but given your lack of special teaching and inexperience, yes, you did well.'

Tina let out a great sigh of relief. She looked limp, as if all the life had gone out of her.

'I want to talk to you,' she said. 'I know I'm a nuisance, but I do so badly need advice. Can I come and see you? Tomorrow afternoon?'

Annis nodded. 'About four o'clock,' she said, and then her attention was claimed by Miss Hurlington, who wanted to introduce her to Rosamund Drew's parents.

Rosamund hovered in the background in an agony of embarrassment. Why couldn't her mother see that one just didn't thrust oneself on someone like Annis Gilroy? And it didn't help that she was being made the excuse for Monica's gushing approach.

14

'We were quite amazed how much Rosamund has come on in the last year,' Monica Drew said in reply to Annis's polite compliments. 'She sings delightfully ... such an asset for a girl.'

Oliver, who thought this a truly Victorian remark, caught Rosamund's eye and gave her the tiniest wink. She looked down, her face even redder than it had been before, but with an involuntary smile on her lips.

'We're near neighbours, Miss Gilroy,' Monica was saying. 'We live in Locksley Green, in Rectory Lane, not five minutes walk from the gates of Rigby House. We were so delighted when we heard you had bought Rigby. I wonder, would you like to come back with us now for a drink? Or, if not, could you come in tomorrow evening? Nothing much, just one or two friends for a pre-dinner drink.'

'I think we could manage tomorrow evening,' Annis said. 'But only for a very limited time, I'm afraid, as I have a dinner engagement in London. Would six-thirty be too early?'

'Not at all,' Monica said, her mind ranging over the telephoning she was going to have to do in the morning. Six-thirty would be ideal, in fact, because even if people were doing something else they would surely spare half an hour in the early evening to meet Annis Gilroy. Really, it could not have been more fortunate, and she smiled with the utmost kindness on her daughter, who had been instrumental in bringing about this meeting.

Annis saw Mr and Mrs Burford standing together and not talking to anyone else. She made her way over to them, smiling broadly.

'Your daughter has a remarkable voice,' she said. 'Tell me, are you a musical family?'

'We were brought up to play the piano, my sister and me,' Mrs Burford said.

'And to sing?'

'Daphne sings.' Reluctantly, Elsie added, 'She's Daphne Durrell.'

'I know the name,' Annis agreed, thinking to herself, *Musical comedy, oh no! Not for Tina!*

'We wouldn't want Tina to follow her example,' Elsie said, almost as if she guessed Annis's thoughts. 'Tina's going to train to be a secretary and get a really good job, or so we hope after all this schooling.'

Unexpectedly, Annis Gilroy seemed to approve of that programme.

'It won't hurt Tina to have a skill to fall back on,' she said. 'She can well afford to take a year off to learn to manage a word processor. It's far too soon to think about serious voice training.'

'I wish you'd tell Tina that,' Will said.

'I will. She's asked to come and see me tomorrow. I'll give her the benefit of my advice and hard experience. Poor child, I don't think she has the slightest idea of what it means to be a singer.'

She nodded pleasantly, summoned Oliver to her side by merely raising an eyebrow and began to move towards the door. Monica Drew, who had been keeping an eye on her, extricated herself from a boring discussion with her daughter's form mistress about Rosamund's A-level chances, and moved to intercept Annis and Oliver.

'I hear you're going to advise that other girl who sang a solo about her career,' she said. 'In my opinion, Rosamund has quite as good a voice as Tina Burford and I hope you won't mind if my husband and I ask for your opinion about the best possible training for her.'

Rosamund, knowing that her mother had never thought of a musical career for her until that evening, was moved to protest. Her face crimson, she murmured, 'Oh, Mum ...! Not here, not now.'

'Be quiet, Rosamund. Miss Gilroy ...?'

Annis looked kindly at Rosamund and took pity on her agitation. 'Come along and see me with your friend tomorrow afternoon,' she said. 'That'll save me the trouble of repeating my little lecture.'

'And we're to expect you for drinks at six-thirty?' Monica said, not entirely liking the way she had been put on one side in favour of her young daughter.

'We'll look forward to it,' Annis said.

As they moved away Oliver said under his breath, 'Liar.'

Annis laughed. 'I know, but we are going to be neighbours and it pays to keep in with the locals.'

16

As he settled her in the car Oliver said, 'You'll find the suburban housewives deadly boring once the novelty's worn off.'

'Don't worry, I know what I'm doing. Sometime this summer I'll give one big garden party and after that I'll refuse all invitations on the grounds that I'm working.'

Oliver said no more until they had left the school car park and were driving away towards Locksley Green, then he remarked evenly, 'I'd like to think you were serious about working again. It's been eighteen months, Annis.'

'I never stopped working,' she protested.

'In the sense of doing musical exercises and keeping your voice supple, I agree; but you're going to have to earn some money soon, my dear. You've spent a fortune on the house.'

There was a long silence and then Annis said flatly, 'I'll never appear in opera again.'

'You could do concerts and recordings. Will you let me take up some of the offers I've had for you? At the moment I'm hardly earning my keep as your so-called manager.'

They were approaching Rigby House. Oliver had to concentrate on negotiating the sharp turn into the drive to which he was not yet accustomed, but that did not stop him realising with disquiet that Annis had not answered him.

As they went into the house he continued, 'You ought to let me do something to justify the salary you pay me. If I just hang around as your companion your new friends are going to start getting sniffy about our relationship.'

Annis shrugged. 'You know how little that matters to me! And I'm the one who'd be pointed at. A woman with a lover fourteen years younger than herself ...'

'Now don't bring that up again. You're as ageless as Cleopatra.'

'A woman of forty-two with a wasted leg ...'

Oliver took her hand and kissed it. 'I grieve over that as much as you do, but put beside the rest of your gifts and beauty it's a very minor thing. When are you going to start using your lovely voice again, my darling?'

Annis sighed and sat down on the sofa, holding on to Oliver's hand to pull him down beside her. 'Listening to those

17

two young things tonight, I wondered whether I could — whether perhaps I *should* — do some coaching.'

'You won't make much profit out of those two,' Oliver remarked drily. 'Time enough to think about giving lessons when you retire — which you're a long way from doing. HMV want you to record *Aida* for them.'

'Ugh! That terrible exposed high C in "*O patria mia*".'

'You could manage it in the recording studio.'

'I could manage it on stage if I worked at it beforehand,' Annis said, offended.

'That's my girl. Can I tell them you'll do it?'

'I suppose so. Bully.'

Oliver laughed and got up. 'Someone has to give you a push. Do you want a drink before we go to bed?'

'A little whisky and water, quite weak.'

As he mixed the drinks with his back to her, Oliver said, 'You know Bruno would have wanted you to go on working.'

'That's true.' Very softly Annis murmured, 'Sometimes I feel him so close to me.'

'Do you think he'd mind — about us?' Oliver asked.

Annis shook her head with a faint smile. 'He'd understand. He would never want me to live alone, grieving for him. I think, wherever he is, he's glad for me to have such a loving, helpful companion. Dear Oliver, you've kept me alive, you know that, don't you?'

In the subdued light of the lamps on the tables, with her radiant colouring, her fine figure and the benefit of her lovely clothes, it seemed absurd to dwell on the difference in age between them. Before he handed her the drink he had poured, Oliver bent over and kissed her on the lips.

'I'm the luckiest man in the world,' he said. 'But the time has come to start cracking the whip. Back to work, back to work, woman. I demand that you earn the money to keep me in the style to which I'm accustomed.'

They laughed together, but Oliver's smile faded as he added, with the utmost seriousness, 'It would be a sad world for me, and for many people, if Annis Gilroy no longer sang.'

Chapter Two

Both Tina and Rosamund would have worn jeans and a T-shirt for their visit to Annis Gilroy, but when they met they discovered they had both been dragooned by their mothers into changing into their best cotton frocks. Tina's was the prettier of the two because Elsie Burford was a talented dressmaker. They had a fresh-faced, well-scrubbed look about them which amused Oliver, who was accustomed to the determined Bohemianism of auditioning musicians.

He had been roped in to play the piano so that Annis could give her undivided attention to the girls. She meant to do it properly and he only hoped that the two youngsters were prepared for the rigorous professional standards she would apply to them.

Annis swept into the room, vivid in emerald green silk pants and tunic, and Oliver saw both girls blink as they took in the stunning chic of an outfit Annis thought suitable for lounging about at home.

'Well, my children! You're punctual, I see, and that's something to be cultivated. Never be late for a professional appointment.'

The two girls nodded earnestly and Oliver, knowing that Annis would never be on time for anything if there were not someone by her side constantly chivvying her, suppressed a smile.

'So you think you would like to sing professionally?' Annis went on. 'How long have you thought this?'

'It's been coming over me gradually for about the last

three months,' Tina said. 'Meeting you sort of crystallised it for me.'

'I hadn't thought about it at all,' Rosamund said honestly. 'It's my mother who's suddenly taken it into her head ... but I do want to do something with my music, really I do, Miss Gilroy, only I'm not sure what and I'd like you to tell me the next step.'

'The *next* step is to go back to school and complete your education.'

'We know we're stuck with that,' Tina said desperately. 'But did you really mean it when you told my mum and dad that I might as well go to commercial school? Won't it be a terrible waste of time?'

'By no means. How else are you going to fill in the time until you're eighteen?'

'Eighteen?'

'At least that. No reputable college of music will start serious voice training until the student is eighteen, nineteen, twenty. For an instrumentalist that would be the upper age limit for admittance, but for a vocalist it is the beginning.'

She looked at their stunned faces and added, 'We're not talking about a violin which is perhaps already a hundred years old before you start to play it, but about an instrument which is new and still growing. It must be treated with the utmost delicacy.'

'If I can't start being a singer until I'm eighteen, I'll have to go to commercial school and then get a job,' Tina said.

'Why not? A year's work experience will do you no harm and it'll certainly show whether you're sufficiently committed to a singing career to give up earning and start again as a student.'

'There must be something we can do for the next three years,' Rosamund said.

'I didn't say you had to stagnate. What musical instruments do you play?'

'We both play the piano,' Tina said hesitantly. 'Mum taught me and I do still practise. Rosamund has lessons, don't you, Ros?'

'I do it as an extra at school.'

20

'What about sight-reading? Tina, sing this. Not full voice, just hum to vocal line.'

Tina looked in horror at the sheet of music that had been tossed towards her. She managed to stumble through a few lines before Annis commanded her to pass the music on to Rosamund. Rosamund performed rather better, but she had had time to get her wits together.

'Not very good is it?' Annis said critically. 'What languages do you speak?'

Tina and Rosamund exchanged harassed glances. This was not at all what they had expected.

'Only French,' Tina said.

'Keep it up, it will certainly come in useful. In addition, you should learn Italian and German.'

'And have singing lessons?' Rosamund asked.

'Certainly. I'll make enquiries and find out whether there's a suitable teacher living locally, one who will teach you technique without allowing you to strain your voices.'

Oliver, who knew who was going to make those enquiries, made a quick note on his memo pad.

'Technique!' Annis went on. 'Do you know what that is? The singer's friend. The thing that gives us the ability to sing in the most adverse circumstances, including having a cold. If you learn good technique at the beginning, your instrument will last your lifetime. Without it, you will fade and die in mid-career. At the moment neither of you has the slightest idea of how the voice should be produced. Where are your lungs?'

Tina and Rosamund cast astonished looks at one another and then both placed their hands on their chests, over their firm young breasts.

'No! Much lower. And at the back as well as at the front. Your lungs go all round, remember. Put your hands *here*.'

They copied her and Annis said, 'Now, breathe in to that spot. No, through the mouth. You are singing while you breathe, remember, and you don't sing with a closed mouth. More, more, deeper, deeper. Good! Now hold the breath.'

Feeling as if they were bursting, the two girls tried to hold on to the air that expanded their lungs.

'Now, purse your lips and breathe it out. Slowly, slowly,

like a long, thin plume of smoke that will reach from here to the wall on the other side.'

She made them repeat the exercise twice more before saying in a grudging way that they were beginning to get the idea.

'And that, girls, believe it or not, is the very first singing lesson you have ever had. I don't profess to be a teacher, but if I can find you someone who understands her job that's the first thing she will make you do. Then perhaps she will allow you to add sound, by hissing. After that, humming. And a most important step, placing the voice and finding the resonance. You know about the little bones here, in your face? Oh, there is so much you have to learn! Muscle! That's what singing is all about — muscle! And stamina. My God, do you need stamina!'

'But ... do you think it's worth our while to go on?' Tina demanded.

She was flushed, almost tearful, bewildered by the unexpectedness of this lecture.

'Ah, that's more than I can say.'

'Why don't you let Tina and Rosamund sing for you?' Oliver suggested.

'You say that because you're getting bored, doing nothing,' Annis accused him. 'Very well. First of all, a few arpeggios to warm the voice.'

Oliver struck a note. Nothing happened. The two girls were looking at him in bewilderment.

'You aren't accustomed to doing exercises first to loosen the voice?' Annis asked. 'But it's essential! I'll show you and you can follow me.'

Obediently, they joined in as her voice ran lightly up and down the scale until she signalled for them to stop.

'And that, let me tell you, is something your singing teacher isn't likely to allow you to do for *weeks*,' Annis said. 'Now, what have we got that you can sing?'

'The duet they sang last night?' Oliver suggested.

'The Handel? Yes, you may not realise it, but that was by far the best thing you did.'

Tina, who had been pleased with her performance of '*Voi che sapete*' swallowed hard and managed to say nothing.

If she had done nothing else, Annis had put them both on

22

their mettle. They had never sung the song better and they knew it.

'Yes, very pleasant,' Annis said when they had finished. 'You both have voices, but as I've told you already, it's by far too soon to judge how they will mature. You, Rosamund, have a lovely, lyrical quality to your instrument, but the lower register will need developing, otherwise your repertoire will be severely restricted. The range may increase as you grow older. If not, you have a great deal of hard work to do on it.'

She turned to Tina. 'As for you, Valentina Burford, what am I to say to you? All power and no music unless you exercise an iron discipline.'

'Didn't I sing in tune?' Tina asked in bewilderment.

'Musicality is what I'm talking about and there's more to that than hitting a note accurately. If you're a true musician you're sensitive to every nuance of every instrument in the orchestra. Do you go to concerts?'

Both girls shook their heads.

'Listen to the radio?'

'Mum and Dad don't like classical music,' Tina said desperately.

'I've got a music centre,' Rosamund put in, anxious to find something that would make them seem less like a couple of philistines.

'I'll stick my neck out and say that if you're both of the same mind in three years' time I'll support your application for admission to college. Preferably the Guildhall, I think. What would your parents say about that?'

'Mine will probably be pleased,' Rosamund said. 'They've been wondering what to do with me. Daddy's been talking about going to university and then into a bank, like him.'

'Does that appeal to you?' Oliver asked, amused by the thought of a future bank manager in a blue cotton frock.'

'Not a bit! I'd much rather do music.'

They neither of them had the slightest idea of what they were getting into, he thought idly. 'Doing' music was not what Annis had in mind at all. A lifetime's dedication, a total single-minded commitment to a gruelling discipline, that was what she was preparing for these two untried children.

'I want to start *now*,' Tina said.

Unexpectedly, Annis was sympathetic. 'I know, darling, I know. I remember ... But all I can do is point you in the right direction and promise to support your application in three years' time, provided I think you're still worth it. In the meantime, join a choir − but don't allow anyone to make you force your voice − take piano and singing lessons, work and work and work on your sight-reading, listen to every concert, every opera, every recital you can.'

Tina was looking at her with a desperate hunger that startled Oliver. So Annis had been right. The child was more than just a schoolgirl with a big voice. She had the makings of that uncomfortable thing, a true artist.

'I shall be working hard this summer,' Annis said. 'Once a week during your school holidays you may both come to me here. Sometimes perhaps you may do no more than listen to me practising, sometimes I may let you sing for me. Prepare some songs, be ready to be called on − and don't be surprised if I tear your performance to shreds.'

They were both radiant and their excitement carried them out of the house and down the drive, chattering and laughing.

'A week ago I was all set to be a secretary and now I know I'm going to be prima donna,' Tina exclaimed dramatically.

'Me, too! At least ...' Rosamund paused and went on honestly, 'We ought not to talk like that until we know whether we're going to be any good.'

'Don't be such a wet blanket. We're going to the top, both of us, and it's going to be *fun*. I love singing, it's the thing I enjoy most in the world. Just imagine making a living doing what you really enjoy!'

'Mm ... well, I hope you're right. Tina, what do you make of Mr Leone?'

'He doesn't do much, does he? He just sat and listened and played a few notes on the piano.'

'And looked bored.'

'Yes, that annoyed me. We may be just a couple of school-girls, but if Annis Gilroy takes us seriously then why can't he? I don't quite understand why he's living with her. Ros, do you think ...?'

'She called him "darling" once,' Rosamund said doubtfully.

'She called us "darlings", too. It's a thing stage people do. She's years older than him, but I reckon there's something going on between them. Of course, she's still awfully attractive.'

'So's he.'

'Do you think so?' Tina paused to consider Oliver, tall and lean and dark. She thought him only moderately good-looking, but there was something about him ... 'He's got a sort of tense look,' she said. 'Like a high-voltage cable that might give off sparks if you touched it. Do you think it's the strain of living with an older woman?'

'Tina, you are awful! How old is she anyway?'

'Over forty. And he must be at least ten years younger.'

'I'd say he's under thirty.'

'Too old for us.'

'Well, of course, Tina Burford, if *that's* all you think about ...'

Rosamund's lofty tone exactly mimicked their form mistress and both girls dissolved into giggles.

'My bus!' Tina exclaimed, as the green double decker lurched round the corner.

There was no time to do more than wave goodbye and run for the bus stop, but sitting on the top deck and travelling homewards Tina began to sober up. Nothing had been said that would make her life any easier. Mum and Dad were set on her taking the secretarial course, and all the more determined because she had secured a free place. All the way home she rehearsed in her mind the words she might use to persuade them to let her go on to complete her musical education, knowing all the time that it would be impossible to make them understand.

She was still preoccupied when she reached home and the sight of a visitor in the kitchen took her by surprise. For a minute she did not know the glamorous stranger sitting drinking tea with her mother and father, but although they had not met since she was a little girl just starting school, she had seen too many pictures of her aunt not to recognise her after the first surprised moment.

25

It was Daphne Durrell who was the more taken aback. 'This can't be Tina!' she exclaimed. 'Tina! I remember you as a sweet little thing about so high.'

'That was ten years ago,' Elsie pointed out.

'I know, I know, but all the same ... she must be as tall as I am, very nearly.'

She stood up, laughing, to measure herself against Tina and then Tina was enveloped in a cloud of perfume as her aunt swooped on her and gave her a smacking kiss on the cheek. With an effort Tina stopped herself from putting up her hand to rub her cheek, convinced as she was that she must have a smudge of scarlet lipstick across it.

She had already blinked at Annis's glamour that afternoon. Now she was encountering her aunt's larger-than-life personality, brasher than Annis's, more obviously 'show-biz', but just as overwhelming.

No one would have thought that Daphne and Elsie were sisters. Involuntarily, Tina glanced from her mother to her aunt. There was a likeness, if you searched for it. They both had good bone structure, but Elsie had gone thin over the years and the eight-year age difference between the sisters showed in the streaks of grey in her hair and the lines on her face. Not that it would be possible to tell whether Daphne was going grey, because the honey blonde colour of her hair undoubtedly came out of a bottle. Her skin had a golden glow and she was skilfully made up, while Elsie never used anything but a pale lipstick and a dash of powder. Daphne's clothes, too, were designed to be noticeable. She wore a white linen suit with large black buttons and very high-heeled black patent leather shoes which matched the enormous handbag that stood on the floor by her chair.

'I simply had to dash down to see you,' Daphne was saying. 'We start rehearsals on Monday – I've got the lead in *Stars Above*, you know – and after that my life won't be my own.'

'You had a part in it in New York, didn't you?' Tina asked.

'Only a minor role, but I understudied Lotte Stedman and played her part a couple of times when she had a bug, so they knew I could do it, and, of course, it makes life very much simpler, having a British star to play in London. No hassles with Equity, for instance. I hope you've seen some of the advance publicity? The "local girl comes home" idea has been played up for all it's worth.'

'We've seen it in the papers,' Elsie said.

'I'll send you tickets, of course,' Daphne said, ignoring her sister's lack of enthusiasm. 'You must all come and cheer me on.'

'If you'd been here yesterday you could have heard me singing in my school concert,' Tina ventured.

'Darling! Don't tell me you've turned out to be a singer, too? Are you planning to join me on the stage?'

Elsie pressed her lips together tightly and it was Will who said, 'Tina's got a very nice voice. It was a pleasure to hear her and her friends last night. And she's just been to see another celebrity. Annis Gilroy, no less.'

'The opera singer? Hasn't she rather dropped out? An accident, or something?'

'She was hurt in a car crash,' Tina said. 'She's going to concentrate on recitals and making records.' The subject was too near the surface of her mind for her to be able to prevent herself blurting out, 'She says if I'm serious about being a singer I ought to go to music college.'

'That's out of the question,' her mother said flatly. 'You're going to that nice secretarial school and that way you'll always have a skill at your fingertips.'

'If I went to music college I'd have a qualification,' Tina said, not really knowing anything about it.

'And how old would you be before you started earning? Nineteen or twenty, I wouldn't be surprised. Do you think it's right to expect Dad and me to keep you all that time?'

The knowledge that she would be at least eighteen before she could even start training kept Tina silent.

'This isn't the time to talk about it,' Will said diplomatically.

'No, just a minute, I'm interested,' Daphne put in. 'Do you mean Annis Gilroy really thinks you've got a voice worth training, Tina?'

'She said it was too soon to tell,' Tina admitted. 'But she's

27

offered to have Ros and me over once a week for coaching during the school holidays.'

'Just a whim,' Elsie said. 'It'll last a week or two and then she'll find she's too busy.'

'I don't think so,' Tina said obstinately.

'Well, come on − sing me something,' Daphne demanded. 'Else, have you still got Mum's old piano?'

'In the front room. Daphne, I wish you wouldn't encourage her ...'

'No harm in hearing what she can do. Come on, Tina.'

She swept out of the room, pushing Tina in front of her. In the immaculately kept front room she sat down in front of the old upright piano, flexing her fingers.

'Goodness, how this takes me back,' she murmured. 'I'm no great shakes as a pianist, but I can still vamp out a tune. What music have you got? Good grief, Mum's old Christmas carol sheets! Try "Silent Night".'

Tina's voice rose effortlessly in the carol. When the last note died away there was a moment's silence.

'Oh, Jerusalem!' Daphne said softly. 'We've got an infant prodigy in the family.'

She swivelled round on the revolving piano stool.

'If you were a couple of years older I could get you into the cast of *Stars Above*, easy as easy,' she said seriously.

Tina shook her head vigorously. 'It's classical music I want. Opera.'

'In that case ...' Daphne turned to Elsie and Will. 'You can't throw away a gift like that. Tina should go to music college. Surely there must be grants available?'

Will and Elsie looked at one another uncertainly.

'It's not just the fees, it's keeping her for years and years,' Elsie said. 'Like as not she'll no sooner get through college than she'll be getting married and all that effort wasted. She ought to have a bit of life, earn some money, enjoy herself.'

'Music is all the life I want,' Tina said.

'I'm getting well paid for *Stars Above*,' Daphne said slowly. 'I could put some money by to keep Tina going while she's at college.'

'No! That's not the life I've planned for Tina and when

she's shaken the star dust out of her eyes it's not what she'll want herself. I've brought her up to be a sensible girl ...'

'Not like me?' Daphne asked softly.

'That's right! Not like you – not like you at all.'

Tina could see that her mother was getting seriously agitated. She was not surprised when her father put his hand on her arm and said quietly, 'No need to upset yourself, Else.'

There was an odd smile on Daphne's face which Tina did not understand.

'You can't actually stop me if I insist on helping Tina,' she said. 'I have the right.'

'You have no rights, none at all,' Elsie said in a way so different from her usual diffident manner that Tina was shocked.

'Oh, yes, I do! Tina ...'

'Stop her, Will. Make her stop,' Elsie cried.

'Tina, go upstairs to your bedroom,' Will said and Tina was so surprised by this uncharacteristic scene that she went without a word.

She sat upstairs on her bed and listened to the voices down below, the two women's raised and agitated and her father's deeper rumble, conciliating them she guessed. She began to feel indignant as time went by. It was *her* future they were discussing. Why was she shut out of it? The only thing that consoled her was the realisation that her aunt, like Annis Gilroy, had thought her voice worth training. Her thoughts wandered back to the time she had spent earlier in the afternoon at Annis's house – the big music room, the grand piano, the atmosphere which she only dimly recognised of a place where the supreme importance of music was taken for granted.

In the room downstairs, just as Tina had guessed, the two sisters confronted one another and Will tried to keep the peace, not very successfully.

'Fifteen years!' Elsie exclaimed, her voice trembling with indignation. 'I've had Tina for fifteen years and now you come along talking about rights! She's *mine*!'

'I'm still her mother,' Daphne put in. 'I take it Tina doesn't know?'

'Of course she doesn't. And neither does anyone else since Mum died. That was what we agreed, all those years ago. I took your unwanted baby off your hands and you promised she'd always be mine.'

'You were glad enough to do it.'

'Of course I was! Not being able to have a child of my own ...'

Elsie choked and Will put a comforting hand on her shoulder, a touch that she shook off as if it were unwelcome at that moment.

'I've brought her up to be *my* daughter,' she said. 'She's a good, sensible girl ...'

'But she's inherited my talent. Queer, isn't it?'

'It's just a passing fad. She'll get over it. Her head's been turned by this opera singer, making her believe she could make a living on the stage. If she's not encouraged she'll get over it. She'll find a steady job ...'

'Meet the right man, get married and start giving you grand-children. Is that the future you've got lined up for her.'

'And what's wrong with it? If I could see Tina nicely settled in a house of her own with a man she could depend on and her own family growing up round her, then I wouldn't want anything better for her. Just because you've never known the satisfaction of a decent life it doesn't mean there aren't plenty of us in the world who ask for nothing better.'

'But Tina wants something different,' Daphne said softly.

'She won't if you don't encourage her. And if you ever tell her you're her real mother – though how you can pretend such a thing when you've done nothing more than give birth and then reject her – I'll ... I'll cut your throat.'

'Now, now,' Will said soothingly. 'You don't mean that, Elsie, you know you don't, any more than Daphne means to give away old secrets.'

'I might,' Daphne murmured provocatively.

'Come off it,' Will retorted. 'What! Give out that you've got a baby that's been brought up by your sister for the last fifteen years? That'll look good in the papers, that will, just as you're going to open in this new musical.'

'You wouldn't tell the newspapers,' Daphne said uncertainly.

'I would! Of course, it'd be hard on Tina, but that's the price you'll have to pay if you insist on putting her in the picture. What Elsie said is true; our Tina is her daughter.'

'And yours,' Daphne said flatly.

There was an uncomfortable pause and then Will went on doggedly, 'Elsie did a generous thing when she took on Tina as soon as she was born. True, she was mad to have a baby; it was still more than most women would have done.'

'And it gives me the right to decide on the best future for her,' Elsie put in.

Her customary timidity was all forgotten in her obstinate fight for what she believed to be the best future for the girl who sat upstairs straining her ears to gather what was being discussed so heatedly down below.

'I won't have her going on the stage, I won't!'

The argument went on for a few more minutes, but Will had taken the wind out of Daphne's sails. Of course it would be a disaster if the story of her old mistake got out. She only went on bickering with her sister because she hated to give in and Elsie's self-righteous air niggled her.

Tina was called downstairs eventually. She looked round, trying to gauge the situation. Her mother was sitting up very straight and she had two vivid spots of colour in her normally pale cheeks. Her lips were tightly pressed together and her hands were clasped in a way that must have made them ache. But for all her nervous strain, she had a triumphant air, and Tina's heart sank as she guessed that for once her mother, with the obstinacy of deep prejudice, had refused to be swayed by any arguments her sister, and possibly even her husband, might have put forward.

None of them seemed to want to tell Tina what had been decided, until at last Will said awkwardly, 'Putting one thing against another, your mum and I have decided you'll do best to stick to taking up your place at the commercial school. After all, it was your teachers' idea, and they must know best.'

'They alway suggest secretarial training for girls who aren't going to college and don't know what they want to do,' Tina said dully. 'Auntie Daphne ...'

'Oh, don't look to me to help you! It's been made quite

clear *my* money's not wanted.' Daphne gave an angry laugh. 'Anyone'd think I'd earned it dishonestly instead of by damned hard graft.'

'There's no need to swear,' Elsie said. 'You may have worked hard. I dare say you did. Goodness knows, I remember the hours you used to keep when you were in the chorus and the way you came home exhausted. It's not the life I want for Tina.'

'I don't want to be a dancer,' Tina exclaimed in despair. 'Mum, you can't do this to me, just when I've discovered what I most want to do.'

'You've had your head turned by a bit of attention. You sing very nicely, I'm not saying you don't, but the day will come when you'll thank me for keeping your nose to the grindstone and making you learn a decent trade instead of flying off after some will-o'-the-wisp. And let me remind you, it was your Miss Gilroy who said it would do you no harm to learn office work.'

'But only as a stop-gap to fill in time before my real training starts. I told you, she's going to let me and Rosamund go to her once a week during our holidays for a lesson. She *must* think we're worth bothering about.'

'You'll have to tell her you've decided not to take up her kind offer.'

'Mum I *can't*. It's my holiday. Surely I can please myself how I spend my time on holiday, can't I?'

'There's no point in starting something you're not going on with,' her mother said, but unexpectedly her husband intervened, struck perhaps by Tina's flat despair.

'Let her go, Else. It'll be an outing for her once a week and I'm sure Tina won't let it go to her head.'

Elsie's lips tightened, but she contented herself with saying, 'You'll have to pay your bus fare out of your pocket money.'

Tina started to agree, eager to cement this small concession before her mother had second thoughts, then she was struck by an idea.

'Auntie Daphne, if you want to give me something – and I haven't said thank you for wanting to pay for my training, but I do appreciate it even if it's not going to happen – would you give me a bicycle?'

'I don't see why not,' Daphne said, with a quick glance at her sister.

'Then I can cycle over to Locksley Green. And I can start cycling to school next term.'

'Winter will be coming on, you'll get soaked,' her mother pointed out.

'Not if I've got a proper cape.' Tina drew a deep breath. 'Don't say "who's going to pay for that", because I am. I'll do a paper round.'

'But you're a girl!'

'Girls deliver papers. And I shall get a Saturday job, too.'

The two angry spots of colour were back in Elsie's cheeks. 'Not with my permission, you won't!'

'Just a minute, Elsie,' Will said. 'Tina, what's behind this?'

'I'm not giving up,' Tina said. 'All right, I'll go to the commercial school, but by the time I'm eighteen I want to be in a position to take charge of my own life. I want that fifty pounds I got as a reward for finding Miss Gilroy's ring put into a savings account. I'm going to save every penny I can earn so that I can have singing lessons, and I don't see how you can stop me if I pay for them myself.'

'Good for you,' Daphne exclaimed at the same time as her sister exploded into an angry, 'No!' Once again Will intervened.

'Elsie, if Tina's got that sort of determination then I think we should let her try. I know it's not your idea of the right thing for her, and maybe in the end nothing will come of it, but I'll not withhold my permission to anyone who wants to work for something they've set their hearts on, especially my own daughter.'

'The roads . . .' Elsie began automatically, reverting to her usual nervousness.'

'Tina can cope,' Will said. 'You'll not begrudge her a bicycle, Elsie.'

'And a gramophone,' Tina added.

'Tina! That's enough! I won't have you asking for presents.'

'Auntie Daphne *wants* to give me something,' Tina argued. 'A bicycle and a gramophone will cost a lot less than putting me through music college, which is what I really want — and will go on wanting, no matter what you may say.'

'Don't get heated. We've had enough arguments for one afternoon,' Will said.

He sounded tired and Tina felt a pang of remorse as she realised how worn he looked. Poor old Dad, caught up in a family row between two sisters and looking as if he'd had the worst of it. All the same, she was not giving up the chance of securing her bicycle and gramophone. She continued to look hopefully at Daphne.

Daphne laughed at her eager face. 'OK, honey, a bicycle and a gramophone it is. Now I'm going. It's been quite a homecoming. I suppose I should have known better than to expect the fatted calf. Perhaps when my name's up in lights in the West End you'll appreciate what it meant for me to take a whole afternoon off to come all the way down here to see you. Tina, will you ring for a taxi to take me to the station?'

'Yes, of course.'

'You're a pet.'

Daphne waited until Tina had gone into the front room to use the telephone and then she said softly, 'You've defeated me this afternoon, but the real battle hasn't even begun. You won't have a moment's peace until you let Tina try for a singing career.'

Chapter Three

All through their summer holidays Tina and Rosamund met in Locksley Green village every Wednesday afternoon and went together to Rigby House for their hour with Annis Gilroy. Contrary to Elsie's prediction, and to Oliver's secret expectation, Annis did not get tired of their visits. She was feeling her way back into the routine of practising and preparing for a recital and for her recording of *Aida* later in the year, and she welcomed their uncritical admiration, as well as taking a pride in passing on some of her knowledge and technique.

At the end of August the Drews went off for a fortnight's holiday and Tina went on her own to Rigby House, riding the bicycle which had given her a freedom she had not possessed before.

'Rosamund's in Jersey,' she told Oliver when she found him alone in the music room. 'Lucky thing! It's almost abroad.'

'Very nearly,' he agreed gravely. 'What about your own holiday?'

'We're going to Eastbourne for a week, the first week in September.'

'That'll be nice,' he said absently, bending forward to making a small alteration to the sheet of music in front of him.

'What's that?' Tina asked, going to stand behind him as he sat at the piano.

'I write the occasional song. This is a setting of a little poem by Victor Hugo called *"Nuits de Juin"*.'

'Goodness, how clever! I didn't know you were a composer.'

Her respectful tone made Olive smile, but there was a wry twist to his lips as he said, 'I'm what is known as a dilettante.'

'I'm not sure I know what that means.'

'I do many little things well, but nothing superlatively well.'

'You ought to concentrate, that's what I'm always being told. Are these the words?'

'Mm. "In summer, when day has fled, the plain covered with flowers pours out far away an intoxicating scent ..."'

'There's no need to translate,' Tina said, offended. 'My French is quite good. Can I hear the music?'

'Well ... yes, I suppose so. I'll play over the accompaniment.'

When Tina had listened, she said, 'I like it. It's ... atmospheric. Is that the right word?'

'I'd like to think so. Of course, without the voice it's nothing.'

'Play it again.'

He half suspected what she meant to do and, sure enough, after the introduction, Tina's voice joined in − "L'été, lorsque le jour a fui ..."

It was, of necessity, a tentative performance, but Oliver was struck by the warm, languorous quality Tina infused into the song. Just the effect at which he had aimed, and she had known it by instinct. It was a little uncanny, but all he said when the song was finished was, 'Your sight-reading has improved.'

'Quite good, wasn't it?' Tina said with a briskness that made him smile at the contrast between her strangely mature performance and her apparent ignorance of what she had managed to do.

He was not quite comfortable when he looked across the room and saw that Annis had joined them unnoticed. She did not give any sign of disapproval, but neither did she comment on Tina's feat, although he was sure she had heard it. Instead, she apologised a little too emphatically for keeping Tina waiting and then set the girl off on a series of exercises which were as demanding as any a fully professional singer might perform.

'Have you been working as I recommended?' Annis demanded. 'I'm not sure you haven't taken it easy since last week.'

'Working? I never do anything else,' Tina said. 'I get up at six-thirty and make myself a cup of tea and then I go out and do a paper round. Mum gives me my breakfast when I get back and at the moment I do an hour's practice after that, but I'll have to cut it to half an hour when school starts again and try to make up the time later in the day. I've been in touch with the teacher you recommended and she'll give me weekly lessons in voice and piano when I stop coming here, but to pay for those lessons I'm going to do a Saturday job in the supermarket. On top of that I'll be put on extra homework because I've got exams coming up next year.'

'What do your parents say about your programme?' Oliver asked.

'They're against it, but it's their own fault because they wouldn't let Auntie Daphne help me. Oh, I forgot to say that I've joined the church choir, too.'

Annis threw up her hands. 'I absolve you from not working. When I said "join a choir", the local church wasn't quite what I had in mind.'

'No, but do you know that you have to *pay* to belong to the Choral Society? I can't manage that, not at the moment. At least it's free at the church and I think it's jolly lucky that they include girls. Some churches don't, you know.'

Whatever resentment Annis might have been feeling earlier had been dispelled in laughter over Tina's ferocious determination to pursue her singing, but once the girl had gone, Annis picked up the sheets of manuscript still lying on top of the piano and looked them over.

'I thought this was to be my song,' she said.

'It is,' Oliver said evenly.

'I was surprised to hear you trying it over with our inexperienced Tina.'

'It just happened. I was still working on it when she arrived and you know Tina − full of curiosity and keen to try anything new. She'd plunged in before I knew what she intended and didn't make too bad a hash of it, I thought.'

'I wanted to be the first to sing it.'

'My dear, you will be. An amateurish run-through with an untrained voice doesn't count, any more than it would if I hummed it over to myself as I composed — which I did, of course.'

Annis did not respond, not until he said, 'Do you want to try it now?'

'If you think I won't "make too bad a hash of it."'

In fact, as he had anticipated, she gave a performance. She had, after all, heard him trying it out many times over the past couple of weeks, and she already knew the words.

'Lovely,' Oliver said. He took her hand and kissed it formally. 'Do you like it well enough to include it in your recital?'

'Of course. And you must write some more songs for me, darling.'

She put her hands on either side of his face and looked at him earnestly, forcing him to return her steady gaze.

'What about the big one? When are you going to compose your opera?'

'What opera? The one Michael Peador stole from me?'

The bitterness with which he spoke shook Annis. She dropped her hands and stepped back.

'You still feel as bad about that as ever?'

'I can't even think about it without feeling physically sick. And when you add to that betrayal everything else that happened that night ...'

'Bruno was beside himself with anger for you,' Annis said.

'If he hadn't been so furious he might have driven more carefully,' Oliver said flatly.

They both fell silent, remembering the horror that had overtaken them.

It should have been a gala evening. It started out that way. The three of them had driven through the Italian countryside to Milan, where they were to attend the first night of a new opera by the ageing Irish composer, Michael Peador. Annis had worn her diamonds and a shimmering gown of green and silver. They had a drink and a snack at the apartment of some Italian friends and then the whole party had gone to La Scala.

The old composer, over eighty and deeply revered, was in a prominent seat of honour. They waved to him and he bowed, but Oliver doubted whether he knew who they were since his sight had been failing over the last two or three years. Perhaps he had been able to make out Annis's red hair. She was a great favourite of his and only her heavy programme of engagements had prevented him from offering her the leading role in this opera, *Astolat*.

'Dear lady, I cannot wait,' the old man had said simply. 'A year, two years perhaps, before you are free to perform for me. My time is running out.'

And Annis, protesting that he was immortal, had shed a few tears and kissed him and the role had gone to an Italian soprano.

Oliver had the greatest respect for Michael Peador, so much so that he had ventured to show him the first few scenes of the opera on which he himself was working. Bruno Marcellini thought highly of it and it was Bruno who had provided the necessary introduction and taken the manuscript sheets to the composer's home. The old man had been indulgent and had promised to examine the music in detail, but it was just as well that Oliver was not expecting an early response because that was the last he heard from Michael Peador apart from a vague message that his work 'showed promise'.

Oliver was disappointed but philosophical. It was well known that Peador had been working on an opera based on the story of Elaine from Tennyson's *Idylls of the King* for some years and that in his old age he worked slowly. Perhaps when that opera was completed he would find time to comment on Oliver's work. In the meantime, Oliver had a copy of the three arias Peador had kept and could go on with the opera he was basing on his father's experiences as a partisan fighting the Germans in wartime Italy.

It was a very different theme from the one Michael Peador had chosen. So different that at first Oliver thought he was imagining it when he detected a likeness to his own music in the new opera he was hearing that night at La Scala. By the end of the first act he knew he was not mistaken. Passionately dramatic, the soprano's voice soared in the aria he had given to the girl who had sheltered his father in the hills. Bruno, seated on the other side of Annis, had leaned forward and muttered, 'Oliver ...'

'Yes,' Oliver whispered. 'Wait ... we can't talk now.'

During the first interval they had huddled together in a corner, ignoring the chattering throng all round them, still more bewildered than angry.

'It must be a mistake,' Oliver said. 'He wouldn't ... not on purpose.'

By the end of the opera there was no doubt. Michael Peador had taken Oliver's music and inserted it at key points in his own narrative. Part of Oliver exulted as he recognised how his own music lifted the opera to a new plane each time it appeared, but for the most part he was overwhelmed by grief and anger.

The opera was a success. Michael Peador went on stage to acknowledge the applause. Looking at him, small and round, with a beaming pink face surrounded by an aureole of white hair, Oliver had a sense of total disbelief that this delighted — and delightful — old gentleman could have perpetrated such a cold and deliberate theft.

Bruno, Annis and Oliver left the theatre as quickly as possible and excused themselves from the celebratory party to which they had been invited.

'I couldn't face him,' Oliver said numbly. 'I wouldn't know what to say.'

'I can think of many, many things,' Bruno said.

'So can I,' Annis agreed. 'Oh, if only I had been free to take that role! I would have *known* ...'

'You'd only had a glimpse of what I'd written, but Bruno ...'

'I knew it immediately,' Bruno agreed. 'Had we not agreed that I was to sing the part of your father? I have no doubt, no doubt at all. Villain, thief ... and it was my fault that you showed him your manuscript. I cannot forgive myself.'

'I feel like a mother who's lost her only child,' Oliver said with a laugh that did not come out quite right. 'Oh, let's go home. I simply don't know what I'm going to do about it. Am I to face him with what he's done? After the triumph he's had tonight?'

They argued about it in the car as they travelled towards

40

the villa Bruno had taken for the season. He became more and more heated and they were all too absorbed to know how the accident happened. A sudden summer storm had overtaken them and the heavy rain had reduced visibility and made the road slippery. A lorry came round a sharp corner, taking it too wide. Bruno had braked, the car had skidded and they were turning over, slithering down a bank, there was glass and broken metal all round them and then, when Oliver had freed himself and was frantically working to get the unconscious Annis out, fire.

The autopsy had shown that Bruno was already dead when the car had gone up in flames. That was the only thing that had saved Annis's sanity. Dealing with her, and his own more minor injuries, and all the red tape of officialdom, had kept Oliver from thinking about his lost music. By the time the memory had come to the top of his mind again it seemed of little importance. Bruno had gone, Bruno who had been his friend, and Annis was gravely injured, to the point where it was feared that she must lose a leg. She had got well, but she needed Oliver, depending on him more and more for the running of her life.

Now, faced with Annis's urging to take up serious composing once more, Oliver knew that he would never pursue his claim to a share in the credit for Michael Peador's last opera. The old man was dead, having lived for less than a year after *Astolat*'s first performance. Most of the obituaries had commented favourably on his achievement in producing a fine opera at the age of eighty-two. The thought of upsetting that verdict filled Oliver with a sense of sick distaste. Let it go. At least with the benefit of Peador's name behind it he would have the satisfaction of hearing his music performed from time to time.

With this cynical thought in his mind he was less than responsive to Annis's encouragement.

'I had a good story and a good libretto for the opera I wanted to write,' he said flatly. 'Nothing else appeals to me — inspires me, if you like. And I can't go back to that story, it's finished for me now. Quite apart from anything else, those three arias Peador used were of key importance. They set the characters, the mood . . .' He raised his hands

41

and let them fall in a gesture of futility. 'Nothing else will do. Be satisfied, my dear, with the little songs I set for you. Perhaps one day ... but that day is a long way off.'

'If only I could be sure I wasn't holding you back,' Annis fretted.

'Without the incentive of writing for you I doubt if I'd be doing anything at all,' Oliver assured her. 'Come on, let's not wallow in self-pity. You like this song, don't you?'

'I love it. Shall we run through it again?'

Annis's recital was the beginning of many engagements. Once it was known that she was available for concerts she was inundated with invitations, and she became so busy that when tickets were sent to her for the first night of Daphne Durrell's musical *Stars Above* she had to return them with a regretful note that she would be singing herself that evening at a concert at the Festival Hall.

Tina and her parents also had tickets. Elsie worried about how they were to get to the theatre and how they were to get home afterwards, but she was persuaded that the trains would be running even if they reached Victoria Station after eleven o'clock. Towards the end of September, they made the perilous expedition to London's West End.

The theatre was full and there was a heady feeling of expectation in the air. The word had gone round that *Stars Above* was a show that ought to be seen and Daphne had been working overtime giving interviews, appearing on chat shows and posing for photographs. Everyone seemed to wish her well on her return from the United States and there was an element of satisfaction that a British star had been chosen to appear in this American musical.

It was a backstage story on a theme that might have been banal, but which was redeemed by a touching and unusual love story, some excellent comic scenes and really outstanding dancing. Daphne looked glamorous, acted sufficiently well and sang splendidly. Tina's critical ear detected slight signs of strain towards the end of her aunt's final song, but perhaps that was to be expected after weeks of arduous rehearsals. Tina thought Daphne had given in to the temptation to belt out her opening numbers too emphatically. Possibly when the strain of the first night was over she would take them a little more easily.

They were invited backstage after the show. Tina had looked forward to this, but it was something of an anti-climax. Daphne, changed out of her last act costume, but still wearing her make-up, was surrounded by other people, all intent on kissing her and assuring her that the show was a raving hit. She was wildly excited, unable to sit down, chattering, laughing, lighting cigarettes, putting them down and forgetting them. The small dressing room was full of flowers, some of them standing in buckets of water, some piled up on her cluttered dressing table. Their scent mingled with the smell of grease-paint, the cigarette smoke, the champagne. The atmosphere was stifling. Will, Elsie and Tina stood in the corner, an incongruous little group, until Will muttered, 'We might as well go.'

'Darlings, you're not leaving?' Daphne screamed from the other side of the room. 'The party ... no, you said you wouldn't come to that, didn't you? Listen everyone, this is my fabulous niece, who sings like an angel. One of these days she's going to sing her old auntie off the stage.'

For a moment everyone's attention was turned on Tina. She turned bright red and shook her head, mutely disclaiming Daphne's extravagant claim. They laughed at her embarrassment, but a minute later she was forgotten as a fresh wave of visitors crowded in.

As they made their way out of the darkened theatre Will said, 'Well, it was certainly a success.'

Reluctantly, Elsie agreed. 'Daphne was very good. She's what she always said she was going to be − a star.'

'She'll have to take care not to wear out her voice,' Tina said.

'You enjoyed it, didn't you?' her father asked.

'I did, and I should think it will run and run ... at least, it will as long as people like you and Mum go to see it. The dancing was fabulous. Apart from that, it's not got a lot in it for younger people. I thought it was bit old-fashioned.'

It was a shrewd judgement and one that the reviews the next day bore out. The critics liked the show, and Daphne's performance was praised, but more than one commented that the story was old hat and only redeemed by the good tunes and excellent choreography. "A good coach party show", one critic summed it up and on that level *Stars Above* settled down for a comfortable run.

If Tina had been given a free choice she would have gone to Annis's concert at the Festival Hall rather than to *Stars Above*, but as she said to Rosamund, she could hardly refuse to attend the first night of her aunt's new show.

'Tell me about the concert,' she demanded. 'Was it good?'

'Fabulous. Have you heard her sing the *"Songs of the Auvergne"*? Absolutely out of this world.'

'Did she sing Oliver's song?'

'Yes, as an encore. It was lovely and it got lots of applause. I think Oliver was pleased. I did happen to mention that he was sitting next to me, didn't I?'

'Yes, you did "happen" to mention it, you clot. You've got a thing about Oliver, haven't you?'

'No, I haven't ... well, perhaps I have, a bit. He's so ... so ...'

'Sexy.'

'Tina! I was going to say enigmatic.'

'Sounds good, but you really mean sexy. You're wasting your time. He never looks at anyone but Annis.'

'That can't go on for ever. She's years older than him.'

'And he's years older than you. He only sees us as a couple of schoolkids.'

'Oh, does he?' Rosamund murmured.

Tina looked at her friend suspiciously. 'You've been up to something,' she said. 'Not with Oliver? Not really? You might have told me.'

'It was sort of precious.'

'Yuck!'

'Oh, all right, I'll tell you. It was the week you were in Eastbourne and we'd just come back from Jersey. You remember I had that fabulous tan? So when I went to Annis's for my lesson I wore my white shorts and suntop and I looked ...'

'Pretty good. I'll admit that. And Oliver noticed?'

44

'You could say so. He looked at me and laughed and said something about gilded youth. Annis didn't like it.'

'I don't suppose she did, you spilling out of that halter top – if you took a deep breath it'd hardly be decent – and her boyfriend getting an eyeful. She's jealous of him, you know. She was quite hard on me after she'd heard me singing his song.'

'She was on me that day, too. She was cross because I admitted I hadn't practised while I was away. Well, how could I, in a hotel? After a bit she said she wasn't going to waste any more time on me and swept out.'

'Leaving you alone with Oliver?'

'Mm.'

'Bad tactics. So, what happened? Something, obviously.'

'I was a bit upset. I was standing by the piano, packing up my music, and Oliver put his arm round me and said, "Cheer up, Rosamunda, it'll blow over". And I turned round and looked up at him and he gave a funny little laugh and said "Rose of all Roses, Rose of all the World" and kissed me.'

'Wow!'

'I nearly swooned.'

'Old-fashioned, but I can see it might take you that way. What then?'

'Nothing really. It was only a *little* kiss. If I'd not been taken by surprise I might have made more of it ...'

'Go on, you wouldn't know how.'

'Well, I could have flung my arms round him or something.'

'Embarrassing if he'd merely disentangled himself.'

'Even worse if Annis had come back. As it was, he moved away and laughed again – but he wasn't laughing *at* me, Tina – and said "Pretty child, go home". So I went.'

Tina considered. 'Not much on which to build a great romance,' she commented eventually.

'No, but it shows that he can be tempted.'

'So, next time you went back ...?'

'He behaved as if nothing had happened and so did Annis. I'd taken a lot of trouble over my preparation during the week and she said she was pleased with me. Oliver just played the piano and said nothing, but I could tell he was *aware* of me.'

'I was there and I didn't notice anything. I bet he's forgotten all about it.'

'Oh, no!'

'Oh, yes! And if he hasn't he ought to and so should you. Ros, you can't let silly romantic ideas get in the way of your career.'

'We're both nearly sixteen. We're bound to fall in love sometime. I wouldn't want to miss out on that side of life, would you?'

'No . . . no, of course not. How can we possibly sing things like *Traviata* and *Butterfly* and all the rest if we don't know what it means to be in love? But it's got to be kept on the sidelines. At least, it has as far as I'm concerned.'

'I feel the same way, most of the time. Particularly at a concert like Annis's at the Festival Hall which was such a triumph. The applause was tremendous and she had masses of flowers. And guess what? One of the bouquets she had brought on stage was ours!'

They both contemplated with satisfaction the result of their efforts to give Annis some sort of thank you for the trouble she had taken over their singing lessons.

'I wish I could have been there,' Tina said. 'It was infuriating that it clashed with Auntie Daphne's first night. Honestly, you'd think her success would make Mum and Dad more open to the idea of a stage career for me, wouldn't you, but they're still against it — especially Mum.'

'It's all such a long way off,' Rosamund said slowly. 'Years and years before we can make a proper start, even longer before there's any hope of having a real career. Sometimes I wonder whether we'll stick it out.'

'I will,' Tina said. 'Don't you dare weaken, Ros. We're both going to get into the Guildhall and we're both going to the top.'

Chapter Four

'I don't know why you don't have a nice perm,' Elsie said above the noise of Tina's hair dryer, vigorously applied to her mane of fair hair.

'Can't afford it. Besides, I like my hair to look natural.'

'Untidy is what I'd call it. Are you going to wear it all hanging loose for your office dance?'

'If I go.'

'Of course you're going! A lovely occasion like that and a nice boy wanting to take you in his car ...'

Tina switched off the hair dryer and put it down.

'Mum, Friday night is my last chance to have a singing lesson before my audition at the Guildhall School of Music. That's more important to me than going to a dance and giving Dick Larson a chance to paw me in his car on the way home.'

'Tina, that's not a nice way to talk. I'm sure Dick is quite serious about you.'

'I know he is and I don't want to give him any encouragement. If I refuse to go to the dance it might actually begin to filter through to him that I'd rather spend time with my music teacher than with him.'

'It's not natural, a girl of your age ...'

'It's my age that's important. I'll be twenty-one in February. I've been waiting five years for this chance. I've got to be super-good to persuade the examiners to take me next September and not make me wait yet another year. I don't think I could bear it, working in that damned office ...'

'Don't swear. There's nothing wrong with the office if

only you'd have a little ambition and get yourself out of the typing pool.'

'I've got plenty of ambition,' Tina said softly. 'But it's not to become a manager's secretary. Working in the pool suits me. I always know what time I'll get off from work so that I can get to lessons and rehearsals. Mum, you've enjoyed hearing me sing, haven't you? You loved *The Messiah* last Easter.'

'It was beautiful,' Elsie admitted grudgingly. 'If you kept your singing as a nice hobby I'd be quite happy. But this idea of being a professional ... look at your Auntie Daphne.'

Tina was silenced. Daphne's success in *Stars Above* had lasted for two years, after which business had dropped disastrously and the show had been taken off. She had not had another starring role since then. She had appeared on television shows and had a supporting part in a British musical which lasted only a few weeks. Now the only possibility of employment for her appeared to be in pantomime at Christmas. She claimed to be amused and enthusiastic about the idea, but even Tina had been aware of an element of desperation in her lively account of the impresario's approach to her.

'My musical career will have a firmer foundation than Auntie Daphne's,' she said. 'That's why it's important for me to get into the Guildhall. I've made up my mind − I'm not going to the firm's dance.'

Tina had applied for the two-year Opera Studies course at the Guildhall School of Music, for which it was required that the applicants should be over twenty-one with developed vocal techniques. She had prepared three contrasting pieces of music, not all of which she would necessarily be required to perform. She was keyed up to a high degree of expectation, urged on by Rosamund, who was already enrolled and taking the four-year Associate in Music course.

On the day of the audition Tina went up to London in a state of frozen composure. She had never felt like this before, not even when performing before the stickiest audience. So much hinged on a good outcome to this day's work. She told herself that if she failed then she would pick herself up and try the following year, but she knew that if that happened something would have gone out of her that she might never recover again. She had trained herself to win this particular race and she felt herself to be so fit and ready for it, so much at the height of her existing powers, that a setback would be a blow that might cripple her long-held ambition.

She had allowed too much time and had a good half hour to wait before she was to be heard. When she saw Rosamund looking for her Tina tried to be grateful, but the truth was that she would rather have been left to suffer her torment of nerves alone.

'How are you feeling?' Rosamund demanded.

'Sick.'

'You can't be sick, ducky. Bad for the voice.'

It was all very well for Rosamund, smiling and confident and already at home in the school. She was looking lovely, too, casually dressed in a long, full skirt and loose jumper, her dark hair cut short in a style that must cost a fortune to maintain.

'Cheer up,' Rosamund urged.

'Go away. You're making me feel worse.'

'I don't know what you're worried about. You've got a super voice, you've worked like blazes, you've got professional experience ... well, semi-professional ... and Annis is rooting for you. Come on, smile! You've got it made.'

'Do you really think I've got a chance? Oh, Ros, if you knew what this meant to me ...'

'I do understand, honest I do.'

'There's so much competition.'

'You'll wipe the floor with them. The teachers here aren't fools, you know; they'll recognise your quality. What are you going to sing?'

'I'm starting with that song of Oliver's, "*Nuits de Juin*" — do you remember him writing it for Annis?'

'Mm ... yes. Have you seen Oliver lately?'

There was something about the extreme casualness of that question that made Tina look searchingly at her friend. A touch of extra colour in Rosamund's face, and the way she looked away, made Tina exclaim, 'Ros, you've not revived that old thing about Oliver, have you?'

49

'No, of course not,' Rosamund said unconvincingly.

'Honestly, the way you fall in and out of love ...! You were mooning over some student last time I saw you, who was much more suitable than Oliver. He's years too old for you.'

'He's thirty-four.'

'And you're the same as me, not quite twenty-one. What about Annis?'

'That must be coming to an end, surely? I mean, she must be getting past it. Last time I saw her she was looking quite middle-aged.'

'Annis will always either be young or old. She'll never be anything so *meagre* as middle-aged.'

'Oliver's writing an opera. Did you know?'

'I didn't,' Tina admitted. 'I suppose you see yourself as his prima donna?'

'Wouldn't it be marvellous? I dream about it, I must admit.'

'Stop dreaming and face reality. We've both got years to go before anyone gives us leading roles, except in amateur productions like the ones I've been in.'

She might have thought that she was not particularly glad to see Rosamund when she had first appeared, but their conversation had passed the time and Rosamund had certainly succeeded in taking her mind off the audition. With a start Tina realised that her name was being called. She jumped to her feet and went forward, forgetting even to say goodbye to Rosamund and not hearing the good wishes that her friend called after her.

Tina had chosen her three pieces of music with care. The song by Oliver because she knew it suited her voice and she had a superstitious feeling that it would bring her luck, '*I know that my Redeemer liveth*' from *The Messiah*, and finally, after much agonising, '*They call me Mimi*' from *La Bohème*. She had doubts about that aria, not feeling herself to be a natural Mimi, but her music teacher had insisted that it was an essentially youthful role and well suited to Tina's ability. She sang it with great simplicity and a lovely tone, trying to see herself as a poverty-stricken seamstress in a big city. The effect was more touching than Tina realised.

She was surprised at being allowed to sing all three pieces, not sure whether that was a good sign or not. There was a brief mutter of voices when she had finished 'Mimi' and then she was asked to recite. For this required set piece Tina, benefiting from the long years of attending services while singing in the church choir, had chosen not a poem, but the passage in the authorised version of the New Testament dealing with 'Faith, hope and charity'. She spoke it clearly and thoughtfully, with an appreciation of the cadences of the fine phrases that brought her a word of approval.

'Nicely spoken,' one of her examiners said. 'I see your application is supported not only by your music teacher, but also by Annis Gilroy.'

'Yes, I've known Miss Gilroy for six years and she encouraged me to follow a career in music.'

'We already have a protégée of hers in the school.'

'Rosamund Drew. She's a friend of mine. We were at school together.'

'You weren't tempted to follow the same four-year course that she is taking?'

'My parents wanted me to take a secretarial course,' Tina said with restraint. 'I've been earning a living in an office for the last three years.'

'Having had that experience, do you think you'll be able to live on the grant to which you'll now be entitled?'

'I'll have to. If necessary, I could do a bit of typing on the side.'

'You may yet be glad of that extra skill,' the examiner said drily. 'Thank you, Miss Burford. You'll be hearing from us very shortly.'

Tina, once again feeling as if her insides were being put through a wringer, went out, leaving a thoughtful silence behind her.

Finally, the examiner who had spoken to her said, 'An interesting voice.'

'And could mature into something really fine,' one of his colleagues agreed.

'Should we make her wait another year — with a strong recommendation that she should be accepted then?'

'I'm inclined to think not. She seems to have worked

51

ferociously hard, from the accounts we've been given of her. She's sung *The Messiah* and the lead in *Die Fledermaus* — and I don't know that I wholly approve of that. If we let her slip through our fingers now she may push herself too hard, too young, and we'll miss the opportunity of training a splendid new singer.'

'She has a certain maturity ...'

'Annis writes that she's been impressed from the first by the girl's determination. A paper round, a Saturday job while she was still at school, and all to pay her own way in the face of some opposition from the family. Let her in. I don't think we'll regret it.'

'I can't go on living at home for ever,' Tina pointed out. Her patience was beginning to wear thin. They had been over this so often, ever since her place at the Guildhall School of Music had been confirmed and Rosamund had told her that there would be a vacancy in the autumn in the flat she shared with three other girls.

'You'd expect me to set up on my own if I were getting married,' Tina continued wearily in the face of her mother's obstinate, silent opposition to her plan.

'You wouldn't be alone, you'd have a man behind you,' her mother countered swiftly.

'I don't *need* a man behind me.'

'That's what you think. You'll find out different one day.'

'Perhaps I will. Until that day arrives I intend sharing with Rosamund and her two friends. Mum, you can't stop me. I'm very, very lucky to have this chance. Rooms are hard to come by and expensive. Like this, I should be able to manage on my grant and, I hope, a bit extra from part-time jobs.'

'You'll work yourself to death. And for what? To end up scraping a living, like your Auntie Daphne.'

'Auntie Daphne isn't doing so badly. She's appearing on television again next week. And, anyway, you can't compare her career with mine.'

'The only difference I can see is that you're getting expensive training and she went right in and earned a living for herself.'

52

'Why can't you believe I might end up like Annis Gilroy – respected, rich and sought after well into my fifties?'

Elsie sniffed, but she was momentarily defeated, so she turned the subject.

'Do these other girls know anything about cooking and housekeeping? Rosamund's always struck me as being the helpless sort.'

'They've been living together for two years, so they must be managing, and what they don't know I can teach them after all the training you've given me.'

She had hoped to please Elsie by that remark, but her mother only sniffed again and said, 'You'll end up doing it all if you're not careful. Don't let them put on you, that's all I can say.'

Tina remembered that conversation when she went to join the three girls in their flat in Southwark at the end of September 1984.

'It's an absolutely marvellous place to live,' Rosamund assured her. 'Daddy talked about buying me a flat in Kensington, but it would have been a poky little place and not really convenient. From here we can hop on the Tube and be at the Barbican in no time. I know it's old and run-down, but it's better than living in a hostel. We're terribly, terribly lucky to have so much space and the walls are fairly soundproof, which is useful when we want to practise.'

They were, indeed, lucky, as Tina came to appreciate in the next few weeks as she listened to the complaints of her fellow students about the grotty digs they were forced to live in. However, she thought privately that their landlord could have afforded to give the place a new coat of paint out of the outrageous rent their flat commanded, not to mention a new carpet to replace the threadbare rag on the living-room floor and a better method of heating water than the ramshackle gas boiler in the tiny kitchen.

The flat consisted of the living accommodation over a shop that sold electrical goods – so much better than food, which might have been smelly and attracted mice, as Rosamund pointed out. They had two attic rooms with sloping ceilings, each of them just managing to hold two single beds, pushed up against one another, a chest of drawers and an inadequate wooden wardrobe. On the floor below there was the living room with the threadbare carpet, which held two armchairs with suspect springs and a convertible settee, so that there was actually sleeping accommodation for five, or even six, but if they actually tried to cram in that many their landlord said he would have to review the rent. Rosamund had also managed to find room for her record player and sizeable collection of records and cassettes.

'Good job none of us plays the double bass,' she remarked. 'Stella's flute and Patsy's violin just about fit in.'

In the kitchen, the gas cooker and the refrigerator were fairly new, but Tina wrinkled her nose at the cracked porcelain sink and warped cupboards.

'We manage,' Rosamund said. 'I know it's not heaven, but I've survived for the last two years and I'm sure you'll fit in, Tina.'

'It *is* heaven,' Tina said. 'It's freedom. I'm fond of my dear old mum and dad, goodness knows, but I've begun to feel stifled at home. I must have a life of my own.'

At first Tina envied Rosamund her established place at the Guildhall. Rosamund knew who everyone was and how everything worked and she had a circle of friends who seemed to live in a perpetual state of irreverent laughter. Tina felt like a new girl at school, which, after having been out in the world and earned her own living, was not easy to take. Nor was it easy to accept direction about what roles she should study and how her development should proceed. Tina was used to following her own line. She had been the one who chose what she should do and then followed it through with single-minded dedication.

Gradually she settled in, becoming reconciled to the things she did not like by the professionalism of the teaching and the obvious progress she was making. Her language classes alone would have been a full-time course for many undergraduates – French, Italian, German and Russian – in addition to her singing and piano lessons; and on top of that Tina managed to get typing work which could be done at home in her spare time – such as it was. It was one of the few things that riled the other girls, that Tina was always sitting hunched over the kitchen table tapping away at her typewriter when they wanted to get themselves a snack.

She already had contacts in amateur musical circles and she also began to receive requests from small churches and choral societies to sing the solo parts in concerts given by the local choirs. It was all experience and the sixty pounds or so she earned each time was more than welcome. Tina began to look on the church festivals with a greedy eye, seeing them more as an opportunity to earn a fee than as a religious experience.

'Tina, you never have any fun,' Rosamund complained.

'Yes, I do. This is fun,' Tina said, taking her fingers out of her ears and looking up from the manuscript she was studying. In the background Patsy was grappling with a difficult violin passage and in their bedroom Stella was practising her flute.

'I heard one of the tutors say the other day that teaching you was like throwing sprats to a shark,' Rosamund remarked.

'Do you think it was meant to be a compliment?'

'Probably. They think terribly well of you, you know.'

'And you. We're the two outstanding sopranos of our year.'

'Lucky old us. I don't know about me, but everyone says you're headed for the top.'

For a moment Tina felt a thrill that went right through her, then she shook her head.

'You should have heard what the Prof said about my Susanna last week. He flattened me to such an extent I didn't bother to open the door when he'd finished, I just crawled underneath.'

'He's a swine, isn't he?' Rosamund said affectionately. 'But he only treats people like that if he thinks they're really, really good and able to take it.'

'I'm a sensitive artist,' Tina complained. 'I need to be coddled and reassured.'

'You won't get that treatment from the Prof. Look, what you need is a change, something different from this everlasting studying. Tom Walden's giving a party this evening and he particularly asked me to get you to come along.'

Tina considered. 'The thing is, Tom might turn into a bit of a nuisance,' she said.

'You can't go on for the rest of your life thinking everyone who fancies you is a nuisance. Tina, you're not human!'

'Huh! Better than being like you, always falling in and out of love. Who is it at the moment? Not that grotty tenor who slurs his notes?'

'If you mean Gordon, no, as a matter of fact that's off. I'm fancy free, which is a very good reason for going to Tom's party.'

'Going on the prowl? You should be ashamed of yourself, Rosamund Drew. What would your mother say?'

'She'd say, "I don't know why you can't find someone with a better *background*, darling",' Rosamund said.

They both laughed, but there was an edge of bitterness in Rosamund's voice and it was Tina's unspoken sympathy that made her change her mind about going to the party that evening.

It was exactly the same as every other student party: a fair amount of booze, a lot of noise and some indifferent food. Tom Walden was Australian, a fine baritone in his final year. Tina had no reservations about him as a singer and she was secretly conscious of finding him attractive as a man, which was why she was wary of him. No commitment was Tina's watchword, and so far she had not been shaken from it.

Tom was a large young man, a full head taller than Tina, who was beginning to find her height something of a trial. He had crisp golden curls which had to be covered by a wig for dramatic roles because, as Tom himself said, whoever heard of a Scarpia who looked like Bubbles? His face was round and his nose was disarmingly snub. He was fun to be with, always laughing, always ready with a drawling put-down in an exaggerated Australian accent, and he was enterprising and adventurous, too.

'Great you could come,' he said, seizing hold of Tina's hand and pulling her away from the main crowd of chattering students. 'My favourite soprano — my favourite *girl*.'

He grinned at her, his blue eyes twinkling, not expecting to be believed, and Tina laughed back.

'You're favourite sheila?' she suggested.

'I've stopped saying that,' Tom informed her. 'I'm more British than the Brits these days.'

'More Pommy than the Poms?'

'Stop taking the mickey. Seriously, Tina, I want to talk to you. I've got a proposition to put to you.'

'And you've said that to a few girls in your time, too. Nothing doing, Tom. I'm only here for the beer.'

'I said seriously. This is a musical proposition. Look, come into the bedroom.'

Tina bit back another facetious retort and followed him into the small back room, away from their chattering friends. It was a warm evening, nearly into July, nearly the end of term. That was partly why she had allowed herself to be persuaded to come to this party; she deserved a bit of relaxation after the last gruelling six months.

She was wearing a cotton skirt her mother had run up for her out of a colourful remnant and a bright green T-shirt. Tom eyed the outline of her full breasts appreciatively as Tina perched on the end of the bed and waited for him to explain himself.

'You know I've made up a party to go in my mini-van to Germany to hawk ourselves round the opera houses this summer?' Tom asked.

Tina nodded. She had heard all about this enterprising idea. All over Germany small towns still cherished their opera houses, and they worked to a system that involved scheduling operas years in advance. Having established *der Spielplan*, the directors auditioned for singers to be cast in these operas. The voices were classified according to the *Fach* system, which divided each range of voice into several types, so that the soprano voice was given no less than seven gradations from 'soubrette' to 'heavy dramatic'. Tom had made up a party of seven assorted voices with a good varied repertoire, he had been in touch with German agents, and he already had several firm appointments with local directors of music with an eye to the budget who were willing to give auditions to experienced students from the prestigious Guildhall which might lead to contracts for the following year.

'Corinne's had to drop out,' Tom said. 'No, nothing wrong. In fact, very much all right. She's been invited to join the chorus at Glyndebourne.'

'Wow! Lucky devil,' Tina said with deep yearning.

To join the chorus of any other opera house was no part of her ambition, though she told herself that if nothing better offered then she would take any singing work and be thankful. Once in the chorus, it was difficult to get out. One did not, in the true sense, 'understudy' a leading operatic role. One learnt it and stood by, ready for the call if the diva fell ill, but the truth was that any opera house would move heaven and earth to fly in a known name to fill the part rather than make use of the talent in the company. Promotion from the ranks was rare, and Tina shuddered away from the thought of ensemble singing for the rest of her days.

Glyndebourne was different. There, every individual in the chorus was a potential soloist, and though there was little chance of being called upon to play a leading role, the entry of a Glyndebourne season on a curriculum vitae was a guarantee of excellence.

'So we've got a vacancy,' Tom went on. 'The point is, we're doing more than just auditioning in Germany. I've organised a tour for us and we'll be paid for those performances. I've been working on it for the past year. We'll be going to all sorts of odd venues – churches, ruined castles, town halls. I'm a bit desperate about losing Corinne because I've offered scenes from *Die Fledermaus* and *The Marriage of Figaro* as part of our programme. I know you've got Rosalinda and Susanna in your repertoire. Want to join us?'

'Oh, Tom!' Tina's mind raced as she considered all the complications involved. 'I'm singing Verdi's *Requiem* at Croydon on 6th July.'

'No problem. We don't leave until the 15th.'

'And then I'm supposed to be going away with my mum and dad for a fortnight's holiday.'

'They'd understand, surely, that your career comes first? It's a good opportunity to get yourself known in a very useful part of the world. Come on, you're not going to turn it down, are you?'

'I don't want to,' Tina admitted. 'Is it ... is it sort of officially approved? I mean, do they know about it at the Guildhall?'

'Sure. It's been done before. I'm not taking you out of the country to perform *The Sound of Music* in a tent. We may be going to places you've never heard of, but that's because you're an ignorant Pom ...'

'Oh, thanks!'

'I've nearly split a gut getting it all organised and although I'm pleased for Corinne and wouldn't stand in her way, I was knocked sideways when I heard she wouldn't be coming. I need you, young Tina.'

'I've got to come, I've just got to.'

'Isn't that what I've been telling you? First stop Freiburg and you can sing Susanna to my Figaro. You know how well we go together.'

A sudden doubt swept over Tina. 'What about money? How are we managing about expenses?'

'We're each putting a hundred pounds into the kitty. That's for things like taking the mini-van on the ferry and petrol and so on. We're going to rough it, I may as well warn you.'

Tom saw her expression and stopped. 'More than you can afford?'

'About five times more than I've actually got at the moment. Of course, I'll get paid for the *Requiem*, but even so, it's going to be a struggle.'

'I'll subsidise you,' Tom said. 'No, don't refuse ... I want you on this trip, Tina. Not just because I fancy you like hell — which I do — but because I want one day to say that I toured Europe with Valentina Burford when she didn't know her own future.'

'You're being kind ...'

'Sure, kind to myself. My family's loaded and I'm pretty well subsidised. A hundred quid is neither make nor break for me. You can pay me back when the Deutschmarks start rolling in.

'I will,' Tina said firmly.

'You're afraid I'll hold the debt over your head and twirl my black moustache and bend you to my wicked will.'

'You won't?'

'Sure I will. It's my number two project for the summer. Number one is to sing my heart out and number two is to get you into bed.'

'Stick to project number one,' Tina advised him. 'It's the only one I'm interested in.'

'You don't know what you're missing.'

He had been leaning against the wall, watching her as she sat on the end of the bed, but now he moved forward, took her firmly by the shoulders, tipped her backwards and leaned over to kiss her. Tina did not avoid the kiss, but she did her best not to respond. Tom settled himself more comfortably, slipped his arms round behind her and lifted her slightly towards him to kiss her more emphatically. Tina put her hands on his shoulders, as if to push him away, but it was a half-hearted effort and after a moment her arms moved up and round his neck. She could feel his warmth and the hardness of his muscles. Her body fitted against his. It was all rather unexpectedly comfortable and it was just beginning to be exciting when Tom laughed softly and took his mouth away from hers.

They sat for a moment with their arms still round one another, his cheek resting against her, and then Tina made a decisive movement to break away.

'You've got a roomful of guests out there,' she said, doing her best not to sound breathless.

Tom stood up and took her hand, pulling her behind him as he opened the bedroom door.

'Listen, everyone,' he said. 'I've persuaded Tina to come to Germany on the Tom Walden Dream Trip Rollercoaster song fest – !'

It was not that easy. Tina went home the following weekend to explain to her parents why she would not be going on holiday with them. It was particularly difficult because they were giving her the holiday as a present. More than that, they were going to Cornwall, which was new ground for the family, and they were staying in a proper hotel. It had been booked for months ahead and Elsie had made herself two new cotton frocks and a quite daring sundress for Tina.

Tina had braced herself for the bewildered hurt when she broke the news that she would not be joining them after all. Elsie went straight to the essential feature.

'We'll lose our deposit.'

'Only for me. I'm sorry, Mum. I'll ... I'll try to pay it back to you.'

Elsie said nothing and they both knew it was a fairly forlorn hope.

'You've worked hard since you went to the Guildhall,' Will said quietly. 'Too hard, I've sometimes thought. Now, it seems, you're going to spend the summer working even harder, and not even in England at that. Do you think it's wise?'

'It won't be like work,' Tina said. 'You know I always enjoy myself when I'm singing. There'll be eight of us in the party and we'll have some fun in between. It'll be wonderful experience for me. Even if it's only a few weeks it means I can say I've sung abroad professionally. It'll help when I'm looking for work.'

'This young chap who's organising it ...'

'Tom's nice. You'd like him. His father's a sheep farmer in Australia. Pots of money apparently. Not that that matters. The important thing is that Tom has a really good baritone voice. The others are good, too. It's an honour to be invited to join them.'

'What about Rosamund?'

'No, she's not coming. I would have liked to have had her along, but there's only one spare place.'

'And what made them offer it to you?'

'I'm the best,' Tina said.

She spoke simply, but it came over her with a rush of pride that it was true. She was not just good, she was the best. Her own contemporaries admitted it. She was not being asked along as a make-weight. She was replacing a girl who had already made the grade and she was taking Corinne's place because she was her equal.

'Please ... try to see it my way,' she pleaded. 'I'm disappointed not to come away on holiday with you, of course I am, especially when Cornwall was my choice and we were looking forward to it so much. But singing's my life and I can't turn down a chance like this.'

'You've turned twenty-one,' Will said. 'You're living your own life. I suppose, when you come to think about it, there's not many girls of your age who go on holiday with their parents. We were looking forward to seeing a bit of you for a change. Still, it's not the end of the world. Cheer up, Else. I don't think you and me have had a holiday on our own, not since ... not since Tina came along. It'll be like a second honeymoon.'

Elsie looked unconvinced, but she recognised, just as Will did, that Tina's decision had been made before she came home that weekend, and there was no shaking Tina, not once she'd made up her mind, not where singing was concerned.

She waited until she and Tina were washing up after the evening meal she still persisted in calling 'tea' and then she said abruptly, 'This Australian boy, is he keen on you?'

Tina concentrated on the plate she was drying, polishing it with unnecessary vigour. 'He is, a bit,' she admitted.

'What about you?'

'I like him, that's all. It's not serious, Mum.'

'No, I dare say not. You want to watch your step.'

'Oh, Mum ...!'

With her hands deep in the soapy water, Elsie looked out of the kitchen window, seeing nothing.

'Are you on the pill?' she asked.

The question, coming from her mother, was so unexpected that Tina almost dropped the plate.

'No, as a matter of fact, I'm not,' she said.

'Maybe you'd better start. I don't condone all this immorality, but living like you're going to this summer, all mucking in together, away from home, away from anything that might restrain you and make you show a bit of sense, something might happen. Better safe than sorry and it's no use saying you can trust a man to take care of you, because the plain truth is, you can't. It's up to you. I don't flatter myself you'll take my advice, but I thought it right to speak.'

'Mum, it's not going to *be* like that,' Tina said. 'Tom and me ... we're just singing partners, that's all.'

'Oh, yes? I've seen the way the colour comes up when you speak about him. Just saying his name makes you smile. I only wish I could believe it might come to something, though an Australian isn't what I'd wish for you. But you've set your mind against marrying and settling down. Just make sure the decision isn't taken out of your hands, that's all.'

62

It was well meant and it had cost her mother an effort to give advice that went counter to her own beliefs and prejudices, so Tina kept quiet and tried to look grateful.

'I'd like to know what Annis thinks about this German trip,' she said, knowing that her mother would be grateful for a change in the conversation. 'I'll give her a ring and ask if I can go and see her.'

It was Oliver who answered Tina's telephone call, but then it usually was.

'Sorry,' he said. 'Annis is away for the weekend.'

'Oh ... pity,' Tina said. 'I wanted to tell her about being invited to join a party of students who are touring Germany this summer.'

'Sounds interesting. Come over and talk to me. I'll buy you a drink in the village pub.'

Tina hesitated for a moment, surprised by the invitation, and then she accepted. Oliver was not Annis, who would have understood her excitement, but he was knowledgeable, especially on the business side, and he might have something useful to say.

He was waiting for her and stepped out of the front door as soon as she arrived.

'Do you feel like a walk?' he asked. 'Across the fields to the Jolly Ploughman? It's no more than a mile if we climb over the fence at the back of the house.'

'Sure, why not?'

He led her round the side of the house and across the lawn at the back. The fence was as easy to clamber over as a stile and they dropped down on to a path which ran along the edge of a field of ripening wheat. A little breeze ran over the field, rustling the ears on their stalks.

'Lovely little noise,' Tina remarked.

'Difficult to reproduce,' Oliver said. 'Just a whisper of sound on the violins perhaps. Very subtle.'

'Are you writing anything at the moment?'

'Trying to. That's why I stayed at home on my own this weekend. I'm suppose to be getting down to some serious work, but it's been sticky.'

63

'Rosamund said some time ago that you were writing an opera.'

'Did she? Whenever did I tell her that? How is pretty Rosamund?'

'Flourishing. As far as I can remember she's not in love with you at the moment.'

'Good God, I should hope not!'

'Well, she does get these passing fancies. Rather often, as a matter of fact. And usually for someone totally unsuitable.'

'Like me.'

'Like you,' Tina agreed. 'Please don't encourage her. It's frightfully bad for her singing.'

Oliver made a choking noise which was not quite a laugh and not quite an exclamation of annoyance.

'Your career doesn't suffer from the same disability, I take it?' he asked.

'I've got more sense.'

'Mm ... perhaps.' They walked on in silence and came to the end of the field. 'Over the stile and bear right through that belt of trees, then we drop down the hill and into the lane.'

The Jolly Ploughman was a small, whitewashed public house isolated from any village, which had once served a community of farm workers. In recent years it had become run-down, but that evening Oliver looked at it and discerned signs that business was picking up.

'Three cars and the sign's been repainted,' he said. 'I'm afraid it's been discovered. Another year and there'll be a proper car park and "pub food". However, in the meantime, let's sit outside and enjoy the tranquillity while we can. What'll you have to drink?'

Tina decided on a glass of cider and sat down on a wooden seat round the base of a horse chestnut tree. Through the leaves the sky was a rich blue. She could hear birds singing all round her and a cricket was chirping in the grass nearby. She felt suddenly regretful that she was going away to Germany. Her father had been right when he said that Tina needed a holiday, and the German trip would be anything but that.

'I suppose I'm doing the right thing,' she said to Oliver when he returned with glasses in his hand.

'Tell me about it.'

He listened while Tina explained and when she had finished he nodded his head. 'You have to do it,' he said. 'It's the kind of opportunity that doesn't turn up twice. And it's something to do while you're still a student. Once you've left the Guildhall you may be too caught up in more serious efforts to build a career.'

'Will it ever happen?' Tina asked. 'Having a career, I mean. There are times when I believe that I'm good, really good, but in spite of that I still look into the future and see an endless programme of singing great music with amateur groups, performing at the back of beyond for a pittance, doing musical comedy, even teaching.

'I'd love your teachers to hear the despairing way you say "even teaching".' Oliver reached over and took her hand in his. 'You and I are suffering from the same disease. We're stale. I've been working my head off at tasks I don't particularly like and trying to come to terms with the fact that a way of life I've followed for rather too many years may be coming to an end.'

'Is Annis going to retire?'

Oliver stared down at the glass of beer in his hand.

'I think she should,' he said in a low voice.

'Oliver ...'

'She's always been her own fiercest critic and yet, now, when there's a real deterioration, she can't seem to see it. Tina, if it ever leaks out that I've said this I'll break your charming neck.'

'Of course I won't say anything,' Tina said, really shocked. 'Oh, Oliver, poor Annis ...'

'Yes, it's tragic. I said that I'd stayed at home to work this weekend and that's the official line, but the truth is we've had a profound disagreement about a very taxing concert she's been asked to do in a few months' time. I advised her to turn it down; she won't hear of it.'

It was a dilemma that made Tina shudder. To lose one's voice, after a lifetime of producing lovely music ... 'Is there someone older, someone whose judgement she respects, who might advise her?'

'The only person who could ever over-rule Annis on musical matters was Bruno and, of course, if he were still alive I wouldn't be in my present difficult position.'

He had no intention of enlarging on that. Oliver was facing something that filled him with a profound disgust of himself: a horror of being tied to someone obstinately proceeding on a downward spiral, an ageing woman for whom he felt a helpless affection and who depended on him to an extent against which he was beginning to rebel. He tried to keep in front of his mind the memory of the long years of love, the laughter, the splendour, and all he could feel was compassion.

It was not a matter he intended discussing with the untried girl who sat beside him with a troubled look on her face and no idea at all of the hopelessness that filled him.

Once I loved Annis as a woman, he thought; I desired her. Now that has gone. And the fourteen years between us is too great a gap for me to resign myself to living with her for the rest of my life as nothing more than a friend. It's sapping me of all the creative energy I once had and if that is to go, too, I don't think I can go on living.

'Oliver . . .'

He turned to face Tina, trying to conjure up a smile.

'Tell me about your opera,' she said.

'What can I say? It's my second attempt. The first . . . I suffered a setback over that, so much so that I thought I'd never try again. And yet . . . there's something there, something that wants to be said.'

'Where have you gone for a story?'

'Back into my own family – not for the first time. My great-great-grandfather was one of the glassmakers of Murano. He made a glass crown for the Great Exhibition in London in 1851.'

'That must have been difficult.'

'Yes, a great technical feat. A bit ornate for today's taste, but a fine achievement for its time.'

'Have you still got it?'

'No, it's disappeared, unfortunately. I've only ever seen pictures of it. He came to London, demonstrating glass-blowing at the Exhibition and, as far as one can gather from the rather scrappy story that survived, fell in love with an opera singer.'

66

'Did they marry?'

'No, but he gave her the crown. I've built my opera round that. In real life they met for the first time in London, but I've made my heroine a girl from his island, who deserts him for a singing career. It's got a sort of theme of the conflict between ambition and love. She becomes a great singer, the mistress of a duke, but eventually goes back to Murano to die.'

'Is she a soprano?' Tina asked eagerly.

Oliver threw back his head and laughed. 'Yes, my self-seeking diva, of course she's a soprano. A tremendous role − if I ever finish it.'

'You *must*.'

'Tell me more about this German trip of yours.'

They stayed another half hour. It was a relief for Tina to talk about her enthusiasm − and her worries with someone who was neither as closely involved as her group of friends nor as hostile as her parents. Oliver knew some of the places they were likely to visit and could comment on what they would find.

'Your Tom Walden sounds an enterprising chap,' he remarked.

'He's not *my* Tom Walden,' Tina said quickly and then stopped, flushing.

'That wasn't what I was implying,' Oliver said, much amused. 'But I see that it's true.'

'He likes me,' Tina admitted.

'And you like him?'

'Mm ... I suppose I do.'

'Bless you, my child. Enjoy yourself.'

'I don't want to get involved. It's too distracting.'

'At your age ... yes, I know, that's a tiresome thing to say ... but, honestly, Tina, it would be unnatural for you not to feel an attraction towards some young man. How can you sing the great romantic roles if you never fall in love?'

'That's Rosamund's argument. I suppose if I looked on it as helping with my singing I could afford to let go,' Tina said doubtfully.

Once again Oliver's shoulders heaved with laughter.

'I think I feel sorry for Tom Walden,' he said. 'Come on, it's time to go.'

They walked back across the fields. The sun was going down, but it was still light and the standing corn was richly gold in the slanting rays of sunlight. The sky had turned a deeper blue by the time they climbed the fence into Annis's garden. In the house the lights came on.

'Damn,' Oliver said softly. 'Annis must have come back early.'

'Does it matter?'

'She won't like me being out.'

Above all, she would not be pleased to learn that he had been out with her young protégée. Wearily, Oliver braced himself for the cold smile and veiled remarks. Dear Annis, he loved her so much. And he was so tired of having to support her.

He saw Tina looking at him anxiously and managed to smile.

'I'm supposed to be at home working,' he pointed out. 'Not skipping off to pubs with gorgeous young sopranos. Come and say hello. Annis will want to hear about your German trip.'

It was a good move. Although Annis greeted them with raised eyebrows and the tightening of the lips that Oliver dreaded, she chose to be pleased when Tina, with unexpected tact, told her how much she wanted her advice about the projected tour.

'The experience will be good for you,' Annis pronounced. 'Of course, you can hardly hope to give of your best, hurrying from place to place, performing without trying the acoustics beforehand, but it will do you no harm, provided you don't allow anyone to make you force your voice.'

'Thank you, that's what I wanted to hear,' Tina said. 'I would have been disappointed to give it up.'

'Would you have done that? Just on my say-so?' Annis asked.

Probably not, but Tina sensed that this was a time to stretch the truth. 'I value your opinion more than anyone's,' she said diplomatically.

Annis was smiling with genuine pleasure and Tina felt Oliver's almost imperceptible relaxation. Somehow, without meaning to do it, she had defused a potentially difficult situation. And she had done it to save Oliver from a scene. Funny, there had been a time when she had not particularly liked Oliver, mainly because she suspected him of sponging on Annis. Now, with greater perception, she could see that his place in Annis's household was not an easy one.

It was Annis who insisted that Oliver must drive Tina home. It took no more than a quarter of an hour and neither of them said anything much during the journey. When they arrived at her home Oliver did not get out. He let Tina open the car door for herself, but before she moved from her seat he put one of his hands lightly over hers.

'Have a good summer,' he said.

'Thank you. You, too. And Oliver ... good luck with the opera.'

Chapter Five

There had never been such a summer. It was an enchantment to Tina, who had only once been abroad, on a school trip to Paris. Now she found herself in the Europe of fairy tales — mountains and forests and gingerbread towns with churches like jewel boxes and small opera houses with unaccountably good acoustics.

Tom had paved the way well for their tour. They were expected, their repertoire of excerpts from operas was understood and they were hospitably received. The camp sites were comfortable and the weather was kind to them. They gave three performances in Freiburg and then went on to Baden-Baden. After that they took time off to visit Stuttgart, where several of the team had auditions. Tina was not competing, not seriously. Her name had not been on the list originally submitted by Tom and the agents were reluctant to put her forward in place of the missing Corinne.

They were a party of eight, four girls — two sopranos, one mezzo-soprano and a wonderful, vibrant contralto; and four boys — a tenor, Tom the baritone, and a bass. The fourth boy was their accompanist, a talented pianist who could also play the organ when their venue was a church. Two of the party played the guitar and the contralto had brought along her flute, so that they could vary their programme.

Tom had insisted that they needed something more than everyday clothes and they had devised costumes which gave them a professional air. The men wore tight jeans and loose tunics sashed at the waist. The girls all had identical dresses with scoop necks, elbow-length sleeves and full, mid-calf skirts. Any colour, Tom had told them, as long as it was bright. Tina had inherited Corinne's dress, hurriedly altered by Elsie to fit. Fortunately, the deep blue suited her well. The costumes were surprisingly adaptable. They had taken along a few props and with the addition of a lacy apron and a saucy cap Tina became Susanna, while a glittering necklace, bracelets and a fan transformed her into Rosalinda.

She made a particular hit in that role in a Sunday afternoon open-air performance they gave in the surviving courtyard of the ruined Schloss Friedestrom in the village of Zons.

'That was *fun!*' she said as she unfastened her sparkling 'diamonds'. 'But I'm getting confused. Where do we go next?'

'We've got a rest day tomorrow and I've fixed a treat for us in the evening,' Tom told her. 'I've got seats for Verdi's *Requiem*. Want to come?'

'Yes, of course. You know I've been singing it myself this year. Who's doing it and where?'

'Berlin Philharmonic with the guest conductor, Ransu Prokopi – the Finn. It's at the Philharmonie in Cologne, but that's only half an hour's drive away.'

'Marvellous. Who are the soloists?'

'Hans Barnin, Gottfried Werner, Mafalda Romolo and the Swedish soprano, Sigrid Hallstein. What you might call a star-studded cast.'

'How on earth did you manage to get tickets?'

'I wrote and asked for them, and I got them cut-price on the grounds that we're students and fellow performers and working for cultural links between the UK and Germany.'

'You've got the cheek of the devil,' Tina said admiringly.

'And you love me for it,' Tom suggested.

They were three weeks into the tour and Tina was still keeping him at arm's length – more or less. There had been kisses and bone-crushing hugs, but Tom was playing it lightly and so was she. She laughed at the idea of falling in love, but as she watched Tom walk away from her to tell the others about the treat in store for them Tina felt a dizzying rush of affection towards him. There was something about

71

Tom that made her feel as if a small, warm fire had been lit inside her, quite apart from his physical attraction, which was considerable. He's got such a nice, straight back, she thought, and grinned to herself at the fatuousness of it.

The seats they had been allotted for the *Requiem* were good ones and Tom instructed his team that they were to make themselves look presentable, on the grounds that they never knew when they might want another favour. Tina wore one of her tiered cotton skirts, patterned in red and black, with a scoop-necked clinging black top.

'You slay me,' Tom said. 'I don't know how I keep my hands off you.'

'You don't,' Tina said, dodging him. 'Come on, Tom, concentrate on your driving or we'll be late.'

In fact, they were settled in their seats a good ten minutes before the concert was due to begin, nor did it begin on time.

Tom glanced at his watch. 'Come, come,' he said. 'Is this professional? Is this right? Why are we being kept waiting, with the chorus all assembled and the orchestra on stage?'

They got their answer almost immediately when there was an announcement that the start of the performance would be delayed owing to the sudden indisposition of Sigrid Hallstein.

'Oh, bother!' Tina exclaimed. 'I particularly wanted to hear her.'

Again they waited and then there was another, completely unexpected, request. Would 'Herr Tom Walden' kindly come forward?

'They're going to ask Tom to sing the soprano part,' someone suggested as he scrambled out of his seat and along the row.

The guess was not far out. Tom came back and beckoned to Tina.

'They want to know whether any of our group has the *Requiem* in their repertoire, so I said you had,' he told her.

'Tom! You fool! I couldn't, not at a moment's notice. And with the Berlin Philharmonic. No way!'

'Come and talk to Prokopi. It's either you or cancel the performance.'

72

'With a choir of this standing there must be someone ...'

'The chief soprano is off with a fish bone stuck in her throat and Sigrid Hallstein collapsed in her dressing room and is believed to be having a miscarriage.'

Ransu Prokopi amplified this when Tina was taken to meet him. He was a small man in his forties with hair receding from a high forehead and a trim, jutting beard. Tina had never heard him conduct, but she could believe that it would be an electrifying experience as he turned his black, glittering eyes on her and she felt the force of his personality.

'We have made three telephone calls, but there is not one suitable soprano available within two hours' drive,' he said. 'If you are capable of carrying this part we will at least give a performance. You have sung it in full, in public?'

'Three times, but not with an orchestra of this calibre,' Tina said.

'With whom are you studying at the Guildhall?'

'Professor Moon and Betrys Jones.'

'This in itself is a recommendation. What roles are you performing here in Germany this summer?'

'Susanna, Rosalinda and Fiordiligi.'

'So ... you have a voice, I'm told. Here is a piano. Your friend, Mr Walden, will play for you and I will listen.'

Tina cast a desperate look at Tom.

'Fiordiligi's "*Come scoglio*",' he suggested.

Tina nodded and went to stand by the piano. She resented having to plunge into an aria cold, but there was no with-standing the Finnish conductor's insistence.

She had sung no more than half the aria when he stopped her.

'Yes, I am satisfied. You have a fine voice. Here is the score of the *Requiem*. Follow it, but above all, watch me. I will carry you through.'

He put both his hands on the tops of her arms and gripped them with such force that Tina winced.

'You can do it,' he said.

He spoke with such conviction that Tina could only nod, as if she were hypnotised. Suddenly it seemed possible, but she knew that she must have time to pull herself together.

'I want five minutes alone,' she said.

'You shall have it. An announcement will have to be made. Come, Mr Walden, leave your friend.' At the door he turned. 'I almost forgot, what is your name?'

'Valentina Burford.'

'Very well, Valentina Burford, I will return in five minutes to lead you on to the platform.'

Tina stood completely still in the middle of the room after they had left her. She knew that Tom had turned to smile and make a gesture of encouragement as he went out, but she was incapable of acknowledging it. She was cold right through; she could observe herself, but she was unable to move, scarcely able to think. So this was it: stage fright. Something completely different from the flutterings in the stomach that had afflicted her on previous occasions. And she had got to get over it.

She moved to the piano and struck four notes, singing them over on an ascending scale: 'I can do it, I can do it, I can do it, I CAN do it.'

She was released from her frozen terror. She could even smile. Of course she could do it. It was not the debut she would have chosen, but in spite of the disadvantages it was a chance most young singers would give their eyeteeth for.

Quickly, Tina ran through a couple of scales, warming up her vocal cords, then again she fell silent, composing herself. When Ransu Prokopi returned she did not speak, but she looked at him calmly and the hand she put in his was steady. He nodded and led her out on to the platform with the other soloists. Mafalda Romolo, a large Italian, billowing in black with a scattering of sequins, gave her a warm generous smile, while the tenor and the baritone nodded encouragingly.

They were in a pool of light with the orchestra all round and the chorus banked behind them. Ransu Prokopi lifted his baton and Tina heard the soft opening chorus ... *'Requiem ... requiem eterna ...'*

She kept her eyes fixed on the conductor and for the first time experienced the magnetism that flowed out from a truly great musician. The score was open in her hands and Tina was careful to keep an eye on it for any special marks that had been inserted at rehearsal, but apart from that she hardly needed it. She knew it, and she never doubted her memory. What she needed, and what she fed on, was the confidence that streamed towards her from Ransu Prokopi.

Her duets with Mafalda Romolo went well and Tina was conscious of the generosity of the older and more experienced singer towards a younger artist. She began to feel exhilarated, but all the time at the back of her mind was the thought of the great *'Libera me'* with which the soprano ended the *Requiem*. Inexorably they moved towards it and then she would be truly exposed, with only her technique and her musicality to carry her through.

She had a moment to think ... *'Libera me ... '* Yes! This was what she had been fighting for ever since a chance meeting with an older singer had turned her mind towards a singing career. God, set me free. Give me this liberty to sing – or let me die.

After that she had no time to think of anything except the words, the music, the placing of every note, the movement of the tip of Ransu Prokopi's baton, the encouragement of his left hand as he lifted her towards a crescendo. The last few bars were on her ... *'Libera me, libera me ... '*

There was a moment of silence and then the applause crashing all round her. Tina stood in bewilderment. Was it over? Yes, it was over. She had got through. She must remember to bow. The other three soloists were bowing. Ransu Prokopi was bowing. He was advancing on her, he was taking her hand and kissing it. There was a rustle of taffeta and then she was enveloped in a large embrace as Mafalda Romolo kissed her on both cheeks.

Ransu Prokopi was leading her forward to take a bow all on her own. The orchestra was applauding, so was the choir. Tina looked round doubtfully, then she began to smile. Instead of a bow she sank into a low, beautiful curtsey, a dancer's curtsey, and the applause seemed to redouble. Bouquets were being brought on and there was one for her. Sigrid Hallstein, in the midst of her own pain and disappointment, had diverted some of her flowers to the young, unknown soprano who had taken her place. Tina could see Tom and her friends in their good seats

75

near the front of the auditorium. Tom was on his feet with his arms high in the air, applauding wildly. She sent him a special smile and hoped he saw it.

They were led off the stage and brought back and again, Tina was forced to take a separate bow. She was beginning to feel the muscles in her cheeks aching from smiling so much, but at last they were allowed to go. Mafalda was exclaiming volubly in Italian, the two German soloists were shaking her hand and kissing her cheek. Tina looked at Ransu Prokopi and raised her eyebrows, silently asking a question.

'It was not the best performance I have ever heard,' he said. 'But you did well, very well. One day, when you have matured, when you have had more experience, you may be a truly great singer. Your preference is for opera?'

'Yes.' Tina could say no more.

'You are right. You have the dramatic ability. Verdi, I think, hm?'

'I hope so, though *Tosca* is one of my dreams, too.'

'Yes, one day that may suit you very well. Perhaps, who knows, I may be your conductor.'

'I hope you are,' Tina said sincerely. 'Tonight ... you were wonderful. I felt ... I don't know how to express it ...'

'I know. I, too, was conscious of your response. We worked well together. We must do it again. I will write to Randolf Moon and tell him I approve of his pupil.'

'You know him?'

'Of course. We are old friends. And now, Miss Burford, what are you going to do for the rest of the evening?'

'My friends in the audience ...'

'Ah, yes, of course. They will be wanting to fête you. Do not drink too much German wine.'

He was turning away. It was all over. Tina felt blank, and completely drained. When Tom came bursting in she flung her arms round him and clung to him, shaking and crying with reaction.

'Now, now, this isn't the time to throw a temperament,' he chided her. 'Tina, you were wonderful. Wonderful, wonderful, wonderful. We're going to paint the town red.

We're so proud of you we could burst.'

The others were crowding in behind him, loud in their praise of her performance.

'What did Prokopi say?' Tom demanded.

'He said it wasn't the best performance he'd heard, but that I did very well.'

'Oh, great praise! Grudging devil. You were *magnificent*. Come on, pull yourself together, girl, and I'll buy you a drink.'

'Has anyone said anything about your fee?' one of the others asked.

'That's a practical question,' Tom said approvingly. 'I shall appoint myself your business manager, Tina, and make enquiries.'

He was back in a few minutes with a limp-looking manager, who seized Tina's hand and shook it with the fervour of great relief.

'We all thank you a thousand times,' he said. 'To step in at such short notice and to do so well! Everyone is overcome with astonishment.'

'And Miss Burford will receive the appropriate professional fee for her services,' Tom said firmly.

'Of course. A cheque will be sent off tomorrow. In the meantime, I would like to take some of your personal details for the benefit of the Press.'

With her head in a whirl, Tina supplied information about her training and her scanty career, and Tom craftily added a word or two about their tour of Germany.

The celebration was joyous. Tina felt her eyes misting over at her friends' generous pleasure in her success.

'Not coming over wobbly again, are you?' Tom asked quietly.

Tina turned to smile at him and then leaned back to rest her head against his.

'Everyone's being so nice to me,' she said.

'Tired?'

'Mm, but restless, too. I'd like to go, but I don't want to spoil the party.'

'Why don't we leave the others to it? I'll give the keys of the van to George and tell him you don't want the long drive back tonight. I'll find a room and we'll stay the night here in Cologne.'

'Together?'

'That's what I had in mind.'

He spoke evenly, but there was an undercurrent of urgency behind his words. Tina began to feel the warm glow Tom always aroused in her beginning to expand until it filled her whole body. She moved her head against his in a little nod of consent.

They left the restaurant followed by knowing catcalls from their ribald friends, but Tina was past caring about that. She let Tom take charge, not without an inner amusement at the cool affrontery with which he engaged a room for a couple without a scrap of luggage between them.

'Not even a toothbrush,' she remarked.

'Are you bothered?'

'I won't make an issue of it.'

The room was impersonal, with every modern comfort, but no character. It was not important, nothing was important except the way Tom looked at her as she began to undress. Tina was surprised to realise that she felt no shyness. With Tom everything seemed natural, even the sight of his own naked body.

'I suppose you're going to tell me you developed those muscles sheepshearing?' she asked, amazed that she could joke with him at such a moment.

'Too right I did. After tossing a few hundred sheep on their backs I can handle a bit of a girl like you with no trouble at all. Like this.'

He caught hold of her neatly and laid her on the bed, sprawling by her side with his arm across her to hold her down.

'No need for force,' Tina said. 'I'm more than willing. Dear Tom . . .'

'My lovely girl,' Tom whispered with his lips against her throat. 'My singing bird. Ah, Tina, Tina . . .'

There was laughter and passion and a beautiful tenderness in their lovemaking. All night, Tina thought drowsily; we've got all night, and I love him, oh, I do love him.

She drifted off to sleep and woke again to Tom's hands

moving over her body to rouse her to love him again. They clung together with little exclamations and grunts of pleasure until Tina heard herself give a strange, hoarse cry she had never uttered before. They were one person, completely charged with one another, so that it seemed as if they would never separate, but at last Tom's hold slackened and he moved to lie, spent and satisfied, with his head on her breast.

Tina could do no more than move her fingers gently against his back, but she knew that Tom understood the meaning of that slight gesture; her gratitude, her delight and her overwhelming love for him.

They slept late into the morning and Tina only woke up when Tom slipped out of bed and went into the bathroom. She heard him moving about and smiled to herself. Nice, domestic noises. When he returned she was sitting up in bed, hugging her knees. Tom had a newspaper in his hand.

'It was pushed under the door,' he explained. 'I asked them last night to be sure to see that we got one. Let's see if they managed to get anything about you into it.'

They found the reviews and between them began to translate.

'"Young English soprano takes over at last minute,"' Tom read. '"Fräulein Valentina Burford, twenty-one-year-old student at the renowned Guildhall School of Music in London was ... um ... removed ... plucked out of the audience last night to sing the soprano part in Verdi's *Requiem* ..."'

'Never mind all that, what does he say about my performance?' Tina demanded.

'"After a tentative start — understandable in the circumstance ..."'

'I was *petrified*.'

'" ... Fräulein Burford gave a performance of ... um ... professional standard ..."'

'So I should hope!'

'"This is a talent and a voice which could well be of world stature in the future. In particular, Valentina Burford's dramatic ability was in front ..." no ... "well to the fore in the demanding *'Libera me'*. which she sang with control and passion."'

Tom scanned the rest of the review. 'Then he says a bit about what we're doing here in Germany,' he said. 'Which should be good for business. And, of course, he compliments the other singers and Prokopi. It's a good notice, Tina, really good. Now, talking about control and passion . . .'

'No, Tom,' Tina said, dodging his clutching hands. 'I must get up.'

'Do you love me?'

'You know I do.'

They kissed gently, but Tina resisted Tom's attempt to push her back against the pillows once more.

'You're not going back to your keeping-me-at-arm's-length policy, I hope,' Tom asked.

'I couldn't,' Tina said honestly. 'Not after this night. Tom . . . tell me, truly, was I really any good?'

Tom rolled over on his back and grinned up at the ceiling.

'Any other man would think from that you were enquiring about your performance in bed,' he said. 'As a fellow artist I know you've got your mind fixed on the concert hall.'

'So, was I any good?'

'Almost frighteningly so. That notice, it's cautious because the critic is an old fuddy-duddy who won't commit himself. You were superb.'

'Prokopi didn't say that.'

'He knew. I've never heard the *"Libera me"* sung with such emotional intensity.' He turned to her and touched her cheek with his hand. 'Don't get too far ahead of me, I want to be with you.'

'And I want to be with you, too. Darling Tom.'

'Incidentally, your performance in bed wasn't too bad either. All you need is a bit of practice. Just put yourself in my expert hands.'

'Not now,' Tina said firmly. 'Who was it called a rehearsal of scenes from *Così* this morning? And who is going to be late for it?'

'Don Alfonso and Fiordiligi. All right, all right, I'll let you get up. Do you want some breakfast?'

'I certainly do. I'm ravenous!'

Tina detected a change in her standing in their little company after that evening. Before, she had been the junior member, in spite of her fine voice. Now she was respected, perhaps even envied. On the whole, it passed Tina by. All her waking moments – and all her sleeping ones, too – were spent with Tom. Their physical need of one another set them apart from their friends. They were still willing to spend a convivial hour talking over a performance or making plans ahead, but the time would come when Tina would feel that Tom was watching her, their eyes would meet, their hands would stretch out to touch one another and they would leave their friends' cheerful company to find passionate solitude once again.

Tina knew what was going to happen when they returned to England and, sure enough, Tom said on the ferry before they landed, 'You'll shack up with me from now on?'

It was only half a question, he was sure of her answer. He turned his head to look at her in surprise when Tina did not agree immediately.

'We're eating one another up,' she said slowly. 'Can it go on?'

'I don't see how we can live apart.'

She had to agree with that. The thought of being cooped up with three other girls while Tom lived alone in his own room was absurd.

'My people won't like it,' she said.

'Don't tell them.'

'I might be able to swing it,' Tina admitted. 'Ros will help.'

She knew her friend well enough to know that Rosamund would be thrilled to hear that Tina had embarked on a full-scale love affair and, sure enough, Rosamund promised to co-operate in keeping her change of address a secret from the Burfords.

In duty bound, Tina went home to see her parents as soon as she arrived in England. She was not aware of how her summer abroad had changed her until they commented on it.

'My word, you must have been having a good time,' Will said. 'I've never seen you look so well. Isn't that right, Elsie?'

Elsie looked at Tina's long, golden limbs, her glowing face and tumbled, unkempt hair, but she saw more than her husband and her lips tightened.

'You've certainly been out in the sun,' she said.

'We had wonderful weather,' Tina agreed. 'And such fun! I've gained a lot of experience ...'

'Yes, I can see that,' Elsie said, and her tone made Tina flush.

'Something absolutely wonderful happened! I sang with the Berlin Philharmonic!'

She plunged into an account of her evening of triumph, hoping to divert her mother's mind, but she could see that neither of them really understood the magnitude of her achievement.

As soon as they were alone, Elsie asked abruptly, 'Are you going to bring your Tom home to see us?'

'Well, I hadn't planned ... I suppose I could ... of course, he's going to be working terribly hard between now and Christmas; we all are.'

'Excuses. If you're not ashamed of him I should think you'd want us to meet him.'

'Of course I'm not ashamed of him! He's wonderful! I mean, he's a fine singer and the way he organised our tour was first class ...'

'And you're head over heels in love with him. Are you going to marry him?'

'We've not talked about it,' Tina said shortly.

'I see. That means there's no hope of it. You'll end up living with him, doing everything a wife does, with none of the standing of a wife and no legal rights.'

Tina opened her mouth to say that she and Tom were already living together and then decided against it. After the elaborate deception she had set up with Rosamund it would be silly to cave in and tell her mother at the first challenge.

She fled back to London, back to Tom, and they fell into one another's arms as if they had been separated for two months instead of two days. Tom had a bed-sitter with a gas ring and a very small shower room. It was wonderful to have him entirely to herself, but after a day or two Tina admitted to missing the kitchen at the flat she had shared with the girls.

'Grotty it certainly was, but at least we had a proper cooker and a fridge and somewhere to do the washing up,' she remarked.

'You don't want to waste time cooking, do you?' Tom asked in surprise. 'Shall I get a microwave oven? Would that satisfy your housewifely instincts?'

'It'd be better than nothing,' Tina said.

They settled into a routine, eating take-aways and reheated food, or cold meat and salads. Once a week Tina bundled together their dirty clothes and their sheets and towels and took them to a nearby launderette. She also bought a duster and a floor cloth, items Tom seemed to think unnecessary, and she borrowed a vacuum cleaner from the girl across the hall and ran it over the room.

'I never figured you for such a domesticated sheila,' Tom remarked idly, using the Australian idiom that meant he was teasing her.

'I'm more my mother's daughter than I ever realised,' Tina admitted. 'Right now I'm thinking of killing you for lying on the bed on my clean counterpane without taking your shoes off.'

'Come and kill me with kindness,' Tom said, holding out a hand.

She went to him, laughing and grumbling, and they spent the rest of the afternoon making love. It was wonderful, as always, but afterwards Tina twisted herself away from Tom and sat back on her heels.

'I ought to be studying,' she said.

'Go ahead. I'll lie here and admire your chest development.'

'You ought to be studying, too.'

'Slave-driver. OK, so we both ought to be doing something different from what we've just been doing. Who's watching?'

'I can't afford to slip,' Tina said. 'The Prof was talking to me yesterday. He'd heard from Ransu Prokopi. It sounded like a very kind letter, but the trouble is that after having had a bit of a triumph ...'

'A total triumph.'

'More is expected of me than ever. He's talking about auditions and ... and ...'

'And?'

'The Gold Medal.'

'My God!' Tom sat up. 'I'm only an irreverent Aussie, but the thought of my girl being awarded the Guildhall Gold Medal makes even me break out in a cold sweat. What shall I do? Go down on my knees?'

'No thanks. What you can do,' Tina said evenly, 'is take the washing to the launderette this week. You did it for yourself before I joined you, why not now?'

There was a short silence and then Tom said, 'Am I being told something?'

'As you'd say yourself, too right you are!'

'Right. OK. I've been behaving like the sort of man back home who expects the little woman to be waiting with a hot meal whenever he chooses to leave the pub.'

'I wouldn't put it like that, but you might perhaps recognise that on career terms we're equal and I don't deserve to be made to do all the household chores while you concentrate on a tricky aria.'

She held her breath, amused but slightly regretful that Tom was not entirely pleased at having his shortcomings pointed out to him. She counted on his fair-mindedness and, sure enough, after only the slightest of pauses he laughed and said, 'I can't argue with that. Get some clothes on, woman, and stop distracting me. I'll take myself off to the Washeteria and you can spend an hour or two practising.'

They were working hard for the Open Days which were to be held at the college in November. Tina was to sing a solo at a concert to which she invited both her parents and her Aunt Daphne.

Quite apart from giving them a chance to see where she studied and to hear how much she had improved, it also provided the opportunity Tina had been looking for to introduce them to Tom without making too much of an event of it.

Tom made an immediate hit, as Tina had suspected he would. His easy good nature and forthright manner put Elsie and Will at their ease and his looks guaranteed his success with Daphne.

'My dear! Those biceps!' she murmured in Tina's ear. 'He's built like a young ox. And a splendid voice as well. Lucky, lucky girl.'

Tina was afraid that her aunt's flirtatious manner would grate on Tom, but he took it in his stride, insisting that she was a household name in Australia and her recording of *Stars Above* had been one of his most cherished possessions.

'You and Tina are very alike,' he remarked. 'Anyone could see there's a family connection.'

'Daphne and Tina both take after my mother,' Elsie said. 'She was tall and fair.'

'And she should have had a career on the stage,' Daphne put in. 'She always encouraged me and she'd have been pleased as Punch at the way you're going ahead, Tina. My news is that I'm branching out into something different. There's going to be a new television quiz show and I've been invited to be on the permanent team. Only half a dozen shows to begin with, but if it takes off it could run and run.'

She sounded complacent, as if sure that the new programme would be a success. The last time Tina had seen her aunt she had thought that Daphne had begun to fade, but now there was an aura of success about her. She was wearing very expensive new clothes, her hair and complexion were perfect and her figure was as alluring as it had ever been.

She was, after all, only forty-one. There was no reason why she should not still be a vital, sexy woman and, judging by the sultry looks she was giving Tom, she still had confidence in her ability to attract a man, even one who was so much younger. The thought of Annis came into Tina's mind. Annis and Oliver ... but that affair had begun to peter out. She must try to see them next time she went home for the weekend. It would interest Annis to hear about her German experiences and Tina knew that she would not be able to resist indulging in a little boasting about the way she had taken over and performed Verdi's *Requiem*.

'Wake up, Tina,' Tom said. 'Aunt Daphne's inviting us all to go and have a slap-up meal at her expense.'

Daphne was laughing in response to his mischievous smile.

'Plain "Daphne" to you, if you don't mind,' she said. 'I refuse to be an auntie to a young man of your size.'

The dinner was more of a success than Tina had expected, and that was mostly due to Tom's tactful handling of her parents. It was Tom who drew out Elsie's chair and saw her settled at the table; it was Tom who relieved Will of the worry of appearing to know something about wine by insisting that they must drink the only Australian wine he could find on the list. He parried Daphne's advances, but adroitly, so that she did not take offence, and only Tina knew that all the time his foot was pressed down hard on hers under the table.

They were all charmed by him. So much so, that Tina was suspicous. When the evening was over and Daphne had been seen into a taxi and Will and Elsie escorted to the railway station, Tina challenged him as they wandered back to his lodgings with their arms wrapped tightly round one another.

'What's going on?' she demanded. 'You've been playing up to my mum and dad as if you wanted something from them.'

'I do. I want them to like me.'

'They do that all right. Mum's so won over she'd probably take it in her stride if she knew we were living together. Was that the idea?'

'Sort of. I wasn't going to tell you, not just yet, but I'm hoping they'll see what a good idea it is for you to come and spend Christmas in Australia with me.'

Tina stopped dead in the middle of the street.

'You never told me. That you were going home for Christmas, I mean.'

'I've been undecided, but then something happened that made up my mind. Tina, come with me. It'll be fabulous and my mum and dad are dying to meet you.'

'You've told them about me?'

'Yes − for a particular reason. Look, we're nearly home. Wait until we're inside and then I'll explain.'

As soon as they were inside the tiny flatlet, Tom took her in his arms and kissed her.

'I love you. You know that, don't you?'

'Mm, and I love you, too. Why do I feel something ominous is looming up?'

'I'm sure I don't know, unless you're going to turn down what I see as a super deal. Mum and Dad asked me what I wanted for Christmas and I said what I most wanted was to have my best girl with me, so they've offered to pay your fare, as a present to me.'

'That's fantastic! It takes my breath away! Tom, the fare to Australia costs *hundreds* ...'

'I told you my folks weren't without a penny or two,' Tom said apologetically.

'Even so ... It's incredibly generous of them.'

'You haven't said yes,' Tom said, watching her.

'I'm still trying to get my breath back.'

But there was more to it than that. 'I've been brought up to look a gift horse in the mouth,' Tina said with a wry smile. 'Tom, we are talking about my *return* fare, aren't we?'

'If you decide that's what you want.'

'Are you trying to tell me you won't be coming back yourself?'

'I've been offered an audition with the Sydney Opera House. If it's successful, I'm very tempted to stay in Australia and begin my career there.'

Tina began to feel herself going cold. Tom permanently in Australia, while she ...

'What about me? she asked in a small voice.

'Apply for an audition, too. You're perfectly ready for it, in my opinion.'

'I've still got a year to do at the Guildhall.'

'Chuck it. Well ... make sure of a place in Sydney and then chuck it.'

'If you knew how I fought to get this two years' training! Tom, I can't ...'

'Why not? Tina, what I'm trying to say is, marry me.

Together we'd be a magnificent team. I wouldn't stand in the way of your career, I promise.'

'Oh, Tom!' Tina felt frantically for a handkerchief. 'You're such a darling and I love you so much.'

'Then will you be Mrs Walden? Please?'

He was holding out his hands to her, smiling and hopeful, but Tina evaded him.

'Let me have time to think.' She pressed her clenched fists against her temples, trying to bring some order to her chaotic thoughts.

'If your audition in Sydney isn't successful, what will you do?' she asked.

'That'd be a facer! Come back to London, I suppose.'

'And suppose I were offered a place and you weren't?'

She had posed a question to which Tom could find no ready answer. The silence between them grew and grew.

'You'd expect me to come back with you, wouldn't you?' Tina asked quietly.

Still Tom did not reply. He sat down on the edge of the bed, his shoulders hunched and a puzzled look on his face.

'It's a contingency I hadn't even thought about,' he admitted. 'Tina, it won't happen. They're genuinely interested in me. I may not get leading roles straight away, I don't expect it, but I'm sure I can get a contract.'

'That's not the point,' Tina said. 'You haven't understood me if you think it is. What I'm saying is that once we're married and have a joint career you'll see me as some sort of appendage. If you come back to London, then I come too. That's what you really think, isn't it?'

'I want to be with you. I can't imagine living without you, not after the way things have been between us since Germany. I'm not playing about, Tina. My whole life is bound up in you. Parting with you ... it doesn't bear thinking about. Come to Australia with me. It'll work out, you'll see.'

'You haven't answered my question. Do you believe that a wife's place is with her husband?'

It cost Tom a struggle, but at last he said reluctantly, 'Yes.'

'So do I,' Tina said, but when Tom looked up hopefully,

she hurried on, 'and that's why I can't marry you. I'm not ready for it, Tom. At this point in my life my career has got to come first.'

Tom was beginning to get angry. 'I didn't realise you were so ambitious,' he said.

'It's not ambition,' Tina said. 'Not exactly. It's a terrible, burning *need*.'

'What about my need?' Abandoning words, Tom took hold of her and held her closely against him. 'I want you, Tina. All the time. It's never been like this before. You can't turn me down.'

For a moment Tina was swept away on a tide of passion as dizzying as it had been on their first night together, but when at last Tom reluctantly took his mouth away from hers, she struggled to free herself.

'I can't do what you want,' she said. 'I'll go on with you like this for as long as you like, but to throw up my training, go and live in another country, commit myself to marriage – no, that's not for me, not now.'

'Then come to Australia just for Christmas. Take up my parents' offer. If nothing else, it's a free ride.'

'It's not free,' Tina said. 'There are strings attached. I'm afraid that if I'm with you over Christmas, in a family atmosphere, I may weaken ...'

'Good! That's what I'm counting on.'

'I know. I dare say we'd be wonderfully happy – for a time.'

'For always. We were made for each other. Oh, sure, I know we can't always live in fairyland, we'll have our ups and downs, but fundamentally we belong together, you and I. Come to Australia and let me have a chance to prove it to you.'

'I daren't.'

Tom drew away from her. 'That's a damn funny thing to say.'

'I know. I don't really understand it myself. I don't know how I can turn down the chance to live with you for the rest of my life, but I know I've got to. Because the day will come when I'll stop being satisfied with loving you and being Mrs Tom Walden. I'm Valentina Burford.'

'I've told you I won't interfere with your career. Of course I expect you to go on singing ...'

'To go on singing! God, Tom, you make it sound like a nice hobby! I want more than that. I want all the leading roles I'm capable of performing in all the great opera houses in the world. I don't just want to make music. I want to *be* music!'

'You want to be famous. The great diva!'

'I don't care about fame,' Tina said slowly. 'Not the outward show. I want acknowledgement, yes, of course I do, but mostly I want it from fellow musicians, people who really know.'

The memory of the rapport there had been between her and Ransu Prokopo came back to her, but she did not want to speak about that to Tom, not while he was so wilfully misunderstanding her.

The argument raged on, sometimes angrily, sometimes with bewildered hurt on both sides, but Tina would not be budged.

They went on living together and even turned to one another and made love in a despairing effort to heal the rift between them, but always afterwards Tom would whisper, 'Change your mind, Tina. Tina, change your mind', and Tina would answer 'No.'

In the end they could neither of them stand it any longer. Tina packed her bags and went back to her old flat with Rosamund and the other girls.

'You look terrible,' Rosamund said bluntly.

'I feel it. I'm split in two, Ros. Part of me is screaming to give in and follow Tom round the world and the other half knows it would be an almighty mistake. If I can manage to hold out until he's gone then I'll be safe.'

Rosamund looked at her friend curiously. 'That's a funny way of putting it. Safe!'

'It's the way I feel. If I once put a foot over this precipice then there's no way back for me. Before I know where I am I'll be domesticated. First a wife, then a mother, and never Valentina Burford, never again. I must fight against it, I must.'

'Poor old Tom.'

'That's the worst thing of all, knowing I'm hurting him. I love him so much.'

Tina put her head down on the kitchen table, the tears that came to her all too readily these days running down her face. 'I mustn't cry,' she said fiercely. 'I've got a class in an hour's time.'

'That says it all,' Rosamund told her. 'Even though you're howling with grief you've still got your mind fixed on your next tutorial.' She gave a little shiver. 'I don't think I could be so strong-minded. I only hope I'm never put to the test.'

Chapter Six

The letter arrived out of the blue at a time when Oliver and Annis were busy settling her programme for the second half of 1987.

'An air letter from the States,' Oliver remarked, tossing it on one side unopened. 'If it's an invitation to go over, how would you feel?'

'Delighted, but if all these plans we've been making materialise then I'm going to be too busy until next year.'

She sounded pleased. Neither of them put it into words, but they both knew she was having to work hard to re-establish a reputation that had been tarnished by a less than successful recital in the autumn of the previous year. Oliver had warned her, but Annis had been determined to attempt everything she had been able to do in her heyday and had refused to acknowledge that she no longer had quite the range or flexibility she had once taken for granted. The critics had been polite in what they wrote, but there was a note of regret for past splendours which had grated on Annis, outraged at a hint that she might be past her prime and unfamiliar with anything but ecstatic reviews. After her first fury had subsided she had become thoughtful. She had never admitted that he had been right, but when Oliver had managed to secure a series of concerts for her during 1987 she had accepted his guidance on her repertoire without any of the arguments she had put forward before that unfortunate evening.

She had attended to her looks, too, losing a little weight, growing her hair and wearing it in a softer style, and spending a great deal of money on new gowns for her platform appearances. She was as lovely and vital as ever and only Oliver knew that the effect was now achieved by an effort and willpower which Annis had once been able to channel solely into her singing.

Their relations had subsided into a loving friendship, without passion, and if Annis regretted that Oliver no longer came to her bed she was too proud to admit it. For the most part they continued to live amicably under the same roof, he was her unvarying escort and he managed her affairs with a dedication she would have found in no one else, but Oliver had acquired a small flat in London and he did not find it necessary to tell Annis everything he did while he was there.

For Annis, approaching fifty, it was a rather more satisfactory arrangement than it was for Oliver. He had tried to break away, knowing that it would be easier and kinder to leave Annis while she still retained a satisfactory career and a radiance that made everyone believe she was years younger than her actual age, but the tie between them still held and Annis resisted his efforts to untie the knot rather than cut through it.

Oliver finished inking in Annis's firm commitments for the coming year on the chart he had prepared for her and then turned to the unopened letter from America, which had been addressed to him.

Annis was immersed in a letter from one of her family in Australia when Oliver exclaimed, 'Oh, my God!'

'Trouble?' Annis asked, looking up.

'The last thing I ever anticipated. Did you know that Michael Peador's correspondence and manuscripts had been acquired by Harvard University?'

'No, that's news to me.'

'This man – Dr Theodore Bayermann – has been sorting and cataloguing the papers and he's discovered Bruno's letter asking for Peador's opinion on my opera. He's sent me a photostat of it.'

Annis came and stood behind him to read the letter over his shoulder. 'A kind and generous letter,' she said softly.

'Yes, I'm glad to have seen it. I never knew what Bruno

93

had written about me. But there's more. Bayermann has also found the copies of the manuscript Bruno enclosed with the letter.'

'Your missing arias!'

'My pirated arias,' Oliver said grimly. 'You see what this Dr Bayermann says – "I was immediately struck by the great similarity between your work and certain passages in Peador's opera *Astolat*. I wonder whether you can offer any explanation for this apparent coincidence." That's academic-speak for "red-hot scandal". What the devil am I to do?'

'Tell the truth,' Annis said without hesitation.

'After all this time? Without Bruno to back me up? You only had a vague idea of what I was doing. He was the only person who *knew* that I'd nearly completed my opera when we went to Milan and heard part of it being performed note for note as Peador's *Astolat*. He was the only one who knew there was no way I could have lifted the music from Peador, it had to be the other way round.'

'Michael Peador is dead.'

'And his reputation is growing. To attack that reputation now – every music critic in the world would be howling for my blood.'

'I can't bear to think of your work being wasted.'

'Hardly wasted,' Oliver said drily. '*Astolat* is scheduled for performance at the Wexford Festival some time in the near future.'

'While you have no recognition at all! It's so unjust Oliver. If you don't write and tell this Dr What's-his-name the truth then I will.'

'I'd rather handle it myself,' Oliver said. 'I suppose you're right. Once the genie has been let out of the bottle there's no stuffing him back in again.'

He wrote a careful letter, setting out the facts without accusations or recriminations, and concluded by pointing out that in the devastation caused by Bruno's death on the first night of *Astolat* his own loss had faded into the background.

He received a cable within a week: 'Immensely excited by revelation. Arriving London next week. Talk to no one.'

'What does he think I'm going to do — hold a Press conference?' Oliver enquired sourly.

Apparently that was precisely what Dr Bayermann did expect. It was beyond his comprehension that a serious composer could stand by and see his work used by someone else without lifting a finger to claim the credit that was due to him, and he said so forcefully when he and Oliver met.

'Cast your mind back,' Oliver said. 'Remember the acclamation that greeted *Astolat*, the fuss that was made because one of the elder statesmen of Western music had produced a major work at the age of eighty-two. Then think what the reaction would have been if an unknown composer in his twenties had upped and said "actually, part of it's by me".'

'You have a point,' Dr Bayermann admitted.

'And remember it was weeks after the first night before I was in a fit state to do anything. That was the night of the accident that robbed us of Bruno Marcellini, crippled Annis Gilroy and injured me badly enough to put me in hospital.'

'Everything conspired against you.'

'It seemed so at the time. And then Michael Peador died. Did you read the obituaries?'

'I wrote one of them.'

'It would have been a brave man who took it on himself to tarnish that reputation. If I'd known that the proof still existed ... but I took it for granted that he'd destroyed Bruno's letter and my music manuscript.'

'I wonder why he didn't?'

'His mind wasn't what it had been,' Annis said. She had been following the discussion keenly and now she offered a suggestion that softened Michael Peador's guilt and made it easier to accept. 'I suspect that he set the words of his libretto to Oliver's music, perhaps as an exercise, perhaps out of surprise that the two fitted together so well, perhaps in a despairing attempt to get his own inspiration flowing again — he'd been working on *Astolat* for years — and then forgot what he'd done.'

'It's a possibility,' Oliver agreed.

'His straggling writing towards the end, the way he

obviously had difficulty in getting anything down on paper, certainly supports that theory,' Dr Bayermann said. 'The question is, what are we going to do about it now?'

'You accept that the three arias are my work?' Oliver asked.

'Oh, sure! It's always been a talking point, the newness of certain passages in *Astolat*, the sudden resurgence of a talent that had faltered. People have mourned the fact that Peador didn't live to exploit the fresh turn his work had taken. This explains everything. Besides, the date of Marcellini's letter, his absolute belief in you and the fact that Miss Gilroy can confirm that you were all stunned by the discovery of your work included in the opera on its first night − it all fits together. What I want to know is, would you be prepared to keep quiet about it until I've had a chance to write the book I'm preparing on Peador?'

Oliver barely hesitated. 'No,' he said. 'That would mean waiting at least another year, more like two probably. Now that the discovery's been made I want it out in the open.'

'At least let me be the one to break the story,' Dr Bayermann pleaded.

'You sound more like a journalist than an academic music historian,' Oliver said with some amusement. 'No, I'm sorry, but that's not the way I intend to handle it. I shall write a letter to a reputable music journal, setting out the facts, and I'll refer them to you for confirmation.'

It started off quietly, just as Oliver had intended, but inevitably the story got into the newspapers and aroused an interest for which he was hardly prepared. He was interviewed by the Press and appeared on the radio and television. He stuck doggedly to the theory Annis had supplied, that the old man had forgotten the origin of the music he had incorporated into his opera, but even that threw an unwelcome light on a composer who had been revered.

'What I want to know, and what no one seems to have asked, is whether Oliver ever finished his opera?' Tina said, scanning the headlines.

'I bet he didn't. He'd been too discouraged,' Rosamund

said. 'It makes me feel quite funny, him having this tre-mendous secret. I always said he was intriguing.'

'You said a lot of daft things about Oliver,' Tina said. 'What I'm thinking about is a Guildhall production.'

'Tina! We couldn't!'

'Why not? If we have to do yet another obscure work by Handel I'll scream. I'm going to visit Oliver next weekend.'

She found Oliver at home and resigned to his notoriety. Annis, on the other hand, was as pleased and excited as if she had written the opera herself.

'I can't think why I didn't insist that he came out in the open years ago,' she said.

Tina suppressed a guilty suspicion that it was because Annis was too taken up with her own career to remember the importance of Oliver's work.

'Oliver, is the opera finished?' she asked.

'All but. I chucked the manuscript into a bottom drawer in disgust, but I can't say I ever really forgot it. Now, of course, all sorts of people are suggesting I should dust it off and complete it.'

'Is it likely to be put on?'

'I doubt it. It's a nine-day wonder, this controversy over Peador. In the end what will happen is that his opera will go on being performed and I'll get a mention as a 'collaborator'. Mounting a new opera is an expensive business and everyone's a bit disconcerted at the idea of performing one with music in it that's thought to belong elsewhere.'

'A concert performance?' Annis suggested.

'That's a possibility. God knows when, because most orchestras and singers are booked up years ahead.'

'What about a student performance?' Tina asked. 'At the Guildhall? An end of term production?'

Oliver and Annis considered the idea while Tina held her breath. Looking at her intent face, Oliver had to smile. 'See yourself in the lead, do you?' he asked.

'Of course. Whatever opera we perform, I'll have the leading soprano role. Or if it's not me then it'll be Rosamund,' Tina said simply. 'We're the best.'

'Oh, the confidence of youth!' Oliver mocked her. 'OK, I'll agree. How do you want to set about it? Shall I approach the Guildhall or will you?'

'You make the formal offer and I'll nobble the Prof. I'm his blue-eyed girl since Ransu Prokopi wrote and said nice things about me. It'll be a tremendous coup for the college.'

'I suppose you're expecting me to waive my right to a performing fee?'

'Please. You know how poor we are. And it'll be great publicity for you.'

'I'm into publicity up to here,' Oliver said, holding his hand above his head. 'Money is rather more difficult to come by. All right, I'll waive my royalties, but I'll expect generous treatment in the way of free seats. Maybe I can get a critic or two to come along, which will be good for you and for me.'

'Brilliant. Do get down to work straight away and polish off the score, won't you?'

'Subject to one or two other little things I have to do.'

'No, Tina is right, you must give this priority,' Annis said. 'When I go to Wales next week you'll stay at home. I insist, Oliver. I've monopolised you for far too long.'

Almost imperceptibly, the break was engineered. Annis toured without Oliver at her side to make sure that all her arrangements went smoothly and was made ruefully aware of how much he had done for her in the past.

Something seemed to have happened to Oliver. The thought of having his discarded opera performed set the adrenalin flowing. He put his second opera on one side and worked in a fever of creative energy to complete *The Partisans*. He went up to London and had talks with Professor Moon and it was agreed that the students should give the first performance of the new work. The Professor saw the score and the libretto and he and Oliver were in agreement that Tina should play the part of Elisabetta, the girl Oliver's father had loved, who died in the mountains, and Rosamund should be Nerina, the novice nun who fell in love with a German she nursed, but who ended the opera by returning to her convent.

'If only Tom Walden hadn't gone off to Australia, he would have been an ideal Ricardo,' Professor Moon said. 'As it is, I can offer you a baritone with a fine voice, but he doesn't have Tom's stature. He and our Tina were heavily involved with one another last term; their scenes together would really have sizzled.'

'When will you start rehearsals?' Oliver asked.

'Not for a few weeks yet. My children have other things to occupy them. It's a good year — two fine sopranos, an excellent contralto and one or two tenors who may make a name for themselves. My only regret is the baritone who got away. I can promise you an outstanding chorus. Fortunately, the set and costumes can be provided very economically.'

'One backdrop of mountains and trees and some old army uniforms,' Oliver agreed.

Once the rehearsals started he was heavily involved in the production, almost too much so, since he had difficulty in thinking of anything else. He realised that he had played down the disappointment he had felt when his work had been plagiarised and he had believed that it would never be performed under his own name. Now it seemed as if a great block had been removed, releasing the creativity he had held back. He was full of energy, full of ideas, and he knew that as soon as the performance of *The Partisans* was out of the way he would take up the composition of *The Crown of Glass* with renewed zest.

Annis was performing in Glasgow, but she flew down specially for the performance and she brought with her a man from the recording company that issued her records. Oliver joined them and was introduced, but the significance of the meeting passed him by.

'Nervous?' Annis asked with a smile.

'About three times as nervous as any of the singers,' Oliver said ruefully.

She took his hand and patted it soothingly. 'It's going to be a great success. I'm impressed by the number of critics who've turned up.'

'You're making me feel worse,' Oliver complained. 'Half of them are here because of the scandal over Peador and even the serious ones will be unable to avoid mentioning it.

I only hope they find something constructive to say instead of just rehashing that old story.'

'It'll be unusual if the papers find any space at all to comment on a student performance,' the man from the recording studio said. 'Your notoriety may yet be useful, Mr Leone.'

The conductor entered and a hush fell on the auditorium. The overture started with a drum roll, like thunder or guns in the distance, rising to a crescendo and then a crash of the cymbals, and all the other instruments joined in for a few bars of the rousing march Oliver had given to the band of partisans. It faded into a more lyrical passage, lifted again to a climax and then the curtain rose.

The band of partisans, holed up in the mountains and descending to the valley only for assaults on the Germans, sang of their hopes and fears and their longing to see their homes again. Tina was magnificent, fiery, passionate and ultimately doomed by her own courage. Rosamund was infinitely touching as the young novice who had been raped by the retreating Germans and who insisted on nursing a prisoner the partisans wanted to execute.

It was an aria sung by Rosamund that ended the opera. She had loved her enemy, nursed him back to life and sent him home to his wife and family; the girl who had befriended her and carried her up the mountainside was dead; the war was over and Nerina had rediscovered her vocation and decided to return to her convent. Her closing aria was a prayer for peace. The lovely melody, which Michael Peador had used in the middle of his opera as a love song, soared in a passionate declaration of belief in a better world, a world in which all men and women would live in harmony, and Rosamund sang it like one inspired. The purity of her voice had never been used to better effect. It had a quality that brought tears to the eyes of the most hardened. As the last notes faded away and the curtain fell there was a moment's hush and then a storm of applause.

Oliver went up on to the platform to take a bow, standing between Rosamund and Tina, holding their hands. He tried to smile, but he felt dazed. The conductor shook his hand and then led him forward to take a bow on his own. Oliver bent his head stiffly. The only thing he was conscious of was a great tiredness and regret that it was all over. He had, he realised, sung every note and played every instrument in his head throughout the performance. Now he wanted to go away and think about it. On his own.

That was something that could not be allowed. He had to attend a party, organised by Annis as a surprise for him. All the cast were there, all the orchestra and, it seemed to Oliver, most of the audience. He saw Will and Elsie Burford and the Drews and remembered to say something pleasant about their daughters' performances. Professor Moon wrung his hand, some tiresome journalist asked him how he felt on seeing his work performed at last and he said it was 'great', a totally inadequate description of how he felt, and then Annis seized hold of him and pulled him to one side.

'My recording man is wild about it,' she said. 'He's talking about getting out a disc quickly to take advantage of the publicity.'

'Oh, Annis, darling, you know that sort of thing takes months and months ...'

'Not if you're using out-of-work students.'

'They'll be breaking up for the holidays.'

'They'll stick together for the chance of making a record.'

'There won't be a studio available.'

'Oh, do stop making difficulties It can be done if we put our minds to it. I've promised to sing Elisabetta.'

For a moment Oliver thought of Tina and the vitality she had brought to the role of the girl who might have been his mother if she had not been shot on the field of battle, but this was not something he could argue about in the middle of a party, not when Annis was paying him the tremendous compliment of wanting to sing his music.

Oliver thought he owed it to Tina to break the news to her himself. It was not the easiest thing he had ever done and was made none the more pleasant by the gallant way Tina bore her disappointment. She went very still and quiet and then, with a stiff little smile, she said, 'Well, of course, Annis ... who could turn down the chance of having Annis Gilroy sing for them?'

'It was the record company which insisted,' Oliver said.

He could hardly say more without disloyalty to Annis, but he wished he could have been more frank with Tina so that she might have known that he had tried to argue in favour of keeping an all-student cast and that he regretted the loss of Tina's fresh young voice in the role of Elisabetta.

Tina kept her head high and a smile on her face, but it was hard to bear with the commiserations of her friends, who were more sympathetic than tactful. She had hardly had time to recover from this blow when Professor Moon asked to see her.

She went along to his room and bore with it while he complimented her on her performance in *The Partisans*. He was leading up to something – the Prof was not a man to waste words, not in the ordinary way.

'You're very highly thought of,' he said. 'Definitely one of our brighter stars. And with a successful future before you, I don't doubt.'

'Thank you,' Tina murmured.

Professor Moon was fiddling with a pen, not looking at her. 'I wanted to see you because I'm afraid that something I said ... I may have raised hopes ...' He straightened his shoulders and stopped shillyshallying. 'A Gold Medal is to be awarded this year, but it will go to Rosamund Drew.'

Tina remembered then that he had spoken of the Gold Medal after her performance with Ransu Prokopi. She had told Tom and he had been enormously impressed. Tom ... For a moment the recollection of his loss gave her more pain than anything the Professor could say.

'It was a difficult decision,' the Professor said hurriedly. 'But Rosamund has been with us for a full four years and her standard has been consistently excellent in all fields. Recently her voice has developed to a point – well, opinion tipped the scales just a shade in her favour. I hope you were not misled ...'

He was waiting for a response. Tina pulled herself together. She had had practice at this.

'I never dreamed of counting on anything so prestigious as a Gold Medal,' she said. 'If it's to go to Ros then it's well deserved.'

The Prof was finding it difficult to look at her. Tina suspected that the grimace she was producing by way of a smile did not deceive him for a moment. It was time to bring the interview to a close. She had to get out of the room before she either collapsed or exploded.

She was glad that she saw no one she knew as she walked the corridors of the college. Of course, it was great news for Ros, and Ros was her friend, but inside Tina's head a rebellious voice repeated, 'I'm *better* than she is! I am, I am!'

The recording of *The Partisans* was made. As Annis had said, a way could always be found if the incentive was sufficient. In the recording studio any slight faults in her performance could be corrected and the result satisfied both Annis and her record company, but it was Rosamund who became the star.

It was not a full recording of the opera, only 'highlights', but, like the stage performance, it concluded with the prayer for peace. With an eye to the popular market, the company also issued this aria as a single with Rosamund singing a duet with her German lover on the other side. It took off slowly and then sales began to pick up. Disc jockeys were inundated with requests for it.

'Imagine me in the charts,' Rosamund exclaimed. 'It's the last thing I ever expected. We've reached number five. If it gets to the top I'll really be in the money.'

'Lucky old you,' Tina said lightly.

She tried to be generous, but it was a bad time for her. She had lost her man, her role and her medal, all in rapid succession. She was not sure which blow was giving her most pain, but she was sure of one thing: the other two disappointments would have been more bearable if she could have had Tom by her side with his ready sympathy and partisan opinion of her ability.

Rosamund was bemused by her unexpected success. It was the last thing she had ever expected, to receive popular acclaim and large sums of money for singing one aria. She tried to keep a level head, but it was very exciting and it led to all sorts of side benefits. She was interviewed for a chat magazine and asked to model clothes for a fashion feature. She also took part in Daphne Durrell's musical quiz show on television.

The show was recorded at the Lime Grove studios, not the main television centre in Wood Lane. Rosamund had had some experience of the ramshackle areas backstage in most theatres, but she was surprised by the run-down air of Lime Grove. In what was called the hospitality room there were one or two low wooden tables with ring-marks from the glasses that had been set down on them and some scuffed chairs. There seemed to be a disproportionate number of young girls with beautiful complexions and long hair who drifted about offering drinks to the team taking part in that day's show. Rosamund asked for a soft drink, but no sooner had she been handed a glass of mineral water than another girl appeared to take her to the make-up room.

'No need to improve on nature with *you*,' the make-up artist said. 'A little more lipstick, perhaps.'

With expert flicks of the brush she painted Rosamund's mouth a vivid shade of pink which Rosamund particularly disliked. She looked at the result doubtfully.

'Blot it on this,' the girl said, pushing a piece of tissue between Rosamund's lips. 'And just a dash of powder.'

Toned down, the result looked much the same as when Rosamund had sat down, but the make-up girl and her assistant and the messenger who had fetched Rosamund murmured, 'Grand ... lovely ... super', and then she was escorted back to the hospitality room where she left most of her newly applied lipstick on the glass of mineral water.

A harassed girl with a clipboard drifted in saying, 'Is Rosamund Drew ... oh, *there* you are!' as if Rosamund had not already been on the premises for half an hour.

'I don't suppose anyone's seen Daphne Durrell?' she went on gloomily.

'I heard my name,' Daphne said from the doorway. 'Now don't you dare tell me I'm late, Lizzie. I must have a good ten minutes in hand.'

'Five, actually.'

'Just time for a tiny G & T. And here's Rosamund, the

girl with the lovely, lovely voice. I've heard your record, of course. It's being played everywhere.'

Rosamund smiled, not quite sure how to respond to this. 'Tina's in the audience,' she said. 'You know she's a great friend of mine, don't you?'

'Isn't it a small world? Is Tina furious that she's not been asked to be on the show?'

'No, I don't think so,' Rosamund said in surprise.

'Poor Tina,' Daphne said, disbelieving her. 'Perhaps we can get together afterwards and make it up to her.'

Daphne poured her drink expertly down her throat and held out her glass for a refill.

'Where's Larry?' she asked.

'He'll be along in just two shakes to brief you,' the clipboard girl said.

'So I should hope. We don't want a fiasco like last week with my team hardly getting anything right. I had to ad-lib like mad to hide the fact that they were all total morons. Never, never put me in a programme again with that so-called pop idol. His entire input boiled down to "Yuh, well ..." and picking his nails.'

She turned her dazzling smile on Rosamund. 'At least we've got one expert on classical music today. Lots and lots of lovely operatic questions, I hope.'

'Yes, we're well up on that side.'

'And Vic Vernon to deal with the golden oldies.'

A middle-aged man who had been talking quietly to the leader of the other team, a comedian with a repertoire of well-rehearsed one-line jokes, moved over to join Daphne and they exchanged airy kisses.

'Actually, my speciality is Bach,' he said smoothly. 'So this is Rosamund Drew. Loved your disc, darling. Of course you realise why our Larry is late? Lunching with our opposition, would you believe. Carlo Cerutti, no less. I think he fancies him, but nothing doing, of course, because Carlo's totally one for the ladies – very much in the plural if one can believe all one hears.'

'He's the finest operatic tenor to come out of Italy for years,' Rosamund said. 'I'm dying to meet him.'

'Looks as if you're just about to expire in that case,

darling. Here he comes. Ooh, yes, *very* nice. I'm sure our Larry's smitten.'

'Larry's a happily married man with three children,' Daphne muttered in Rosamund's ear. 'Vic's jealous because he wasn't invited to the producer's lunch party. Neither was I, come to that, but do I care? Well, yes, actually, I do feel a bit put out. Larry's beginning to take me for granted. He's making a mistake if he thinks he can pass me over for a greasy Wop warbler.'

She held out her hands with her warmest smile.

'Carlo Cerutti!' she exclaimed. 'I can't tell you how thrilled I am to meet the finest operatic tenor to come out of Italy for years.'

The Italian lifted first one hand and then the other to his lips and kissed her fingers.

'And for me, too, this is a very great privilege,' he said. 'I have seen all your films, of course, and as many of your stage appearances as I have been able to catch. I fell in love with you when I saw *Stars Above* in New York and my devotion has never wavered.'

His English was perfect, with just enough of an accent to give charm to his every word. He was not a tall man, but above middle height, with an olive skin and dark, expressive eyes. His hair had receded slightly, but the effect was attractive, giving his forehead a height it would otherwise have lacked, and he emphasised it by wearing his hair brushed back very smoothly.

Rosamund bit back a smile as she saw the way Daphne succumbed to his outrageous flattery. Carlo Cerutti looked over Daphne's shoulder and caught her amusement. His own smile deepened and he went on, 'And this is our young singer? An appearance that matches the voice – how rare! The English operatic stage is indeed fortunate. What do they plan for you, Miss Drew?'

'I'm going to do some broadcasting – a programme of English songs,' Rosamund said. 'And I have three auditions promised. I want a career in opera, of course. Meeting you m-means a lot to me.'

The producer clapped his hands. 'Everybody! Could I have your attention, please. Briefing time. You've all seen the programme, I hope, those of you who've not been on it before?'

There was a murmur of agreement, which Carlo Cerutti did not join. He stood a little on one side with the air of one about to join a game to amuse the children, and his gaze was fixed on Rosamund. She had a lovely wild rose flush of colour in her cheeks, not because she was about to appear on television for the first time, but out of excitement at meeting him. By the side of her young, serious ardour, Daphne's flattery was shallow and meaningless.

Rosamund was surprised by the amount of information they were given about the types of questions they were likely to encounter during the quiz. Not the answers, not exactly, but one would have to be fairly stupid not to make a guess at what might crop up. Rosamund concentrated, anxious not to make a fool of herself, especially not in front of Carlo Cerutti.

As they were shepherded out of the room towards the studio he caught her hand and gave it a tiny tug.

'Afterwards,' he said in a low voice. 'We must get together. You and I, we have more in common than anyone else here today. You agree?'

'Oh, yes ... yes ... please ... thank you,' Rosamund stammered, and then they were on the set, which looked curiously shabby until it was lit, with the audience already in place and the compere going through his warming-up patter.

It was one of the show's more successful editions. The jokes succeeded, the audience was appreciative, and Rosamund scored a hit by identifying a snatch of music from a little-known early opera by Tchaikovsky. It happened to be one she had studied at the Guildhall and she had a suspicion that someone from the BBC knew this and had included it on purpose, in which case full marks to them for doing their homework. Carlo had the women eating out of his hand, with his delightful accent, his air of being slightly above the present company, and the slumbrous looks of his dark eyes.

The performance ended in a storm of applause. The teams smiled and nodded as the camera panned round them and then stood up and stretched and talked amongst themselves as the audience filed out.

'Oh, is that man ever sexy,' Daphne muttered to Rosamund, watching Carlo. 'I wonder if he'd like to take me home?'

'You said you wanted to see Tina,' Rosamund pointed out.

'Darling, I can do that any old time. Men like Carlo don't come along every day of the week. How old do you think? Younger than me, alas, so let's hope he goes for older women.'

She moved purposefully towards the Italian, but Carlo extricated himself with torrents of regret. He had no time to spare, no time at all. He was leaving London, almost immediately.

Disappointed, Daphne drifted off in search of a reviving drink. Rosamund hesitated, looking towards Carlo, and again he caught hold of her hand.

'Come, we must run,' he said. 'The delightful Miss Durrell must not know that I am standing her up − turning her down − which is it?'

'Giving her the brush-off?' Rosamund suggested.

'Exactly! Unfortunately, it is true that I have no time. My car is waiting downstairs to take me to the airport. Will you ride out with me, help me to pass the tiresome waiting time and then allow me to send you back in the car?'

Rosamund felt almost as disappointed as Daphne. He was leaving. She agreed to go with him to Heathrow, unaware of how expressive her face had been.

She had never been in the VIP Lounge at Heathrow. How the other half lives, she thought, looking round at the space and comfort and free refreshments. One day ... yes, one day she would be entitled to use this facility in her own right. It was a heartening thought and it helped her to overcome her natural diffidence. After all, she was, in her small way, a celebrity too. And Carlo Cerutti admired her.

He treated her like a queen, leading her to a seat, fetching the glass of wine she asked for with his own hands, talking to her as if she was the only woman on the planet. The warm, caressing voice flowed over her and the casual touch of his hand made her catch her breath. When he saw that what interested Rosamund was his operatic career he spoke of roles he had sung, opera houses he had known, great singers, great orchestras, great conductors.

'And you,' he said. 'With your exquisite voice you are obviously destined to be one of our leading prima donnas. What is your ambition? What roles do you most covet?'

'I'd love to do *Tosca*,' Rosamund said, which made him smile, because that was the opera in which he had just sung at Covent Garden.

'Why not? You are perhaps a little young yet for the sophisticated diva. You would be a delightful Mimi and a most elegant Violetta.'

'There's so much,' Rosamund said yearningly. 'In some ways I dread it and in others I long to do it all!'

Carlo laughed at her earnestness. 'It will come, *carissima*, it will come. Alas, for now we must say goodbye. That is my flight being called.'

He took her hand and bent over it. 'I am in New York for one week only,' he said. 'Then I return for three more performances at Covent Garden. May I see you again when I am in London? Give me your telephone number and I will call you. We will talk about your future.'

'That will be wonderful,' Rosamund said, scribbling hurriedly on the piece of paper he handed her.

He was going. 'I hope you have a good flight,' she said.

Carlo shrugged. 'Nothing is more boring than a flight over the Atlantic. How I wish you were coming with me! *Ciao*, Rosamund, we will meet again soon.'

Tina looked up from the book she was reading as Rosamund drifted into the flat. One look at her face was enough to tell Tina that Ros was in a dream.

'You were last seen getting into an enormous limousine with Carlo Cerutti,' she said. 'What happened? Tell!'

'We went to Heathrow.'

'Oh, dead romantic.'

'It was wonderful. He's gone to New York, but he'll be back next week and we're going to meet again. Isn't he divine?'

109

'I haven't been given the full treatment,' Tina pointed out. 'But I'll admit that he's the sexiest thing on two legs I've seen in a long time. If the part were transposed he'd be the perfect Don Giovanni.'

'Mm,' Rosamund said, obviously not hearing a word Tina was saying. 'He's quite simple and natural and easy to talk to. He thinks I ought to sing Mimi and Violetta.'

'Chance'd be a fine thing. At the moment you look as if you've been cast in the part of a lovesick cow.'

'Tina! I say, I was supposed to see you after the show, wasn't I? I'm sorry, but as you saw ...'

'You got carried away. I was taken out by my Auntie Daphne, who also saw you getting into the classy Limo and was not pleased. She gave me quite a decent meal, but I think she drinks too much.'

'She was knocking it back a bit before the show,' Rosamund agreed. 'What did you think of it?'

'Entertaining. Very slick and well done and you all performed your parts to perfection. Ros, don't get sidetracked into becoming a show biz personality, will you?'

'Oh, no!' Rosamund said, shocked. 'Especially not now, with Carlo Cerutti taking an interest in me.'

'What Carlo's interested in lives rather lower down than your agile larynx,' Tina informed her. 'Watch yourself, Ros.'

'Of course! But you're wrong, Tina, he really does mean to advise me about my career. He said so.'

Chapter Seven

'You're stark, staring, raving mad,' Tina said. 'You can't go off to Italy with Carlo Cerutti. You just can't, Ros.'

'He's promised to get me an audition at La Scala.'

'He doesn't run the place.'

'He's got a lot of influence. I have to go, Tina. I have to be with him. Carlo ... he's the most wonderful thing that's ever happened to me.'

'He's married.'

'I know. And he's got a family. I can't say I don't care, because I do, but Carlo has explained it to me. He was married very young, before his career took off, and he and his wife have drifted apart. They have a perfectly amicable arrangement. He has to travel the world because of his singing commitments and she stays at home, which is what she prefers. There can't be any question of a divorce, of course ...'

'Why should there be when he can wangle girls like you into bed without having to marry them? Oh, God, I sound like my mother.'

Her dismay made Rosamund smile, but only for a moment.

'Do try to understand, Tina,' she pleaded. 'I love him so much everything else is blotted out. I'd walk over red-hot coals to be with him. Flying to Milan and staying in an apartment and ...'

'Making yourself available when he wants you.'

'It's a small thing to do to enjoy the bliss of being together.'

'In other words, he's a super lover and you've never had

it so good. Ros, grow up! There are other men in the world who can make the earth shake without the liability of being a self-centred Italian tenor with a wife and three children.'

'You didn't talk like that when you went off to live with Tom.'

'That was different,' Tina said. 'He was my own age, we were equals and we were both free of other ties.'

'Have you forgotten what it was like − already?'

'No,' Tina said. Her hands gripped together so tightly that the knuckles showed white. 'I haven't forgotten.'

She let her breath out in a long sigh. 'OK, Ros, I can see it's no use talking. You go off and learn your lesson the hard way. Just remember I'm always here if you want me. What are you telling your mum and dad?'

'Only that I've been offered an opening at La Scala. They're mildly impressed, but not as much as they were when I appeared on TV!'

'I know. My mum was green with envy over that. She's been nudging me ever since to get Auntie Daphne to give me a similar spot.'

Rosamund went off to Milan and Tina, of necessity, took in another student to share the flat, which meant that Tina was the only old hand of the original four sharers. What was more, she was now the only one who was not a music student. She was doing occasional concerts and waiting for a response to various applications to opera companies. It was a humbling experience, after having been at the top of the heap during her years at the Guildhall. It would be even more humbling if Rosamund's gamble came off and she really did get taken on at La Scala.

Reluctantly, because she had to eat and pay the rent, Tina took a few weeks' work as a temporary typist.

'Typing!' her mother said disbelievingly. 'All that study and you've gone back to typing?'

'Just to tide me over,' Tina said. 'After all, that was why you made me go to secretarial college, wasn't it?'

'Do you want to come back home to live?' her father asked.

'Thanks, Dad, but I'd rather stick it out at the flat if I can.'

'You miss Rosamund, I expect,' he said.

'Yes, I do. The new girls ... they're all right, but they're very young.'

Tina smiled to herself, remembering the time when she, too, had believed that she only had to open her mouth to have the opera houses clamouring for her services.

She had a postcard from Rosamund, giving her address and saying everything was 'divine'. Tina frowned over that, wishing her friend had written a proper letter, but by the same post she had a reply from Covent Garden inviting her to attend an audition the following week, and that drove everything else out of her mind.

Rosamund closed her Italian grammar and glanced at her watch. Carlo had said he would call in to see her at about six, on his way to the theatre. He had spent the whole of the previous afternoon with her, all the long siesta hours, filled with love and laughter. She shut her eyes and smiled, remembering, and stretched herself like a languorous cat. Everything was wonderful ... except that she was just a little bit bored.

The promised audition had not yet materialised, but Carlo was still sure that he would be able to arrange it. In the meantime, Rosamund practised assiduously, doing her exercises every morning and studying the score of *Madame Butterfly*, in which Carlo was to sing Pinkerton as his next role at La Scala, interspersed with performances of the Don Carlos for which he was already famous.

He came to her whenever he could and they made love with mutual delight, but he never spent the night with her and the hours she passed alone seemed very long. She went out sightseeing, visiting the Cathedral and the arcades, doing a little shopping, but not a lot because she still shrank fastidiously from spending the money Carlo gave her. He was paying the rent of the flat, that was enough, she insisted, but he laughed and poured lira on to the bed and told her to go to a fashionable hairdresser and get her hair cut or buy herself some wonderful perfume to make herself alluring to him.

113

She made another effort when he arrived that evening.

'I want to work,' she said wistfully.

'*Cara*, I will speak to the director again. Don't frown and spoil your pretty face. Come, we have so little time and I have been thinking all day of how we will make love before I have to go off to the theatre.'

There was, as he had said, very little time, and Carlo did not waste it. Rosamund lay on the bed, sleepy and lazy, after their tumultuous lovemaking, and watched him as he dressed.

'I don't know how you can be so energetic and then go off and sing a demanding role,' she said.

'It relaxes me. *Carissima*, you were delicious. I love you. Have I ever told you that? Ah, if I could only stay!'

'The demands of your art come first,' Rosamund said with mock solemnity. She was tickled when Carlo took her seriously.

'You are right,' he agreed. 'My audience is waiting for me. *Ciao, bambina*!'

'Tomorrow.'

Carlo hesitated. 'Alas, no. I shall not see you again until Monday.'

'Oh, Carlo!'

'I know, my beloved. I, too, shall count the hours. But what must be, must be. Until Monday. *Arrivederci*!'

He was gone and Rosamund was left with the prospect of a long, empty weekend in front of her.

Looking round the next morning for a way of passing the time, it occurred to Rosamund that the apartment could do with a really thorough clean. She had the services of a cleaning woman who came in twice a week and gave the surfaces a desultory wipe over, but Maria was not given to shifting furniture, nor to using polish. Rosamund covered her hair with a scarf, put on an old pair of jeans and a T-shirt and prepared to amuse herself with an out-of season spring-clean.

She sang softly as she worked. It was satisfying to be doing something constructive. The flat was not big. There was a bedroom, a living-cum-dining room with a balcony, an antiquated bathroom and a minute kitchen. The bedroom contained a very large bed, a very small wardrobe and a dressing table with a mirror which could be tilted so that the occupants of the bed could see themselves, something Carlo liked to do and which Rosamund still found embarrassing.

The back of the dressing table had obviously not seen a brush for some time. Rosamund wondered whether she could manage to shift the wardrobe out as well. It was not very large and once she had taken all the clothes out and piled them on the bed she managed to manoeuvre it forward. As she had suspected, behind it she found a drift of dusty fluff and a couple of dead spiders.

Feeling really zealous, she fetched a chair and stood on it to dust the top of the wardrobe. On the top, concealed by the raised edge, there was a large photograph album, which had obviously been long forgotten. Rosamund dumped it on the kitchen table to be looked at later.

She spent the whole morning on the bedroom and bathroom and then decided she had had enough of hard manual labour. She would have a bath, even though she was reluctant to soil her newly gleaming bathroom, a snack lunch and a rest. The kitchen and living room could be saved to fill up the next day. If only she knew someone in Milan who would join her for a meal in the evening. For a moment she thought of her flat in London and her congenial companions with real longing. Above all, she would have liked to have had Tina there to talk to. Except, of course, that until she had something a little more concrete to report she was not anxious to talk to Tina at all.

She had almost forgotten about the album she had found on top of the wardrobe. When she went into the kitchen, fresh from her bath, tying the belt of her thin cotton robe, the album looked excessively dusty. She lifted it with the tips of her fingers and put it on the floor until she had eaten.

She had cheese and tomatoes and a fresh bread roll with a tall glass of white wine mixed with mineral water and followed by a few grapes. It was not a meal that created a lot of washing up so she dumped the plates in the sink, made herself a cup of coffee – black and strong in the way Carlo had taught her to take it – helped herself to a delicious chocolate-covered cherry from the box he had given her and took the dusty album into the living room.

She had expected to be amused by a glimpse into the lives of complete strangers, but this was far from being the case. The photographs were of Carlo. Carlo and his family. The very first photograph was of Carlo and a young girl, standing side by side with their arms linked, and a caption written underneath saying, in Italian, 'The day of our engagement.'

Slowly, Rosamund turned the pages. There were wedding photographs, holiday snaps, christenings, birthdays, anniversaries – the record of a married life. A happy married life. Looking at Carlo's smiling face, at the three delightful children and, above all, at Carlo's wife, grown a little older, a little plumper, but still recognisably the pleasant, loving girl he had married, Rosamund could not doubt that the marriage had been successful. In which case, what was she doing in this flat, longing in every pore of her body for Carlo to come back and make love to her?

The photographic record stopped abruptly about two years previously, which was possibly how long the book had lain unseen on top of the wardrobe. The final photographs were particularly painful, since they showed a series of groups taken at a large family party to celebrate Carlo and Lucia's tenth wedding anniversary. The last picture was almost a replica of the first, the two of them alone with their arms round one another. Carlo still smiled, Lucia still smiled; he looked sleek and successful; she was better groomed and her gown was more expensive; apart from that, they seemed to be as much of a couple as they had been at the time of their betrothal.

Rosamund shivered and shut the book, pushing it away from her. It was obvious that until a fairly recent date Carlo and his wife had been in accord with one another. And then, Rosamund told herself, they had drifted apart. Carlo had told her that was what had happened. Then she and Carlo had met and he had fallen overwhelmingly in love with her and known, just as she had known, that it was absolutely impossible for them to live apart. It was the scenario she wanted to believe, but now a cold, niggling doubt was squirming about in her mind. She had always known that there could be no question of a divorce, but she had believed that was because of the question of religion and the difficulties of Italian law. It occurred to her now, and the thought would not go away, that perhaps, as Tina had suggested, Carlo did not want a divorce; perhaps he was just as happy to stay with his wife and to have a pretty young mistress on the side. Perhaps Rosamund was not the great love of his life, but just a passing fancy and not even unique, but one of many.

She got up stiffly and took the photograph album and hid it at the bottom of a drawer. She was being morbid. It was the result of spending so much time on her own. Two years had elapsed since the last picture in the book and a lot could have happened in two years. Carlo and Lucia could have quarrelled. Lucia might have been unfaithful, though that plump, satisfied matron looked an unlikely candidate for an illicit love affair. Perhaps the photographs were a lie, but that was not a pleasant idea either, since it would have made both Carlo and Lucia into hypocrites. It was worrying, it was upsetting, and it was making her head ache.

Rosamund told herself she would put it out of her mind, but she tossed and turned all night and when she slept she had troubled dreams of a laughing man holding a small child high in the air while his wife and two older children looked on. In the background lurked a menace that would spoil the idyllic picture, and the menace was herself.

Carlo bounded back to see her on the following Monday, looking fit and brown and pleased with himself.

'*Carissima*! Have you missed me? Say yes, say yes!'

'Of course I have,' Rosamund said, weak with relief that he was unchanged. She had been imagining things. Carlo loved her, of course he did.

'I have wonderful news,' Carlo said. 'Shall I tell you now or tease you by making you wait? I think I will tell you now and then you will love me twice as much. Why are you wearing all these clothes? Off with them, off with them. Come, *bellissima*, I want you so much.'

'Tell me your news,' Rosamund said, laughing and dodging his eager hands.

'You have an audition at La Scala at six o'clock this evening.'

'Carlo!' Rosamund paused, clutching at the dress which was sliding off her shoulders. 'But it's four o'clock now!'

'We have plenty of time.'

'But I ought to prepare ...'

'You are as ready as you ever will be. *Cara* ...' Carlo hesitated and then he said carefully, 'There is little they can offer you. You must be prepared for that.'

'Of course. Just to be heard, that's marvellous. Oh, Carlo, I am grateful.'

'Show me! You know how I like to be thanked.'

'Yes, I will, I will. Six o'clock! It's an odd time for an audition.'

'Benno is fitting it in before the evening's performance.'

'Benno ...? But he's not the director.'

'His assistant only, but with the power to pronounce on singers. He is hearing you as a special favour to me. Come ... I will wait no longer.'

They arrived at the theatre with a scant two minutes to spare. Rosamund felt dazed with love, exhilarated and frightened, and rather hastily put together, since a bath shared with Carlo was no suitable preparation for an interview which might decide the course of her entire working career.

The theatre was still dark, but Carlo led her in by the stage entrance. She followed him, resisting an impulse to catch hold of his jacket. He left her in his dressing-room and went in search of the man who had agreed to hear her sing. After waiting for some minutes, Rosamund went to the door and looked out uncertainly. Somewhere she could hear raised voices, but that meant nothing in Italy where a kind enquiry about a neighbour's health could sound like a threat to cut his throat.

Carlo came back looking rather less pleased with life than he had when he left her. Rosamund looked at him fearfully, waiting for him to tell her that the director's assistant had gone back on his promise, but he said, with a curtness that increased her nervousness, 'Come, Benno will see you now.'

118

There was a rehearsal room, with a piano in it. A man was sitting at the piano, looking bored. He gave her a long, hard look as she came in. Rosamund lifted her head and looked back at him. Damn it, she might be inexperienced, but she was no green novice. She had done a long training, she had been awarded the coveted Gold Medal, she had played one of the leading parts in a brand new opera and she had made a successful record. She walked forward and held out her hand. For a moment she thought he was going to ignore it, then he got to his feet and shook hands.

Rosamund had got Carlo to tell her a little about him. He was a second-generation American-Italian who had returned to his father's country to gain experience at La Scala, having already built up a reputation as a producer in the United States. He was not much over thirty, but looked older because of the deep lines which ran from his nose to the corners of his mouth and his air of world-weary cynicism.

'I've brought my curriculum vitae with me,' Rosamund said, handing over the folio.

Benno Neroni took it and flicked through it in a perfunctory way.

'What roles have you studied recently?' he asked.

'Since I've been in Milan I've been practising *Madame Butterfly*, because ...'

'Because Carlo is to sing Pinkerton. So, what are you going to sing for me? "One Fine Day", I presume?'

'It's not in my usual audition repertoire, but I'm prepared to sing it if that's what you would like,' Rosamund said evenly.

'It'll do as well as anything else.'

It was cruel, and it was not good for her voice, to make her plunge straight into singing such a testing aria, but Rosamund saw Carlo nodding encouragingly and she did not quite have the courage to refuse.

She thought that, in the circumstances, she did reasonably well. It was not the performance she would have liked to have given, but she could see no reason for Benno Neroni to frown quite so fiercely when she finished. Carlo broke into applause and not even the look of derision the director's assistant turned on him was enough to quench his exuberance.

'I can't take you into the cast of *Butterfly*,' Benno Neroni said.

'I didn't expect it,' Rosamund replied.

'In fact, all the contracts for the year have been awarded.'

She ought to have anticipated that, knowing how far in advance of productions an opera house had to work.

Carlo made an impatient exclamation. 'You can find a corner for this talented girl,' he said.

'This talented girl has no work permit,' Benno Neroni pointed out drily.

'That can be arranged. With a contract from La Scala in her pocket, a personal request from you and a little ... persuasion — perhaps the promise of a couple of good seats for the first night of *Butterfly* — it can be done, you know it can.'

'Oh, please ...' Rosamund said, in an agony of embarrassment, ' ... please, I don't want all this fuss!'

'Be quiet! You are my friend and my protégée. I have promised that you will sing at La Scala ...'

'You only promised to get me an audition and I've had that — after a fashion.'

She looked desperately at Benno Neroni, who was leaning back in his chair with an air of boredom. He sat up at Carlo's next words.

'I have made a promise. I, Carlo Cerutti! I will not be thwarted. Benno, I tell you, unless you find Signorina Drew a place I will not sing, not in *Butterlfy* and not in *Don Carlos* either.'

'You can't break your contract.'

'I shall see my doctor immediately. Already I feel my throat tightening. To sing, I must be happy. I must have people round me I can trust. You — with your petty rules — you are not my friend. My heart is pounding, there is a band round my head. I am ill.'

He collapsed on to a chair, with one hand clutching his chest. Benno Neroni sat for a moment, his lips pressed together in a thin straight line.

'There is one possibility,' he said at last.

'Ah! You see? Always there is a solution when you put your mind to it!'

Benno Neroni ignored him and spoke to Rosamund.

'I can't take you into *Butterfly*, that's quite impossible. Nor can I add you to the chorus, not without all the singers turning on me. However ... have you had German measles?'

'Yes, as a child,' Rosamund said in bewilderment.

'The super who's been playing the Countess of Aremberg has gone down with it and the fool who should replace her refused to put on the costume for fear of infection. You can do it.'

For a moment Rosamund was puzzled. In her mind she ran through the characters in Verdi's *Don Carlos* and could not remember a soprano part for the Countess. Then it came to her. She was shattered. All her careful composure deserted her. She could only look pitifully from him to Carlo, her lips quivering. He was offering her a non-singing part.

Before she could pull herself together, before she could even think of the words with which to refuse this offer she could only look on as an insult, Carlo had put his arm round her shoulders. She expected him to be as angry as she was, but he said, 'It's not much, but we shall be together, *cara*. And this is La Scala, the greatest opera house in the world.'

'Other opera houses might dispute that,' Rosamund said coldly. 'Am I to understand you expect me to accept this part?'

'Of course! Say thank you nicely to our good friend, Benno.'

Rosamund turned to Benno Neroni. She wanted to fling his offer in his face, but there was something in what Carlo said: they would be together, she would be earning, a pittance, it was true, but she would have some degree of independence. And one day she would make Neroni grovel for what he had done to her today.

'Thank you — nicely,' she said.

They look at one other coldly and then a faint smile appeared on Benno Neroni's lips. He knew everything she wanted to say and he was not completely unadmiring, especially when Rosamund went on in a business-like way, 'Will you be wanting me to cover for anyone else?'

It was a slight hope. If she was 'covering' another role

she would at least learn it and attend rehearsals. But Neroni shook his head.

'All that is already arranged,' he said. 'Think yourself lucky to be offered anything at all.'

He was putting her in the part because his leading tenor wanted his girlfriend with him and was threatening to throw a temper if he were thwarted. Rosamund felt that humiliation could go no further. And Carlo did not see it. He was nervous of her reaction, but otherwise he was well pleased. Rosamund left him at the theatre and went home alone, feeling cold and sick. She had not brought up the question of the photograph album and now she felt that she probably never would. It would remain at the bottom of the drawer, an ever-present, never quite forgotten reminder of Carlo's other life.

Nothing in her previous experience had prepared Rosamund for the factions and jealousies at La Scala. She had worked with a troupe of students, all much of an age, all with the same high ambitions and all friends with one another. Now she found herself in a world in which rivalry was taken for granted and the organisation of a claque who could be relied on to applaud their chosen star was a serious business.

No one at La Scala thought of anything except the opera. Even the stagehands would stand in the wings to hear their favourite arias rather than slip away for a game of cards as she suspected they would have done in other theatres. Rosamund admired the total dedication of everyone concerned. She, too, she thought wistfully, could have been as single-minded if they had let her into their enclosed world, but she was an outsider, very much an outsider, and treated as such.

She was not liked and that, for Rosamund, who had never known what it meant to be unpopular, was a shrivelling experience. The cast made no secret of their knowledge that she was Cerutti's mistress. Rosamund, who had thought that she gloried in her place in Carlo's life, found that she was humiliated when her situation was common knowledge.

She kept herself aloof, too proud to make overtures of friendship that would clearly be unwelcome, and she gained the reputation of being 'above herself'. Those who knew about her recording of the 'Prayer for Peace' joked about her pop star status and it seemed to occur to no one that she could actually sing.

'You are not happy, *cara*?' Carlo said, in apparent surprise.

'How can I be?' Rosamund asked. 'I didn't come here to play a walk-on part which any girl off the street could do.'

'But to be with me? That makes you happy?'

He was persuasive, but Rosamund was no longer quite so sure that their love was the unique experience she had once thought it to be. It was not Carlo's fault, she thought, trying to be loyal to him, but she was surprised by his lack of sensitivity, particularly when he began making love to her in his dressing room.

Gradually it had come to be a habit for her to go to the theatre, even on the evenings when *Don Carlos* was not being performed. Carlo liked to have her there, especially when the opera was *Madame Butterfly*. The part of Pinkerton was not an obviously appealing one for a tenor of Carlo's standing. The fact that he was not a likeable character was of less importance than the fact that he was off the stage for the greater part of the opera.

'I agreed to do it because it is a role which makes fewer demands than *Don Carlos*, which I have performed all over the world, and *Otello*, which I am now preparing,' Carlo explained. 'Three performances of Pinkerton each week, that leaves me time for other work, and also it is pleasant for me to be in Milan and to spend some time at home.'

That jolted Rosamund. She told herself that he meant no more than that he liked to be in Italy, but in her heart she suspected that when he said 'at home' Carlo had in mind his wife and children.

With an hour or more to spare between appearing on the stage at the beginning and end of *Madame Butterfly*, Carlo sometimes passed the time playing cards, but more often he took Rosamund into the dressing room, locked the door and made vigorous love to her.

The first time it happened she responded eagerly. They had been apart for nearly a week and she thought that it

123

was their separation that had brought his desire to fever pitch, just as her own longing for him had increased with every day they were apart.

It was when this interlude of lovemaking became a habit that Rosamund began to dislike it, especially when making love at the theatre began to replace Carlo's visits to the flat.

'You know how hard I am working,' Carlo said reproachfully when she complained. 'Is it not wonderful, *bella mia*, that we can be together like this? Are we not the most lucky people in the world?'

It was all very well for Carlo − back in costume, his make-up touched up and apparently refreshed by his bout on the dressing-room couch − he did not have to face the knowing looks and whispers of a jealous and hostile company. He went on to the stage and sang, gloriously, Rosamund had to admit, while Rosamund remained in the dressing room to pull herself together, trying not to notice the knowing smirks of Carlo's dresser.

It was better on the evenings when *Don Carlos* was being performed and Rosamund, silent and beautiful in black taffeta and velvet, joined the entourage of the Queen of Spain on the stage. Once, and only once, a member of the cast put out a foot to trip her up. The crowd surrounding her and her own long skirts disguised Rosamund's stumble. She was in the wings when Benno Neroni turned on the offender with a snarl that distorted his face into a mask of rage and a threat in Neapolitan argot that drew a shocked gasp from the chorus. It never happened again.

Neroni was a man Rosamund had difficulty in understanding. She had thought him hard, cold − even cruel − when he had taken her into the cast of *Don Carlos* as the Queen's French friend, banished from her side by the King's jealousy. She did her best to support the singer playing the Queen, reacting to and enhancing her sad farewell aria, and was rewarded by being totally ignored. Her only word of commendation came, surprisingly, from Neroni, who remarked, 'At least you look like a gentlewoman.'

He disliked her relationship with Carlo, but in a different way from the sneering disdain of the rest of the cast. It seemed to Rosamund that Benno Neroni was reluctantly on her side. Certainly he was on the dreadful evening when she went to the theatre to join Carlo, as he had requested her to do, and found him playing cards in his dressing room with three other men, one of whom was Benno.

Carlo looked up and saw her and said, with his charming smile, 'Not this evening, *carissima*; I'm on a winning streak. I'll call round tomorrow.'

Rosamund felt paralysed. One of the men looked down at his cards and she thought he was embarrassed, the other glanced at her with a knowing smile, and Benno laid down his cards and came to open the door for her. Did he know that without his intervention she would not have been able to get herself out of the room? Perhaps he did. As she passed him, he said in a voice that was no more than a breath, 'Leave him'. Glancing up, Rosamund saw that his eyes were glittering with anger.

Outside in the corridor Rosamund leaned against the wall, shaking all over. 'Not this evening, *carissima*,' she thought bitterly. Like some cheap joke about Napoleon – 'Not tonight, Josephine'. As if she were no more to him than some call girl who came and went at his command.

It was one of the rare occasions when Rosamund made a scene. The storm that broke over Carlo the next day took him by surprise. It also, in some curious way, seemed to please him.

'I am all contrition,' he said. 'See, I go down on my knees to you, my queen. Forgive your Carlo. Truly, it was only because my cards were good and I was gripped by the gambler's fever. Did it hurt you so much, to be sent away from me?'

'Like a woman off the streets,' Rosamund said.

'That is not what you are to me and you must not say it! You are my Rosamund, my sweet delight. Forgive me. I will *make* you forgive me.'

He swept her into his arms and Rosamund cried against his shoulder and allowed herself to be consoled. She felt weak with anger and hurt, and her head ached, but she did not refuse to go to bed with Carlo, and the ardour with which he made love did go some way towards reassuring her.

'If only we could be together all the time,' she whispered.

'Ah, if only! But that is not our fate, *cara*. All next week I shall be away from you. I am to give my *Fidelio* in Madrid.'

'Can't I come with you?' Rosamund asked.

'Not this time, Rosamunda *mia*. Perhaps when I go to the States . . . you would like to see New York?'

'Very much. With you.'

He laughed and kissed her. 'I will try to arrange it.'

What Rosamund longed to know was whether his wife was going to Madrid with him. It would be unusual if she did. Lucia stayed at home and minded the children. She was rarely seen in public and apparently she did not mind her subservient role.

Rosamund's curiosity about this woman Carlo had married had intensified as her own commitment strengthened. How could Lucia possibly be content to let him roam the world without her? Did she know about Rosamund? With everyone at La Scala knowing, was it possible that no rumour of her husband's infidelity had reached Lucia?

With Carlo away and her own services not required at the theatre, Rosamund had even more time on her hands. The thought of the photograph album hidden in the drawer began to nag her. She took it out and turned the pages once more until, at last, she came to a decision. She would go and visit Lucia Cerutti, using the album as an excuse.

The villa where the Cerutti family lived was well outside Milan. After looking at a local map Rosamund decided to take a train to the nearest station and then hope for a country bus or taxi. When she arrived she found that there was, indeed, a solitary taxi, an ancient and battered car whose driver looked as surprised to have a fare as she was to discover him drowsing at the wheel.

November in northern Italy could be as dreary as it was in England. A thin, chilly rain began to fall as the taxi coughed and lurched its way over the uneven surface. It took twenty minutes to reach the Villa Cerutti and, since Rosamund had no mind to find herself marooned in the rain in this out-of-the-way spot, she asked the driver to wait for her. Philosophically, he parked the car against the wall and resumed his siesta, while Rosamund tugged at the bell pull outside the formidable iron gates which seemed to be the only way into the property.

There was some surprise when she asked for Signora Cerutti. Rosamund sensed an air of suspicion and guessed that this was a place where Carlo guarded his privacy. She produced the photograph album and explained in the Italian that now came easily to her that she had found it and believed that it belonged to the Signora, and she would like to return it to her in person.

Still the gate was not opened to her, but she heard a telephone call being made to the house and then there was a clash of keys and a creak from the hinges and she was inside.

There was a garden, formally laid out with box hedges and cypress trees, and a short gravel drive which led up to a white house with a flight of shallow steps in front of it. Rosamund felt her throat going dry and there was a sick churning in her stomach. She wished she had not come. It was absurd, calling on her lover's wife like this. What did she hope to gain by it?

Her steps slowed. She was on the point of turning round and handing the book over to the keeper of the gate before fleeing back to the city, but then a figure appeared at the top of the steps and she saw that it was Lucia Cerutti. She had seen Rosamund, she was waiting for her to approach, it was impossible to get away.

Lucia looked much the same as she did in the photographs. She always seemed to wear her hair drawn back into a smooth chignon and even though she was informally dressed she wore large gold earrings. She was no longer young, and her body had thickened with childbearing, but her face was smooth and unlined except for sun creases at the corners of her eyes.

Her smile as Rosamund drew near was warm and unsuspicious. More than ever Rosamund wished that she could turn and run away.

Lucia Cerutti's voice was low and musical. Had she

once been a singer herself? The question passed through Rosamund's mind, but then she had to concentrate on what was being said to her and what she had to say in reply.

'Signorina! I am told you have something that belongs to me? I am most intrigued.'

Once again Rosamund produced the album and Signora Cerutti exclaimed in pleased surprise.

'You must come in and tell me how you came across it. Please ... this way.'

Helplessly, Rosamund followed her into the house, across a marble-floored hall, down a short passageway and into a warm conservatory full of scented plants. The glass doors of the conservatory opened on to a covered swimming pool and from the pool came the sound of excited young voices.

Signora Cerutti smiled as she closed the door. 'The children make so much noise in the water,' she said. 'We will sit here, I think. May I offer you some coffee?'

Rosamund accepted the coffee, though she thought it would choke her if she so much as sipped the hot, dark liquid. The children ... she could see them: a boy, a fine-looking child, a little girl and a baby about two years old. Carlo's children. Lucia's children. Not hers, never hers.

'The photograph album,' Lucia prompted her.

'I found it on top of an old wardrobe in the flat where I'm ... staying,' Rosamund said.

'So that is where it went! I recognise it, of course, and I'm very pleased to have it back again. But this flat – is it in the Via Morello? Number 15, on the top floor?'

'Yes.'

'Oh, what memories that brings back! It's the apartment where Carlo and I lived when we were first married. Francesco – *our* son – was born there. Later, when Carlo became successful, we bought this house which, as you can see, is more suitable for a growing family. Carlo kept the flat on ... it's so useful for him when he is kept late at La Scala ...'

A puzzled look came over her face and Rosamund said hurriedly, 'I'm only a temporary tenant.'

Inside, she was in turmoil. The flat she had thought Carlo had rented for her was already his. He had lived in it with his

wife, had conceived a son there, had kept it as a convenient
pied-à-terre and finally, inescapably, she knew that he had
kept other mistresses there.

'May I ask your name?' Lucia was probing gently.

Rosamund was too overthrown to do anything but answer
truthfully, 'I'm Rosamund Drew.'

'Of course! I thought I knew your face. I have your
delightful recording of the "Prayer for Peace". How I
would like to see that opera performed! My own family
was caught up in the Resistance during the War. You know
Oliver Leone?'

'Yes, I know him well,' Rosamund said.

'And what are you doing in Milan? Are you singing at
La Scala?'

Rosamund tried to pull herself together. 'I've had an
audition,' she said carefully. 'Unfortunately, at this time
of year the casting is already arranged. Benno Neroni heard
me, but he could offer me nothing but ...' She took a deep
breath and came out with it ' ... I'm walking on as the
Countess of Aremberg in *Don Carlos*.'

'My dear! That Benno, he can be so cruel. But to give
a singer of your quality such a part, that is unforgivable.
What does Carlo say about it?'

This was terrible. Again Rosamund told the simple truth.
'He advised me to take the part.'

Too late she saw how suspicious it was, that Carlo
Cerutti should take the slightest interest in who was playing
a silent part in the opera in which he sang the title
role. Lucia was watching her silently. To hide her con-
fusion Rosamund took a hurried gulp at the unwanted
coffee, but one swallow was all she could manage because
she had to tighten her muscles to hold back the telltale
tears.

Lucia, looking at her chalk-white face, the hollows in
her cheeks, the enormous shadowed eyes, was unexpectedly
kind.

'Did Carlo bring you to Milan?' she asked gently.

'Yes.'

'And he put you in our old flat?'

'Yes.'

Lucia sighed, the long, slow sigh of a woman who had heard it all before.

'Sometimes I think I could cut out his cruel heart and chop it into little pieces,' she said. 'But he is my husband and I love him. In spite of everything, I love him. As you do, too, I think.'

'I did.' Rosamund said.

'Ah, yes ... now you are disillusioned and perhaps you think you hate him. I, too, have hated him. And yet, in his way, he is not altogether a bad husband and he is a most loving and generous father.'

'I know. When I saw those photographs ...'

'The record of a long relationship. An unbreakable relationship, Signorina Drew. Carlo will never do anything to harm his children. He is weak and he has a certain vanity which needs to be fed. He does not like to think of growing old, he likes to have beautiful young women adoring him, and he has a temperament which drives him to excess. It is the same temperament which makes him a great singer. He *is* a great singer.'

Rosamund could not bring herself to speak, but when Lucia went on, 'To such an artist much must be forgiven,' she cried out,

'How can you say that, knowing that he has been unfaithful to you? And if I am not the first ...'

'The first!' Lucia laughed and for the first time her composure showed signs of cracking. '*Cara mia*, I doubt if you are the tenth! Of course, I don't know everything he gets up to when he goes away to other countries, but I can guess.'

'How can you stand it? How can you possibly forgive him?'

'It's not a question of forgiveness or of condoning his conduct. I accept that this is the manner of man I have married. If tears and reproaches would change him then perhaps I might indulge myself, but such conduct would only drive him away from me. Signorina, in spite of all his other diversions, we are still husband and wife. Look around you at what I have – money, position, a fine house, servants and the children, above all the children. I have my place and, no matter what you may think, that place is the centre of

130

Carlo's life. He comes back to me — always. I shut my eyes to what he does elsewhere. Oh, yes, it causes me great pain. I spend much time in prayer because I fear for his soul. But I am still his wife and I always will be his wife.'

'I must go,' Rosamund whispered. 'I shouldn't have come. I'm ... sorry.'

'Go back to Milan, give up that absurd position at La Scala and return to England. Forget Carlo.'

'How can I, how can I?'

'Which hurts most — your betrayed love or your humiliation?' Lucia asked shrewdly.

'Everyone *knows*!'

'Only a very small circle, I think. Carlo is usually discreet. Some people at La Scala perhaps ...'

'Everyone, from the director to the stagehands.'

'So? They will soon forget. As you must forget.'

It was useless for Rosamund to explain to her that this was a wound that would never heal. How could she possibly understand that Rosamund felt as if she had been flayed? Every inch of her shrinking flesh winced away from the realisation that all the love she had poured out had been misdirected, that she was nothing more than one of a long line of silly girls who had pandered to the vanity of a man with an over-active libido and a heartless determination to satisfy it. He had not been worth it. That was the thing that made her want to shriek aloud. She had given herself to him body and soul and he had not been capable of understanding the value of that gift.

Rosamund had no recollection of parting with Lucia, but she must have said or done something because the next thing she knew she was stumbling down the drive towards the gate.

The taxi was still waiting and the driver was too sleepy to notice her condition. It was not until she tried to pay him and her fingers shook so much that all the coins fell through her hands on to the ground that he looked at her curiously.

She had half an hour to wait for the train. Time passed. It might have been five minutes or five hours for all Rosamund knew. The rain stopped and a ray of sunshine lit up the grey sky, but she felt icy cold. All she wanted was to get home, even though home was the flat that was now contaminated by the knowledge that Carlo had enjoyed other women there.

When at last she reached the solitude she craved, she crawled on to the bed and lay there, curled up into a tight hunched ball, until morning.

'Tina, there's a friend of yours at the door and she's got a suitcase with her. If you're having someone to stay I do think you might have given us a bit of notice.'

Tina removed the headpiece through which she was listening to a recording of *Carmen* and uncoiled herself from her bed with a sigh. The aggrieved note in her flatmate's voice was all too familiar and she longed for the days when she and Rosamund and their two fellow-students had all mucked in together and someone extra turning up for the night was just a matter of shoving over and making a little extra room.

By the time she had clattered down the stairs from the attic room she now shared with a seventeen-year-old oboe player who had recently won a major competition and thought that the heavens moved when she played, Rosamund was in the living room, sitting on the battered couch which she hoped to claim as a bed for at least a night or two.

She looked up with an attempt at a smile as Tina came in and Tina, recognising her fatigue and making an accurate guess at her heartache, greeted her with casual warmth.

'Hi! This is great. I ought to have guessed it was you. Are you going to stay? I'd love to have you, though you know the place too well to imagine that you're going to be comfortable.'

'Could I? Just for a night or two. I realise it's not convenient, making up a bed in the living room, but I do need ...'

Her voice shook and she looked down.

'Somewhere to hole up while you pull yourself together?' Tina asked.

'That's it, of course. I can't go home.'

'No, I wouldn't want to myself, even though they'd be kind if they saw I was unhappy.'

'You know how it is with my parents. They only really like me when I'm successful, at least Mum does, and she's the one who does all the talking. She'd go on and on about throwing away my opportunities and I couldn't tell her why I've left La Scala. Even Mum's heard of La Scala.'

'It didn't work out?' Tina asked gently.

'Oh, it worked out very well – for Carlo. He had everything he needed, including me in his dressing room every night. And his wife ... his wife is *nice*, Tina. I want to hate her, but instead it's Carlo I hate.'

'What about work?' Tina asked, hoping to divert her mind.

'I've been playing a mute role in *Don Carlos*.'

'My God! Not even understudying?'

'Not even that. I've completely wasted my time. I don't know if I can sing any more. I'm not even sure that I want to.'

Tina sat down beside Rosamund and put an arm round her shoulders to give her a quick hug.

'You'll get over that,' she said. 'And, of course, you're staying here until you're in your right mind again. I'd give you my bed, but that would mean sharing with that little pain who let you in.'

'Thanks, Tina. I'm ... I feel battered. And Carlo doesn't even know I've left him. He's in Madrid. He'll be furious when he finds out I've gone. At least, I think he will. On the other hand, he may have found himself a fiery Spanish gypsy and be glad to have the bed free for her.'

'So in the end you saw through him?'

'Mm, and if you say "I told you so" I'll never speak to you again.'

'I'd better not say you'll get over it either, although it's true.'

'The fact that I was able to organise myself to buy an airline ticket and get to London means that I'm in a better state than I was when I first realised ... but it's been coming on for a long time, the *knowing* that nothing between us was true. And it was so perfect at first.'

'I know. I've never seen anyone so incandescent. Tears before nightfall, I thought ...'

133

'Oh, Tina, don't! Don't try to make me smile. I'm not ready to treat it as a joke.'

Rosamund jumped up and began moving restlessly round the room until she came to a halt by the fireplace, fingering the ornaments on the shelf.

'He's a great singer,' she said.

'Yes, I have to admit that,' Tina agreed. 'A shit with a wonderful voice.'

'How can that be? A great artist – and he is that, his *Don Carlos* is untouchable by anyone else at the moment and his *Otello* is going to be wonderful – how can he have such gifts and know how to use them and yet ... he has no integrity, not in his personal life. I can't tell you what it costs me to say that out loud and to know that it's true.'

'He's not alone,' Tina pointed out. 'If you read the lives of the musicians, for instance, or great painters, they're not renowned for their high moral tone.'

'It's not just the sex,' Rosamund said in a low voice. 'It's the belittling of me as a person, as a woman.'

'As a singer.'

'That, too. He never took me seriously. And I believed that he was going to help me! Oh, Tina, Tina, I can't bear it!'

With an exclamation of sympathy Tina jumped up and led Rosamund back to the couch again.

'Poor old Ros. There's nothing I can say that will be much help. Hang on, love, and the worst of the pain will die down. When I lost Tom ...'

'It wasn't the same. You sent him away, it was your choice, and he still loved you. Carlo ... Tina, do you think I've got it wrong? I was overwrought after I'd seen his wife. I never gave him any opportunity to defend himself. Perhaps he'll come after me, perhaps it'll be all right ...'

'I could shake you. If Carlo comes here – and God knows I think it's pretty unlikely – then I, for one, will show him the door. You know it's not going to happen, Ros. Show a little sense.'

Rosamund collapsed, her shoulders shaking, the tears she had held back overwhelming her. Tina gave her a helpless pat on the back and then she stood up.

'I'm going to fetch you a a box of tissues and put the kettle on,' she said. 'You can have a good cry and a cup of tea and after that we'll start thinking positively about your future.'

'What future?' Rosamund muttered.

'That glittering future we both know you've got in front of you. How about this for a beginning – the Wexford Festival have rearranged their schedule so as to put on the Peador and Leone operas on alternate nights next November, and Oliver won't hear of anyone but you and me playing the soprano roles.'

Chapter Eight

'I do think you might have asked me if I wanted to play Elisabetta,' Annis said.

'But, darling ... you've said many, many times that you would never perform on stage again,' Oliver protested.

'This would have been different. The girl is a partisan. We could have explained away my limp as a war wound. After all, I did create the role.'

'On record,' Oliver said evenly. 'Tina was the first Elisabetta on stage.'

'A student production,' Annis said impatiently. 'That hardly counts. Everyone associates the role with me.'

'You gave a wonderful performance and I'll always be grateful to you for lending your prestige to my unknown work, but I think the Wexford production would be too taxing for you.'

'How? Physically? Apart from this wretched leg I'm perfectly fit. Perhaps you have doubts about my voice?'

There was a long, terrible silence.

'That's it,' Annis said in a whisper. 'You think I can't sing any more.'

'You can and do sing magnificently in concert. I doubt whether you could sustain a full-length role such as Elisabetta.'

It was said, the thing he had been dreading having to say for the last two years. Oliver closed his eyes, in weariness and horror at his own cruelty. It was impossible to look at Annis, knowing how he had wounded her.

'You're wrong,' she said at last.

'Think how long it is since you had to carry an entire opera. You recorded *Aida* and *Tosca* and they were superlative, but can you really pretend that what you did in the recording studio could be repeated on stage, night after night?'

'We're not talking about an entire season,' Annis said. 'Ten days in a small opera house – and not even performing every night. I wouldn't expect to take part in *Astolat*, only *The Partisans*. I should have been asked.'

What Oliver did not want her to know was that the idea had been suggested and he had turned it down. He wanted Tina to sing his Elisbetta, just as he had secretly wanted her to take the part when it was recorded. Annis was wonderful, but she was not twenty-five. She was fifty-two, and it showed.

'I'm sorry you're disappointed,' he said. 'Truly I didn't think you would consider the idea.'

'Liar! You think I'm too old for the part. I am, of course, but my voice would have carried me through. That, and my acting ability. Is it too late to make a change?'

'Yes, it is.'

'Oh, you came out with that very quickly! Not so much as a pause to pretend to think it over.'

'Be fair, Annis. The part has been offered to Tina, the announcement has been made. We can't withdraw all the advance publicity.'

He had hoped to silence her, but Annis gave a sniff.

'Tina! A singer who has never yet taken a full-length role, not professionally. What makes you think she can do it?'

'I have faith in Tina. And so have you when you're not feeling annoyed with me.'

'Annoyed! That's a little word to describe the deep, deep hurt you've inflicted on me. Are you in love with her?'

'Of course I'm not.'

'No, it was always Rosamund you favoured, wasn't it?'

'I look on both those girls as our protégées, nothing more.'

'There must be *someone*. It's years since you and I . . . and you never understood how much that hurt me either.'

'Annis, really! You as good as turned me out of the house because you said you were holding me back.'

'You didn't contradict me.'

137

'Up to a point it was true. If I was to make any progress with my music I had to give up being your manager.'

'And my lover.'

'That, too, seemed to move naturally to an end. We parted, I thought, with goodwill and affection.'

'And relief on your part because I let you go so easily.'

Since that was true, Oliver could find nothing to say. He was dismayed at the turn the conversation had taken. He had come down to the house at Locksley Green for the weekend, full of news about the forthcoming performances of *The Partisans* at the Wexford Festival, and the last thing He had expected was to find Annis seething with jealous rage because she had no part in it. Perhaps he had been tactless. He had known at the back of his mind that Annis resented the younger, fresher voices coming along to take her place in the operatic world, but he had thought that she had too much pride to voice her jealousy.

Helplessly, he tried to think of a way to placate her.

'I'm lonely,' Annis said in a low voice.

He went to her then and sat beside her on the couch, taking one of her hands in his.

'My dear, what can I do?'

'Not take up our old relationship, I quite see that's out of the question. I should have told you, I suppose, that I was expecting to take on Elisabetta in *The Partisans*, but I didn't realise it was necessary. I expected you to see it the same way.'

'I'm not clairvoyant, my dear.'

'Nor particularly understanding when it comes to my feelings.'

'I've offended you − the last person in the world I would want to hurt − and there's nothing I can do about it. It's far too late to make any alteration to the programme.'

He said that with some firmness, determined to stamp on any idea Annis might have of substituting for Tina even for one performance. The opera was going to be given three times: three performances of *The Partisans*, three performances of *Astolat*, interspersed with a little-known work by Handel.

Annis shrugged her shoulders with a mulish air of being

unconvinced, but Oliver was relieved that she did not argue with him.

'You'll still come to Wexford?' he ventured to ask.

'Of course. I wouldn't be so petty as to stay away. I just hope your faith in these two untried girls is justified. Has Rosamund recovered from that disastrous affair with Cerutti?'

'I hope so,' Oliver said fervently, relieved that the conversation was taking a different direction. 'I could murder that man.'

'He's a great artist.'

'I'd like to fit him out for singing castrato roles.'

'I said you had a soft spot for Rosamund,' Annis said. 'You could do with a wife. Why don't you marry her?'

'*Marry* ...?' Oliver exclaimed, wholly taken aback. 'I'm not thinking of marrying anyone.'

'You should. It's high time. You need a companion.'

'I've got plenty of friends.'

And a satisfying, if somewhat hectic, sex life, but that was something he had no intention of discussing with Annis.

'Friendship isn't what I'm talking about — although it's part of a good marriage, as I knew with my dear Bruno. It's time you settled down. Leave it a few more years and you'll be nothing but a selfish old bachelor trying to make it with girls years younger than himself.'

'It's an unattractive picture,' Oliver agreed. He still smiled, but he was beginning to be irritated by Annis's persistence. 'What do you want me to do? Draw up a list of suitable candidates and work my way through it?'

'I've given you the name that should head the list,' Annis said, ignoring the edge on his voice. 'Think it over. You'll be seeing a lot of Rosamund at the Wexford Festival.'

'And Tina.'

'You can't marry Tina.'

'Why not? I would have said she was just as eligible as Rosamund — if I were thinking of marrying at all, which I'm not.'

'Tina is single-minded to the point of obsession. Don't tangle with Tina or you'll end up hurt. Rosamund is softer, more pliable. She, if she really loved you, would let her career

139

take second place and go in for making a home and having children.'

'Children! Are you arranging a family for me as well?'

'Certainly. You'll make a very good father, provided you don't leave it too late.'

There was no deflecting her. Oliver abandoned the argument.

'Let me get this Wexford thing behind me,' he said. 'I can't think about anything else with the performances of *Astolat* and *The Partisans* hanging over my head.'

Annis's remarks about Rosamund's affair with Carlo Cerutti would have horrified Rosamund. Because it had all happened in Italy and because it had seemed to her that La Scala was such a closed community, she had imagined that both her foolishness and her heartache were known only to a few people in Milan. She had not made allowances for the international operatic network. Annis had heard of the disastrous affair and had told Oliver about it. To other people Rosamund was just one more of Cerutti's little girls, but Annis had raged over her loss of face and the damage to her reputation as a singer. She had paid less attention to the emotional upheaval. That, to Annis, was one of the hazards of being human and vulnerable. One fell in love, one suffered, one recovered. Only occasionally did a man come along who was entirely satisfactory, such as her Bruno; someone to be mourned to the end of her days. Carlo Cerutti certainly did not come into that category, and if Rosamund had given her the opporunity Annis would have told her so, briskly.

As it was, she took more practical steps to rehabilitate Rosamund, recommending her as a soprano with a beautiful voice to several impresarios, with the result that Rosamund had concert engagements all over the country. What she had not achieved was a contract with any opera house.

Tina, on the other hand, was under contract to Covent Garden for fifty performances a year, each rehearsal to count as a third of a performance. She had special permission to be absent in order to perform at the Wexford Festival. She was delighted to be given an opportunity to repeat the role of

Elisabetta she had created as a student, and never suspected that Annis wanted the part. The only regret, for Tina, and she tried to suppress it, was that while she had only a minor role in Michael Peador's *Astolat*, Rosamund had been given the leading role.

'"Elaine the pure, Elaine the loveable, Elaine the lily maid of Astolat",' Oliver quoted. 'Who could it be but Rosamund?'

'I could do it,' Tina said, unable to stop herself.

'I know you could, but your Elaine would be a tiger lily. Be content, Tina; your time is coming.'

'I've been promised some proper roles next year,' Tina admitted. 'Oscar in *The Masked Ball*, Zerlina in *Don Giovanni* and Micaela in *Carmen* — that swine Cerutti is singing Don José; I shall probably throw up all over him.'

She pulled herself up and looked uncertainly at Oliver, expecting him to ask for an explanation of her hostility to the tenor.

'I know about his affair with Rosamund,' Oliver said.

'Damn, I did hope it hadn't seeped through to this country.'

'Annis and I won't talk. Has she got over it?'

'Not really. She shuts people out. What she really needs is a new love affair with a nice boy of her own age.'

'Someone like Tom Walden?'

'Bloody hell! Have we no secrets?'

'Not many. I brought up his name because I wanted to warn you that he's been engaged to sing the part of your lover in *The Partisans*.'

They had walked across the fields to The Jolly Ploughman and were enjoying a leisurely drink outside. It had become something of a ritual on the rare weekends when Tina was at home and Oliver was visiting Locksley Green.

'Well?' Oliver prompted when Tina did not respond to his news.

'I thought Tony Briggs, who did it on the recording, was to sing it at Wexford.'

Oliver shook his head. 'He's got problems. His voice has gone off alarmingly and he's been advised to rest it. Tom was approached – not by me, of course – and is eager for the chance.'

'He might have let me know!' Tina exploded.

'Do you write?'

'Not often. Well, not at all, actually. I stopped him writing because in every letter he urged me to go out and join him. Oh, heck, I feel all churned up at the thought of seeing him again. Why on earth does he want to come back to Europe? He's done terribly well in Australia.'

'His own back yard. Perhaps he wants wider recognition.'

'Yes ... I suppose. It's a bit soon. He's only just established at the Sydney Opera House. I do hope it's not because of me. I couldn't bear to go through that again.' She frowned ferociously. 'Bloody men, they're nothing but a nuisance.'

'I'm sorry,' Oliver said meekly.

Tina turned to him, a broad smile breaking out.

'I don't count you,' she said.

Oliver put his head down in his hands. 'Annis has been warning me about my age,' he said in a muffled voice. 'And I see she was right.'

He looked up and Tina was relieved to see that he was laughing.

'Having Tom opposite you won't make any difference to your performance, will it?' he asked.

'Of course not. It might even give a bit of an edge to it.'

'He's singing Lancelot in *Astolat* as well.'

'Don't remind me about *Astolat*,' Tina begged. 'I don't like that namby-pamby Court lady I'm playing; it's a silly little role.'

'A pity Peador made Guinevere a mezzo role,' Oliver suggested, keeping a straight face.

'Absolutely!' Tina agreed. 'But, of course, he was right. Musically, the contrast between the two voices is needed. I'll just have to grin and bear it. It's good news about Micaela for me next year, isn't it? I can really get my teeth into that.'

The Wexford Festival was a time of delight. The small Irish seaside town was charming, the people were friendly and there was an agreeable eccentricity about the entire festival.

On the afternoon of the first performance of *Astolat* Tina and Oliver found themselves meandering round the town together. They wandered down Monck Street to the waterfront and then across New Bridge. In late October the sun went down early and when they turned back and looked towards the town it seemed to be held in a bubble of shimmering light. The harbour water glowed crimson, a few lighted windows were softly golden, the town climbed up the hill until the top houses were silhouetted black against a sky that was banded in rose and gold, a clear cold green and pellucid blue.

'"Dear God, the very houses seem asleep",' Oliver quoted.

'Wordsworth,' Tina said vaguely. 'But that was morning, wasn't it? Still, morning or evening, it's very lovely.'

'Are you enjoying it?'

'Mm ... the place has got a lot of charm. I don't trust charm.'

'There's solid musical achievement here, too,' Oliver protested. 'Come on, Tina. You have to admit the performances are first-rate.'

'Including mine?'

'Of course. For me, you're the only Elisabetta.'

'Annis ...'

'Was too old for the part. She sang it beautifully, of course. When did Annis ever give a poor performance? All the same, if it hadn't been for ... circumstances, I would have insisted on you recording the role.'

'You mean, if she hadn't been your mistress?'

'As you said yourself, have we no secrets?' Oliver enquired evenly.

'And as you replied, not many,' Tina retorted. 'I've annoyed you. Can't you see how unfair that is? You can probe into my relationship with Tom, but it's hands off when I speak of you and Annis.'

'For the very good reason that Annis is on a different level from Tom Walden. She deserves your respect, young Tina, and don't you forget it.'

In spite of Oliver's opinion of Tina's performance as

143

Elisabetta, once again it was Rosamund who was the star. She repeated the role of Nerina, singing like an angel, but it was her Elaine that was the real revelation. The story of the lovely, betrayed girl whose love for Lancelot could not be requited because of his own illicit love for his Queen, might have been written for her. Rosamund admitted to Tina that she lived in dread of the night when she would find herself singing the words from Oliver's *Partisans* to the music Michael Peador had purloined for his own opera, but although she said it both girls knew it would never happen. When Rosamund sang Elaine she was too immersed in the role to run the risk of confusing it with the quite different Nerina.

Tom was in magnificent voice as her Lancelot, though Tina was critical of his acting.

'A bit wooden,' she said. 'He's better as Ricardo with me.'

The role of Lancelot, the tormented, guilty lover, was a difficult one. Oliver was inclined to agree that it was rather beyond Tom at that time.

'He'll mature into it,' he said.

'Maybe,' Tina replied doubtfully.

She and Tom circled round one another, outwardly friendly, inwardly wary, both reluctant to admit that there was still a powerful attraction between them. He had filled out and there was a hint of bulk about him which Tina criticised.

'You're developing what's known as a commanding presence,' she remarked.

'Meaning I've put on weight?'

'Must be that diet of mutton chops and kangaroo steaks they feed you on down under. What's the Sydney Opera House really like, Tom?'

'Oh, great! I'm having the time of my life. You should have joined me, you know.'

'I'm doing fine at Covent Garden, building a reputation. Slow but sure.'

She spoke hurriedly and breathlessly, too aware for comfort that Tom had drawn close enough for his breath to stir the hair touching her cheek. They were strolling along

144

the sea front in the magical gloaming on their free Sunday evening.

'Just look at that light on the sea,' Tina said, speaking at random. 'Realms of gold.'

Tom's fingers were touching the back of her head, playing with strands of hair in a way that sent a reminiscent shudder down Tina's spine.

'As gold as your hair,' he said. 'You're as gorgeous as ever, Tina.'

Of course she knew what was going to happen, had known ever since they had walked out together to stare at the setting sun. She made an inarticulate murmur of protest, but it was stifled as she was engulfed in Tom's embrace and her mouth opened under his. For a moment she gave in to a tide of remembered passion, then she began to feel stifled. She struggled to free herself and Tom reluctantly let her go.

'You may fight it, but it's still there,' he said. 'We were meant for one another. Come back to the hotel with me, Tina.'

'No,' Tina said. 'No, I can't go through that again. A week ... two weeks ... and then you'll go back to Australia. I'm not coming with you, Tom. I won't break my Covent Garden contract.'

'I'll settle for two weeks and no pressure to change your mind,' Tom said. 'It's better than nothing.'

Tina shook her head, holding him off as he tried to take her in his arms again. 'If we start making love it'll be a very short-lived happiness. If we stay apart I can just about bear to say goodbye to you a second time. Our parting nearly broke me last time. I can't afford that terrible emotional drain, it's too weakening.'

'You mean it has a bad effect on your singing?' Tom asked sarcastically.

'On my whole constitution, like getting over a really bad bout of flu.'

'Oh, great! If you look on me as nothing more than a nasty flu germ I can see there's no way you'd want to go to bed with me.'

'I've upset you,' Tina said wretchedly.

'Upset me? I *love* you, Tina. Standing here I ache all

over with wanting you. I'd ask you again to marry me if I thought you'd listen.'

'I can't do it,' Tina said. 'We'd better part, Tom. Dear Tom. I wish I could give you what you want, but the cost is too high.'

'To you, Tina. Too high for you. I'd give everything I had to possess you.'

With that scene between them Tina worried about their next performance of *The Partisans*, but to her relief they both proved professional enough to put their personal difficulties behind them while they sang. If there was an added tension between that night's Elisabetta and Ricardo and a touch of roughness in the way Tom handled her, it did nothing to detract from the atmosphere of the partisan camp. They both sang magnificently. Tom's voice had matured, Tina decided in a moment when she had time to think about it. As for her own performance, she was almost satisfied with it, although she would have liked a longer rehearsal and a few more performances to bring it to the peak of which she thought she was capable.

She was back in her dressing room, taking off her make-up, tired but happy, when Oliver looked in.

'Well done!' he said, 'You were stupendous. I'm more grateful to you than I can say.' He leaned over and gave her a careless kiss on a cheek still greasy with cold cream. 'And guess who was in the audience tonight? Ransu Prokopi!'

'I'm glad I didn't know that beforehand,' Tina said. 'Did he enjoy it? Has he said anything . . .'

She stopped, not wanting to sound too egocentric, but Oliver understood and smiled as he said, 'About your performance? Not yet. Annis and I are having dinner with him. I'll report anything he says – anything favourable, that is.'

'Either way, good or bad,' Tina said. 'He's a man whose opinion I really respect. If he's got any criticism then I'd like to know about it.'

She was just slightly aggrieved that the eminent conductor had not come round to see her. Perhaps it was too much to expect, but she had got him out of a hole once and he had

146

thought well of her. He might, she thought, have had the grace to look in and say something nice. In fact, it wouldn't have hurt him to have added her to the dinner party.

She would have been gratified to know that the idea had occurred to Ransu Prokopi and the reason he had rejected it was because he wanted to talk about Tina with Annis and Oliver.

He complimented Oliver on *The Partisans* and added one or two shrewd comments about details of the production.

'I was here for *Astolat* last night,' he said. 'It's been an interesting experience, comparing the two operas.'

'Tell me what you really think of both of them,' Oliver said.

Prokopi hesitated for one moment and then he said, 'Without the addition of your music, *Astolat* would be nothing. With that addition it's the better opera of the two.'

Annis exclaimed in protest, but Oliver smiled.

'It's my own opinion,' he said. '*The Partisans* is the work of a very young man. I've been privileged to see it produced here, but I doubt if it will survive as anything more than a musical curiosity, whereas *Astolat* could find a place in the repertoire of any opera house.'

'You're too hard on yourself,' Annis protested.

'I hope to do better next time.'

'You've got something in hand?' Prokopi asked.

'Yes, and I think now that I shouldn't have allowed myself to be diverted from it to complete *The Partisans* and see it into production.'

Prokopi nodded. 'Get it finished. I'd like to see the score when you feel ready to show it to me.'

Oliver's polite inclination of the head revealed nothing of the exhilaration he felt at that quiet request.

'You were well served by your singers,' Prokopi said.

Oliver felt Annis stir restlessly at his side.

'Our dear Annis might have been persuaded to repeat her Elisbatta,' he said.

To his relief, Ransu Prokopi was adroit enough to pick up the hint.

'Your performance on record could hardly have been

147

bettered,' he said smoothly to Annis. 'But Valentina Burford did well. I've come across her before and I was interested to have the opportunity to see her on stage, as compared with a concert performance.'

'We've all heard the story of how Tina saved the Berlin Philharmonic from an ignominious cancellation – of course,' Annis said.

'It was a performance that did her great credit. I knew when she told me you supported her career that it was worth gambling on her, and she did not disappoint me. Tell me, is she ready, do you think, for leading roles?' He turned to Oliver with a rueful smile. 'I'm sorry, that sounds rude. She has, of course, been singing a leading role tonight. I mean, is she ready for the classical repertoire?'

For a moment Annis's envy struggled with her musical integrity and then, to Oliver's relief, her natural honesty won.

'The voice is maturing nicely,' she said. 'It's not quite at the peak it will reach in perhaps five years' time. In the meantime, yes, Tina could sing major roles, provided she doesn't overstretch herself.'

'*Traviata* in a year's time?'

'Yes, she could do that,' Annis said. A smile broke over the face that was strained with the effort to be fair. 'She'll be a very healthy-looking Violetta.'

'She'll act convincingly,' Oliver said.

'Yes, that's going to be Valentina Burford's great strength,' Prokopi agreed. 'She can act. Whereas the other girl, for all the beauty of her voice, has a more restricted emotional range.'

'She reduces people to tears at the end of *The Partisans*,' Annis objected.

'A natural lyric soprano with great purity of tone. She's infinitely touching, just as she is as Elaine. The two roles, juxtaposed, have the effect of making her seem a better actress than she really is. She will be a heart-rending Mimi and she might tackle Butterfly, but whereas Burford may go on to tackle the lighter Wagnerian roles – Elizabeth, Eva, Siegelinde – I doubt whether Rosamund Drew will ever be up to anything so weighty.'

148

'Her voice will carry her through,' Oliver said.

'That might have been true in the past. Today we ask for so much from our prima donnas – looks, acting ability, the stamina to fly around the world and, on top of that, a flawless voice.' He cast a thoughtful look at Annis and added, 'In other words, we ask that every major singer should be an Annis Gilroy and, alas, such marvels are few and far between.'

It provoked Annis into laughter. 'That's shameless flattery and I love it.'

'What are your own future plans?'

'I've several recitals to give over the next few months and then ... I may do something I've not yet discussed with anyone.'

For a moment Oliver thought with dread that Annis was about to announce that she had decided to attempt a return to the operatic stage, but to his surprise she went on, 'I've spent a lot of time in the last week talking to our young baritone, Tom Walden, and it's made me homesick. I may go back to Australia.'

'Permanently?' Both men spoke together.

'I think so. I want to go home.'

'After all these years?' Oliver asked. 'Can you really call Australia home?'

'I've still got family there,' Annis reminded him. 'My two brothers and their wives and children. I think I'll find somewhere nice in the Australian sun and settle down.'

She glanced at their faces, pleased by the sensation she had caused.

'I may allow myself to be coaxed into doing an occasional concert,' she said. 'But there'll be no more touring. Just think! No more boring journeys, no more draughty dressing rooms, no more difficult conductors ...'

'Thank you,' Ransu Prokopi said with a smile.

'Dear Ransu, you know I don't mean you. If you knew how I regret that you weren't conducting operas when I was still performing! What music we could have made together!'

'The regret is all mine. Will you be doing any coaching?'

'If anyone seems to want me.'

149

'They'll be fools if they don't beat a path to your door. Settle in Sydney, dear Annis, I beg you, and offer your services to the Opera House. In the meantime, I was wondering whether, nearer the time and provided you haven't already deserted us, you would coach Valentina in *Traviata*.'

As Annis hesitated, he added, 'It was one of your own great roles.'

'Yes ... my Violetta was a triumph. Very well, I'll give our Tina the benefit of my experience – if she'll accept it. Tina's very independent.'

'I shall make it a condition of offering her the role. Thank you, Annis.'

After Ransu had left them Oliver said to Annis, 'Your idea of going back to Australia was a real bolt from the blue. Are you serious?'

'Perfectly. I'm tired Oliver. And I'm finished. The fact that you wouldn't badger the festival authorities to fit me into a performance of your opera told me that. Time was when a composer would have moved heaven and earth to have Annis Gilroy sing for him.'

'Don't hold it against me, Annis.'

'I don't ... oh, well, perhaps I do. It's made me realise that my day is past. It's a hard thing to accept. I think I'll be happier away from the European scene, watching the young ones coming up to take my place. I'll do my best for Tina – damn her! After that, I'm going home.'

'Violetta!' Tina said disbelievingly. 'Violetta with Prokopi! Oh, glory, glory halleluiah! And I've still got Micaela to look forward to before that.'

'Lucky you,' Rosamund said lightly. 'I wish my own prospects were as good.'

'With Christmas coming along you must be booked solid with oratorios.'

'I'm singing a lot of Bach,' Rosamund admitted. 'And, of course, *Messiah*.'

'God bless Handel. What would a budding soprano do without him? Seriously, Ros, your turn will come.'

'I don't know. My only experience of the operatic stage,

150

apart from here at Wexford, which has been so much fun it hardly counts, was at La Scala. I can't say it was a happy time, quite apart from the fiasco with Carlo. Sometimes I think I'd prefer to stick to the concert platform.'

'I can't imagine it,' Tina said. 'Dramatic roles are the breath of life to me.'

They went back to London and at last were able to take on the expense of sharing a flat without any other tenants. It was in Kensington, which was a relief to Mrs Drew, who thought it a better address than Southwark, and it was once again in a big old house with walls thick enough to stand two sopranos practising every day.

Tina was soon busy with rehearsals for *Carmen*, not always happily.

'I wish I could say I liked Rosa Manella,' she said one evening. 'But the truth is, the woman's a bitch. In fact, she's a proper Carmen. Still, I'm getting on well with Benno Neroni.'

'With who?' Rosamund said, her head jerking up.

'Benno Neroni. He's the producer. Surely you knew that?'

'I didn't. It just happens to have passed me by. He was at La Scala when I ... when I ...'

'When you were temporarily out of your mind. I know. He was the one who made you Countess of Aremberg. Perhaps that's why I haven't mentioned his name before. I can't help it, Ros. I rather like him.'

'He was cruel to me,' Rosamund said in a low voice.

'Perhaps he resented being used.'

'Perhaps. Oh, well, as long as he's not my producer I don't have to worry. Tina, I've got news. An audition at the Coliseum.'

'English National Opera? Ros, that's splendid. Go in and wow them. What are you going to sing?'

'Not Oliver's "Prayer for Peace", I think. It's getting too hackneyed. I thought it would be less obvious if I did something from *Astolat*. Elaine's aria when she realises that Lancelot loves Guinevere. What do you think?'

'Good choice. And it's still Oliver's music, as it happens. What else?'

'How about *"Questa cosa accorder"* from *Il Matrimonio Segreto*? You know, where Carolina goes on about how unsuited she is to marry into nobility.'

'It would be a good contrast to Elaine.'

'And the third thing, just in case they should ask?'

'A song?'

'No, I'd rather stick to opera.'

'I suppose you couldn't bear to do Butterfly?'

'I'm afraid my throat might close up. Stupid, I know, but it still makes me feel sick to think what I went through while Carlo was singing Pinkerton.'

'Do you remember I sang *"Mi chiamano Mimi"* for my Guildhall audition? I never felt it was quite me, but I've heard it said that you'd be a perfect Mimi.'

'Yes, that's something I know well and it would make a reasonably well-balanced programme. I don't suppose I'll get beyond one piece, but I'd better be prepared. I think I'll get on the telephone to Betrys Jones and see if she'll give me a couple of lessons beforehand.'

'Good idea. Remember me to her. Funny what a long time ago it seems now since we were under her at the Guildhall. Ros, talking of Carlo, you do know he's doing Don José in my production of *Carmen*, don't you?'

'I do. Don't worry, Tina. I shan't attempt to get in touch with him. I've well and truly recovered from that illness.'

Given her low opinion of Carlo Cerutti, it was not easy for Tina to endure the rehearsals of *Carmen*. The renowned tenor was not involved in the early rehearsals, which was a relief to her. She was able to put him out of her mind and concentrate on her own music and Benno Neroni's conception of the role.

'Micaela is a peasant,' he said to Tina. 'A good, plain, simple girl straight out of the earth. You can make your sound as refined as you like, but don't come tripping on like a tart in Mayfair. Remember you've come miles to find your sweetheart and you've probably walked most of the way. I want you sturdy and strong and healthy, though I won't mind if you're a bit hot and weary. But *good*, that's the key to my idea of the girl.'

'"*Bon comme le pain*"?' Tina suggested.

'Right! Wholesome as bread – and not much more interesting – a real contrast to Carmen, who's larks' tongues and ortalans. Personally, I'd rather have bread.'

He gave her his wide grin. As Tina had said, they got on well together. She saw that he watched warily to see the effect of Carlo's overwhelming charm when she first met him.

Carlo took her hand and kissed it lingeringly.

'Valentina Burford! One has heard of you. One of England's most promising singers. Ransu Prokopi is interested in you.'

'Aren't I a lucky girl?' Tina said in dulcet tones.

'Lucky? It is talent, not luck, I think. And you are to be my Micaela. So often one wonders why poor Don José prefers the terrible Carmen to the charming Micaela.'

You wouldn't say that if Rosa Manella were anywhere within earshot, Tina thought cynically.

'He's dazzled,' she said out loud. 'People do get dazzled by tinsel and gilt and mistake it for silver and gold.'

'How true that is! Benno, we have a philosopher here! But you, Valentina, you, I am sure would never be so foolish.'

'No.' Tina said. 'I can tell the false from the true.'

Her tone was very gentle, but there was something in the quality of her smile that made Carlo Cerutti drop the hand he had insisted on keeping in his, and later in the day he said to Benno, 'I suppose the Burford girl really is up to the part?'

'Well up to it,' Benno replied. 'Don't worry, Carlo, she's quite equal to what's required.'

When he had an opportunity, Benno remarked to Tina, 'It seems you're immune to the Cerutti charm?'

Tina hesitated and then she decided that it might as well come out. 'Rosamund Drew is my closest friend. We share a flat.'

'Then you can put me in touch with her,' Benno said.

'Not likely! She's just beginning to get over that awful time in Milan and seeing you will do her no good at all. You were miserably unkind to her.'

153

'Look at it from my point of view. I was in a real dilemma − the director away and our leading tenor threatening to quit unless I gave his girlfriend a job. I couldn't give Rosamund a singing role, not without having the entire cast at my throat.'

'Put like that it sounds almost reasonable,' Tina said.

'It's not my fault that Carlo is a swine about women.'

'You did nothing to help when everyone else treated her badly.'

'Honey, we're talking about Italy, where the man who plays the triangle holds his place because his mother's the first violin's father's second cousin. Bring in an outsider and you have to have a damn good reason to justify it. Being Cerutti's latest lay isn't enough. She was resented, even though she did nothing more than walk on the stage looking remote as the moon − and as beautiful.'

'Ros is a lovely girl, but she's more than that. She's a fine artist.'

'I admit it. I was dumbfounded when I heard her voice. For once Carlo had picked himself a singer with real talent. I would have used her if I could, but my hands were tied. Fix up for me to meet her again and I'll do my own apologising.'

'Not until after she's had her audition with the ENO. That's next week and she's pinning all her hopes on it.'

'Is that so?' Benno looked thoughtful. 'Maybe I could put in a good word.'

'No! Don't interfere.'

He smiled and said no more, but Tina was on tenterhooks until Rosamund returned from her all-important audition.

Tina was at home and she looked up as Rosamund came in, not daring to ask how it had gone. Then Rosamund smiled and flung her arms out wide and Tina jumped up and hugged her.

'They offered me a contract,' Rosamund said. 'Then and there, on the spot. They'll be doing *The Tales of Hoffman* and I'm to be the Muse of Poetry.'

'Oh,' Tina said blankly, remembering the briefness of that role.

'And covering the part of Antonia.'

'Well ... that's a step in the right direction.' She looked suspiciously at Rosamund. 'You're keeping something back. A few lines in *Hoffman* wouldn't make you all pink and pleased-looking.'

'A new production of *The Huguenots* and I'm to play Valentine.'

'Ros! That's really, really good. I couldn't be more pleased for you.'

'There's just one drawback. Guess who's the producer?'

A suspicion formed in Tina's mind. 'Not Benno Neroni?'

'How on earth did you guess that?'

'I see him nearly every day,' Tina pointed out. 'Something he said ... when you asked that question the idea darted into my mind.'

'I suppose I shall be able to bear it, though I'd rather it was almost anyone else. You get on all right with him, don't you?'

'He's an arrogant bastard, but I respect him. He's a very, very good producer and the Foreign Office ought to send their diplomats to watch the way he handles Rosa Manella. If I were you, I'd put the past behind me and treat him as if you'd never met before.'

Tina sped off to rehearsal the next day and cornered Benno.

'Rosamund will be singing Valentine in your production of *The Huguenots*,' she said. 'You recommended her, didn't you?'

'I merely said I'd come across her and been impressed. Tina, I may be the prospective producer, but I don't do the hiring and firing.'

'You did in Milan.'

'I was in a different position there.'

'Ros must never, never know that you spoke for her. She *must* believe that she got this contract entirely on her own merits.'

'She did.'

'She won't believe that if she knows you put your oar in and it would shake her confidence terribly.'

'OK, OK, I hear what you say. Now can I get to meet her?'

155

'Why? You've done your bit.'

Benno seemed to have difficulty in answering. 'She haunts me,' he said at last. 'I want to lay my ghosts.'

'I'm having no part in it,' Tina said. 'If you want to make contact with Ros then you must do it yourself.'

She expected that to be the end of the matter, but a couple of mornings later Rosamund opened a letter at the breakfast table and exclaimed in surprise.

'Would you believe it! Benno Neroni says he's heard I'm to be his Valentine and he wants me to meet him for a drink.'

She looked at Tina in sudden dread. 'You don't think he's going to tell me he won't have me, do you?'

'Of course not! He doesn't do the hiring and firing,' Tina said, quoting an unimpeachable source. 'Can I see the letter?'

She glanced at the scrawled lines, curious to see how Benno had expressed himself, and gave him full marks for tact.

'The Savoy! He's doing you proud. Don't be daft, Ros. That's not the place he'd choose to tell you he was having you chucked out. Sounds more like he wants to mend his fences. Scribble a reply to say you accept and I'll take it to the theatre and see that he gets it.'

Rosamund was not familiar with the Savoy lounge, but her stage training stood her in good stead. She walked to the edge of the steps which led down into the big room with its armchairs and low tables and stood looking round with apparent poise and calm, until a tall figure she recognised rose to its feet. She went down the steps with the grace instilled by dozens of classes and walked towards Benno.

He watched her come, more nervous than she was, if she had only known it. It was true, she had haunted him; and here she was, the slim, pale girl with troubled eyes, coming up to him without smiling − wary, as she had every right to be.

She looked very elegant in a plain, dark dress with a long silk scarf thrown carelessly round her neck. Benno held out his hand and Rosamund put her own fingers into it. Only their coldness betrayed her nervousness.

'I'm glad you were able to come,' Benno said. 'What'll you have to drink?'

156

'A glass of white wine, please.'

'And I'll have Bourbon and water.'

The order was given. Rosamund sat in expectant silence, not helping him.

'We're going to be working together. I wanted to put things on a friendly basis,' Benno said abruptly.

'It'll be months before we start rehearsing *The Huguenots*,' Rosamund said.

'Sure, it's going to be a long time before we get together, and once *Carmen* is launched I'll be leaving England for a visit to the States, but I've got you on my mind and I wanted to talk to you.'

'What about?'

'You're not making it easy, are you? About Milan, and La Scala and the lousy deal you had.'

Their drinks arrived, just as he was getting up a head of steam. Conversation lapsed. Rosamund picked up her glass and took a sip of cold wine. She was beginning to think she could have done with something more warming.

'I owe you an apology, actually,' she said. 'I walked out in the middle of a season.'

'It didn't matter. The original girl had recovered and went straight back into the part. What I appreciated was that, in spite of what you were going through, you took time to write me a note saying you were leaving.'

'Was it readable?'

'Only just. It gave me a fair idea of your state of mind. I never came closer to murder.'

'Oh, you wouldn't kill off your tenor, not after you'd been so obliging to him.'

'Rosamund don't be like that. I did what I thought was best in a difficult situation.'

'You were in a steaming rage at having a pistol held to your head and you took it out on me.' She struggled with herself for a moment and then she said, 'I've always wanted to know, how did Carlo take it when he came back and found me gone?'

Benno drained his glass and looked round to order a refill. 'That's a hell of a question,' he said.

'He was relieved.'

'I guess you could say so. These little affairs of his, they don't last long. Usually the girls know the score. They make what they can of it while it lasts and shrug it off when they get dropped. You were ... different.'

'I believed he was the love of my life.'

'He never deserved that. Rosamund, you've got one of the loveliest voices I've ever heard; you've got beauty, you've got presence and there's a quality about you that touches the heart. You could have a great career. I'm thrilled you're going to be in an opera I'm producing. What more can I say? I want us to be friends.'

Rosamund smiled and held out her hand. In spite of the fact that she had been twisting her cold glass between her fingers, it felt warmer than it had when she arrived.

'All right,' she said. 'Friends.'

She laughed suddenly. 'I was afraid you'd asked to see me to tell me you wouldn't work with me.'

'Whatever gave you that idea? I'm delighted to be working with you. Do you know *The Huguenots*?'

'I've never seen it performed,' Rosamund admitted.

'It's hardly ever done in this country; more often in France and occasionally in Germany. I think we can make something of it. It's the fact that it's not well known that made me accept the offer from the ENO.'

'When did you switch to producing? I mean, that's not what you were doing when I knew you in Milan, was it?'

'I went to La Scala to get general experience, but I'd been producing in the States. I wanted to go to Italy − back to my family's roots. I learnt a lot and most of the time I enjoyed it. Say, didn't you once say that you knew Annis Gilroy? Is it true she's retiring?'

'So she says. She's going back to Australia.'

'I've got all her records. I certainly regret never having seen her on stage.'

'It was through Annis that Tina − you know, Valentina Burford, your present Micaela − Tina and I went into singing.'

She told the story of the summer afternoon when Tina had found Annis's diamond ring and Benno sat and watched the play of expression across her face.

158

'Have dinner with me?' he asked.

'Well ... not here,' Rosamund said doubtfully. 'I'm not dressed ...'

'You look a million dollars. There's a place upstairs where we can get an informal meal. Overlooking the forecourt rather than the Thames, I'm afraid, but it's quite pleasant.'

Tina was getting ready for bed when Rosamund got home.

'Pleasant evening?' she asked.

'Mm. Tina, he's *nice*! We've both got the wrong idea about him. He's not arrogant at all. In fact, at times I thought he was quite unsure of himself.'

'Wait till you start working with him. Benno Neroni knows what's right and Benno Neroni is going to get it, even if he has to spill blood.'

'I suppose ... yes, he's got terribly high standards. But tonight he was sweet.'

'Sweet,' Tina said disbelievingly. She looked more closely at her friend. 'Rein it in, Ros. Don't start one of your things for Benno. Remember the Nero in Neroni.'

To her relief, Rosamund laughed with genuine amusement.

'Don't worry, Tina. I'm just relieved that the man I thought was a monster has turned out to be human. I shan't object to a bit of bullying for professional purposes.'

She stretched luxuriously. 'I could sleep for a week. At last my career is moving in the direction I always wanted. It makes everything seem worthwhile.'

Chapter Nine

Benno's production of *Carmen* early in 1990 was well received and Tina had particularly favourable notices for her Micaela. Because she thought it was an opera her parents would enjoy, Tina arranged for them to have seats for the first night.

'We recognised lots of the tunes,' Will told her afterwards. 'You sang beautifully. It was a treat to hear you.'

'Pity they made you look so plain,' Elsie said. 'Your pretty hair all scraped back in that tight little bun and those clomping great boots, whatever was the costume woman thinking about?'

'It's this year's peasant look,' Tina said cheerfully. 'I was quite happy with it.'

'Your Aunt Daphne was a bit narked not to have been invited,' Will said.

'Oh, dear! I never thought of it, to tell you the truth. It's ages since I saw Auntie Daphne.'

'That was what she was complaining about.'

'If Daphne wants a ticket she can pay for it,' Elsie said. 'She ought to be able to afford it, the money she's raking in with that TV programme of hers. Mind you, I think it's gone off. I watched it the other evening and it wasn't a patch on what it was when it first came on. I wish she'd found you a place on it, Tina. It seems wrong to me for Rosamund to have been a guest and not you.'

'I'm too busy to be fooling around with quiz shows,' Tina said.

She was supremely happy. The three small roles she was

singing at Covent Garden were all regarded as stepping stones to better things in the future; Annis had promised to coach her in the part of Violetta, a role Tina looked forward to with eager anticipation; she and Rosamund had settled amicably into their flat and Rosamund was going to have a career that matched Tina's own.

The only thing that troubled her at all was the thought of Tom. She missed him with a small, dull ache as if an old wound had been freshly bruised. She had never found anyone to take his place. Plenty of friends; even an occasional thrill of attraction, but never anyone who came near filling the void left in her life when Tom had gone off to Australia. It had been hard, seeing him once more in Wexford, wanting him and making herself turn him down all over again. Tina told herself that what she had done had been right, for her at any rate. It would have been quite impossible to turn her back on the opportunities that were opening up for her, but that did not stop her lying awake at night wishing that Tom could be by her side.

She took a cynical view of Rosamund's nervous, edgy relationship with Benno Neroni. Rosamund was fascinated by him, that was obvious, and Tina came to believe that Benno himself was being drawn into an intimacy that went deeper than he had ever intended. It did not make him any easier on Rosamund when rehearsals for *The Huguenots* began in the autumn of 1990.

The Huguenots, with a complicated plot and music by Meyerbeer which was no longer quite so highly regarded as it had been in the nineteenth century, was a difficult opera to stage, particularly since its theme of conflict between Protestants and Catholics was uncomfortably topical. Benno was determined to highlight this aspect and to bring out the futility of one faction warring with the other. Rosamund was playing the part of an aristocratic young Catholic, offered in marriage to a leader of the Protestants in the hope of effecting a reconciliation. Having been rejected by him, she marries her original Catholic fiancé, but too late she and the Protestant, Raoul de Nangis, realise they are in love.

'Pity they weren't a bit more clued up,' Tina remarked critically, reading the libretto. 'Just think, according to this version of history, if Valentine and Raoul had got together earlier then the St Bartholomew's Day massacre might have been averted.'

Rosamund laughed at her irreverence, but she still looked anxious. Benno was pinning a great deal on her long duet with Raoul in the fourth act, when he sought to be released from a locked room to warn his fellow Protestants about the forthcoming massacre and Valentine pleaded for her relatives and the cause they regarded as holy.

'It's all very dramatic,' she said. 'Benno keeps on at me to give him more − but more of what? I'm already singing my heart out, not keeping anything in reserve. He talks about broader gestures, more body language, but I feel a fool waving my arms about. My idea is that the music should carry the message. We're singing in English, after all − and I don't find that easy. He says it's because I like to hide behind a foreign language, but I sang both *Partisans* and *Astolat* in English, so I don't know what he means.'

'They were both rather *cool* girls, Nerina and Elaine,' Tina said slowly. 'Nerina because of her religious vocation and Elaine because she had to suppress her love for Lancelot. Valentine is highly emotional. I can see what he means about having to throw yourself into the part in order to give it conviction.'

'He's giving me some special coaching,' Rosamund said. 'I suppose I ought to be grateful, but it makes things very tense between us.'

'In your personal life, you mean? I don't want to probe, but how does that stand?'

'He's attracted, but holding back because he doesn't think it's a suitable time to start an affair with one of his leading sopranos − at least, that's my reading of the way he behaves.'

'And you?'

'I'm attracted, too,' Rosamund admitted. 'More than I would have thought possible after my Carlo fiasco. I resent the way Benno bawls me out at rehearsals, but I'm dependent on his guidance.'

'He's a first-class producer,' Tina agreed. 'What's his next project?'

162

'He'll be around for the next three months, working on a production for the Welsh National Opera. After that he'll be in Paris.'

'And presumably your little affair will fizzle out.'

'It's not an affair − not yet. And if I have any sense it never will be.'

'Be strong,' Tina said flippantly.

'Easy to say, but if he really presses me ... Tina, I don't think I'll be able to hold out against him. He's ... damn him, he's got into my blood and I think about him all the time.'

Tina was sympathetic, but Rosamund puzzled her. Considering how easy she seemed to find it to fall in love, one would have expected her to be able to convey that emotional intensity on stage, whereas it was Tina, who prided herself on being level-headed, who seemed to be able to put across the anguish of thwarted love.

By the time *The Huguenots* opened Tina was deep in rehearsals for her own debut in *La Traviata*, but it would have been unthinkable not to go to Rosamund's first night.

It was a stirring production, with plenty of Benno Neroni touches to keep the action going. It was also an exceedingly long production, since he had managed to retain the fifth act. Rosamund had obviously benefited from his personal tuition and she sang with sufficient passion to make her Valentine truly dramatic. Her sound was always lovely and rather better, Tina thought critically, than the voice of the other main soprano in the role of Marguerite de Valois. But the triumph of the evening went to the two leading men − Raoul, the tenor, and the Count de Nevers, the baritone. What a part that would have been for Tom.

The opera was not as obviously popular as *Carmen* had been. Tina detected a note of unease amongst the audience when it was over, with Valentine shot dead on the unwitting orders of her own father. She died praying for him, but the Catholic soldiers were still swearing to wipe out the Protestants. It was not a comfortable conclusion, nor had Benno intended it to be, the programme notes made that clear, but he did allow them to suggest that a modern opera

163

might have hinted at reconciliation.

There was a party after the first night for the cast and friends and the sponsors of the opera. Tina was invited, as was Carlo Cerutti, who was back in London for the last two performances of *Carmen*.

It was the first time that he and Rosamund had met since she had run away from Milan. She managed it well, allowing him to kiss her first on one cheek and then on the other, and accepting his compliments with aplomb. It helped that Benno was by her side, with one hand under her elbow, steadying her. She turned to him with a grateful smile as Carlo moved away.

'Thanks for the support, but I truly think I'm over that disaster,' she said. 'Benno, you haven't said, were you pleased with me tonight?'

'It went better than I dared hope.'

'Rather a backhanded compliment. Did you think I'd let you down?'

'I knew you'd sing wonderfully, but I was afraid that nerves might betray you into forgetting all I'd told you about acting the part. That didn't happen. You were great.'

On the other side of the room, Tina watched uneasily as she saw them looking deep into one another's eyes.

'What are you scowling about?' a familiar voice enquired.

She turned to find Oliver watching her with amusement.

'Svengali,' Tina said darkly.

'You think Benno has got our Rosamund hypnotised, as in the Du Maurier novel?'

'Sort of. He got a great performance out of her in this opera. I just wonder whether she'll be able to repeat it in something else when his influence isn't there.'

'Rosamund isn't a natural actress, as you are, but she'll get by.'

'Do you really think that about me? I wanted Annis to give me some pointers about acting Violetta, but she will only talk about phrasing and pauses and so on.'

'Very important.'

'Yes, of course, and all a help towards building the part. What I haven't quite worked out yet is how to convey that Violetta is frightened.'

'Is that how you see her?'

'I think so. Frightened of the illness she knows she's got, frightened of losing her looks, frightened of not having money, of being sick and destitute and alone.'

Oliver was watching her with the smile that seemed to come naturally when he was talking to Tina.

'We're here this evening to congratulate the cast of *The Huguenots*,' he suggested.

'I know,' Tina said guiltily. 'It's just that *La Traviata* is so much on my mind. Who's that man talking to Rosamund now?'

'That's Jeremy Bilchester, known to his friends as Jerry, as they say in the gossip columns.'

'Does he feature in the gossip columns?'

'What do you think? He's rich, he's clever, he's got a title and he's unmarried.'

'Sounds worth cultivating,' Tina remarked mischievously.

'Very much so. He's chairman of the company which sponsored *The Huguenots*. Rosamund seems to have him eating out of her hand, which is all to the good. Always be nice to your sponsors, young Tina.'

'Not so much of the young,' Tina retorted. 'I'm coming up twenty-six and old enough to be taken seriously.'

'Oh, I take you seriously,' Oliver said. 'You're my favourite soprano. Didn't you know that?'

'Thank you, darling.' Tina looked thoughtfully across the room to where Rosamund was still talking to Lord Bilchester. 'I think I'll go and cut Ros out. I could just do with a nice, rich man in my life and Ros has more than enough to cope with at the moment with Benno Neroni at her feet.'

She moved in an apparently purposeless way to the other side of the room and caught Rosamund's eye. Rosamund, not at all deceived by her casual approach, did what was expected of her and made the introduction.

'How nice to meet someone from outside our closed musical world,' Tina said, all wide-eyed innocence. 'But you must be an opera lover, Lord Bilchester, because it's your company which sponsored *The Huguenots*, isn't it?'

'Yes, indeed, and a very worthwhile investment it has turned out to be.'

He was a tall man and thin, with a narrow head and sleek dark hair. He had an air about him – like a Spanish grandee, Tina thought, with a vague idea of *Don Carlos* in her mind – as if he could rule the world if he chose and it was only a whim that made him stand to one side and watch everyone else making a mess of it. Not handsome, not even particularly good-looking, but his long-boned hands were beautiful and his spare body had the careless control of an athlete. An interesting man, and a formidable one.

They talked over one or two points concerning the opera and Lord Bilchester showed himself to be well informed and discerning.

'You must be a model amongst sponsors,' Rosamund remarked. 'You really know what you're spending your money on.'

'We all do that,' he replied coolly. 'Publicity! Don't be misled by my display of knowledge, Miss Drew. This is a commercial venture and the success of the opera is tied up with my company's success. You both look surprised.'

'We're used to thinking of everything from the artistic point of view,' Tina said.

'Of course, that's your role. Mine is to provide the money – and to make it. Unless it comes rolling in I can't push any of it in your direction. Things aren't easy in the business world at the present time and I'm profoundly thankful that a venture I urged on my directors has proved to be so worthwhile. An unusual opera, very well done. Something that will make people talk. The reviews tomorrow should be interesting.'

'Don't remind me,' Rosamund begged. 'I dread them.'

'No need. You were first class.'

Rosamund's attention was claimed and she moved away.

'What else do you do, besides sponsoring opera?' Tina asked.

'Where shall I start? I'm head of the company that was founded by my grandfather. That's where my title comes from. Quite honestly, I'd just as soon be without it in this day and age, but it seems churlish to discard something that gave him such tremendous pride. He was an engineering genius, my father was a financial genius and I spend my time holding together what they passed on to me.'

'No spark of genius of your own? I find that difficult to believe.'

'You flatter me. I moved into electronics at the right time and we're leaders in the communications field. I suppose that called for a certain amount of forethought. I have a seat in the House of Lords, I'm a Justice of the Peace, a minor landowner, I sit on the board of a couple of charities and I'm a governor of the local school near my home in the country.'

'Stop! That's enough to be going on with,' Tina exclaimed, laughing. 'You have a busy life.'

'I keep occupied. And when I have a spare evening I spend it listening to music such as the splendid occasion we've had tonight.'

'You enjoyed it?'

'Very much, especially Miss Drew's performance.'

He looked across the room to where Rosamund was standing. It was obvious that she was receiving compliments. She was flushed and smiling, but to Tina, who knew the signs, it was plain that Ros was exhausted.

'She's done in,' Tina said under her breath. 'I ought to rescue her and take her home.'

'You live together?'

'Yes, we've shared a flat since our student days.'

In her concern for Ros, Tina was unaware that she was being studied, nor did she appreciate the contrast between her glowing vitality and the draining effect of an arduous performance which made Rosamund look almost drab.

Lord Bilchester glanced at his watch. 'I asked my chauffeur to call for me in ten minutes' time,' he said. 'May I take you both home?'

'That would be kind. I'll go and speak to Ros.'

'Ah ... but I want something in return for giving you a lift. I'm bringing a party of friends to see *Carmen* next week. Will you join us for supper afterwards?'

'Of course, I'd be delighted,' Tina said demurely.

The ride home in a chauffeur-driven limousine was a treat. The thought came into Tina's mind that if she and Ros went on rising in their profession the day might come when they could afford such luxuries for themselves. It seemed strangely remote from the hard work and hard times of their student days, as if they had become two different people, but her feeling of disorientation righted itself when they let themselves into their pleasant, shabby flat and Ros collapsed on to the sofa.

'I'm almost too tired to undress and get into bed,' she said. 'Tina, was it really as good as everyone says or are they just being kind?'

'It was very, very good and you were superb,' Tina said stoutly.

'I thought it was probably all right when Benno said he was pleased.'

'He really does go in for the superlatives, doesn't he?'

Rosamund smiled. 'You know as well as I do, that's high praise from Benno.'

'Is he still giving you trouble?'

'Depends what you mean by trouble. In between telling me I've got a voice like a train whistle, move like a cow in labour and have the temperament of Minnie Mouse, he does occasionally press me to go back to his hotel for a bout of lovemaking, yes.'

'I recognise the style — except for the lovemaking,' Tina said. 'So you haven't given in yet?'

'Not yet,' Rosamund admitted.

'It might be a terrific experience,' Tina said thoughtfully. 'All that nervous energy ... the trouble is, I can't see it lasting, not on the level Benno would demand.'

'Nor me,' Rosamund agreed. 'Give me a hand, Tina. I'm so tired I don't think I can stand up on my own.'

As she tugged her friend to her feet Tina said, 'There's never been anyone for me but Tom. I live like a nun.'

'Oh, yes?'

'Well ... a *worldly* nun,' Tina admitted with a grin. 'I could do with a bit of romance.'

'Maybe it's coming your way. You seem to have hijacked my millionaire, you rotter.'

'Is he really a millionaire? How nice.'

'You want to watch your step. You wouldn't be the first singer he's kept.'

'Really? I say, what do you think he'll offer me? Diamond necklaces? A discreet villa in St John's Wood? A yacht?'

'Those days are past, unfortunately,' Rosamund said. 'A year's supply of luncheon vouchers and a flat in the Barbican, more likely – easy access from the City, you know.'

'I'll sell myself more dearly than that,' Tina protested.

Rosamund yawned. 'What was the matter with Oliver?' she asked. 'He looked really down in the dumps.'

'He was all right when he was talking to me,' Tina said idly. 'I say, perhaps I can influence our wealthy friend to sponsor *his* opera.'

Tina remembered that conversation as she got ready to join Jerry Bilchester and his friends after her performance as Micaela the following week. She could not change out of her costume, but in the interval between her last appearance and the final curtain she was able to unpack the dress she was going to wear and lay out fresh underclothes. As soon as the curtain calls were over she hurried back to the dressing room, carrying the bouquet Jerry Bilchester had sent her, a lovely arrangement of white flowers, slipped out of her plain peasant costume and sat down in front of the brilliantly lit looking glass to remove her make-up. She felt pleasantly excited at the thought of an evening out, buoyed up by the exhilaration of her performance and not too tired to enjoy herself.

She brushed her hair out of the tight braids in which she wore it in the character of Micaela and decided to leave it loose about her face. Her skin glowed from the vigour with which she had removed her stage make-up and she applied no more than a dash of foundation, a flick of powder, some bright lipstick and a careful application of mascara, and then she was ready to slip her dress over her head.

She had chosen it with Rosamund's assistance and it had cost more than Tina liked to remember. 'A very discreet little number', Ros had called it approvingly. The navy blue chiffon skirt was calf-length, the neck was high and the sleeves were long and tight. The top was sparsely spattered with minute multi-coloured sequins. Tina added a pair of gilt earrings set with red, blue and green stones, slipped her feet into navy blue sandals, tossed a long red silk scarf round her shoulders, picked up her handbag and was ready when a discreet knock on the door announced that Lord Bilchester was calling for her.

They were a party of eight, split between two cars.

'I've brought the Rolls this evening, but there's no point in being crowded,' Jerry Bilchester remarked.

'How nice,' Tina said, and nothing about her betrayed the yelp of laughter she was suppressing. A Rolls Royce! This is the life, girl. Live it while you've got the chance.

They went to Le Gavroche, which was new to Tina. It was all very civilised and pleasant and conversation flowed, but Tina was shrewd enough to realise that she was being sized up, certainly by the women, and perhaps by the men, too. Jerry Bilchester was important to them, she could sense that, and they were curious and just a little wary of the new woman in his life.

There was a suggestion that they should go on somewhere else for dancing, but Tina said, 'I'm sorry, but I'm singing Zerlina tomorrow. I mustn't have too late a night.'

'A charming role, but when are we going to hear you as Donna Anna or Donna Elvira?' Jerry asked with a smile.

'Oh ... one day, I hope. *Traviata* is my next hurdle.'

They dropped the couple who had shared the Rolls Royce with them off at Annabel's and Jerry directed his chauffeur to Tina's Kensington address. In the back of the car he took Tina's hand in his. She let it rest loosely in his clasp and tried to ignore the way his thumb delicately stroked the inside of her wrist.

When they arrived Jerry got out of the car in a leisurely way and saw her to the front door.

'When shall I see you again?' he asked. 'Have you any free evenings next week?'

'I'm not doing anything on Thursday,' Tina said. 'After that, I'll be plunged into rehearsals for *La Traviata* and, quite honestly, unable to think about anything else.'

'I understand. I'll pick you up on Thursday about seven. I suggest we might drive out of London and have a quiet meal in a country pub.'

'That would be lovely.'

Tina hesitated, but Jerry had no doubts about the next move. He slipped one arm round her, put his other hand on the back of her head and drew her forward to be kissed. His lips were firm and warm and unparted. Tina stood quite still, not so much kissing as letting herself be kissed. After a moment, Jerry let her go and stepped back. He was smiling.

There were flowers for her every evening she was at the theatre and a particularly lovely bouquet delivered to the flat at the weekend.

'I say, you are being given the treatment,' Rosamund said. 'What about the diamond necklaces?'

'No sign of them as yet,' Tina said. 'Of course, Thursday is only my second date with him.'

'Better put your toothbrush in your handbag. If he comes without his chauffeur I bet he asks you to stay the night in this country pub he's taking you to.'

'If he does, I'll say no. I think I'll say no,' Tina said. 'Actually, I don't believe he'd be so crass. A very subtle gentleman, our Jerry.'

'And rich, and charming and unattached,' Rosamund said. 'Some people have all the luck.'

She had recovered from her exhaustion after the first night. Her notices had been uniformly good. There were some doubts about the choice of opera, but all the critics thought that Rosamund Drew had performed to perfection. As a result, Rosamund was on a high that transformed her. She went around the flat singing, she lost her haunted look and she put on weight and regained the colour which had drained from her cheeks. About her relations with Benno Neroni she said nothing, and Tina thought it better not to ask. His work on *The Huguenots* was finished, he must be leaving London soon. Perhaps then Rosamund would escape from the fascination he exercised over her.

Jerry Bilchester picked Tina up punctually on the following Thursday evening. He was, she noted, driving himself. A Jaguar this time. The range of cars at his disposal seemed to be endless. Had he put an overnight bag in the boot? If so, Tina decided, he was going to be disappointed.

She thanked him sedately for the lovely flowers he had sent her and he passed it off lightly.

'This pub we're going to isn't exactly in the heart of the country,' he said. 'About a forty-minute drive if the roads are reasonably clear. I discovered it a week or two ago and thought that food was rather good. It makes a change from the round of London restaurants.'

'Yes, indeed,' Tina said, as if she dined at Le Gavroche every day of the week.

He asked about the performances she had given since they had last met and Tina spoke about them and about the impending rehearsals for *La Traviata*.

'I've been studying the role for months, of course,' she said. 'But the actual stage rehearsals begin next week.'

'You're looking forward to it?'

'Very much. My first real leading role, you know.' She paused with a smile and said, 'I'd like to ask you about your work, but I understand so little of what you do that I don't know what to say.'

'You'd probably find it excessively dull if I told you.'

'But you enjoy it?'

'The management of people is endlessly fascinating.'

'It must be,' Tina said. 'That isn't what I thought you'd say.'

'In the end, that's what my job depends on. Will this man — or woman — perform as well as we think, will the department or company they run achieve the goals that have been set, and are the goals, in fact, realistic.'

'In other words, will the profits still come rolling in?'

'Precisely. There's no better indicator of performance.'

It sounded a far cry from the world Tina knew. She fell silent as the miles rolled by.

The way looked familiar. They were going down the A3, she realised. Home territory, almost. How would his lordship react if she suggested they should drop in on her mum and dad? The idea diverted Tina so much that she had to fake a cough to hide an impulse to laugh out loud.

She was not so amused when they pulled up outside The Jolly Ploughman. Because they had approached it from the opposite direction from the one she was used to, over the fields from Locksley Green, she had not realised where they were going. Nor did she immediately recognise the unpretentious public house where she and Oliver had sometimes enjoyed a drink. It had, as Oliver had once forecast, been taken over and improved. If you could call it an improvement, Tina thought sourly, taking in the new lattice windows, the white paint and the rustic porch over the door.

She wondered for a moment whether to pretend that the place was new to her and then decided it would be a mistake.

'How strange,' she said as they got out of the car. 'I actually know this pub, but it's been very much altered since I was last here.'

'New people took it over and decided to open a restaurant, I believe,' Jerry said. 'I'm disappointed that it's not a novelty to you. I discovered it only a few weeks ago, and of course, as one does, I assumed it would be new to everyone else, too.'

'It is, in that it's completely different,' Tina said. 'In the old days you might have got a wedge of bread and cheese or a ham sandwich, but certainly nothing more.'

'I think you'll find the present menu an improvement on that.'

Inside, the pub was still unpretentious, but it had unmistakably been done up. The walls were newly white-washed, there were gleaming horse brasses on the beams and the previous tatty notices about meetings of the darts club had given way to tasteful prints and a framed history of the house about which Tina was profoundly sceptical. It was not exactly bogus, in that the original fabric was untouched, but something had gone out of it, something honest and plain and down to earth.

The food, Tina had to admit, was outstanding. At least Jerry had got that right. Good wine, too, which was something that would have been unthinkable a few years earlier.

They were halfway through their second course when two new people came into the restaurant and were shown to a table on the other side of the room. Oliver and a girl Tina recognised as a top stage designer. Tina waited until they were seated and then set about trying to catch Oliver's eye.

He looked up from shaking out his napkin and glanced round, as if his attention had been caught. When he saw Tina he went very still for a moment, then he made what Tina thought of as a typical Oliver face: the maximum of communication conveyed with the minimum of muscular movement. She knew from the slight wrinkling of his forehead that he was surprised to see her and slightly sardonic about her companion, while a quick glance at the ceiling and a twitch of the eyebrows told her that he shared her opinion of the way their pub had been altered.

'Someone you know?' Jerry asked, catching her smile.

'Oliver Leone and Simone Milford. I haven't met her, but I recognise her. Oliver I've known for years and years, ever since Annis Gilroy first encouraged me to take up singing. He lives in Locksley Green, at least he used to, though he doesn't spend much time there now. That's the village Rosamund comes from, and my own home is only a few miles away.'

'So I've really brought you to your own back yard. How old were you when you first realised that you wanted to be a prima donna?'

'Fifteen.' Tina plunged into a lively account of her early struggles, resolutely ignoring the couple across the room.

They were invited to take coffee in the lounge. The lounge! Tina recognised it as the old public bar and wished she could share her amusement. Better not to say anything to Jerry. He was already just a little bit put out that this had turned out to be familiar ground to her.

They could have left the restaurant without passing by Oliver's table, but Tina was determined to speak to him and she resolutely led the way.

Oliver got to his feet at their approach and she said, 'Jerry, do you know Oliver Leone? Oliver, this is Lord Bilchester.'

'We have met,' Oliver said. 'And I expect Lord Bilchester knows Simone because she worked on one of the operas his firm sponsored.'

Jerry agreed and turned to speak to the dark-haired woman on the other side of the table. While his attention was diverted, Tina murmured under her breath to Oliver, '"The old order changeth ..."'

'"Yielding place to new",' Oliver agreed. 'The nosh is good.'

'Superb, but ...' She broke off as Jerry turned back to her.

'We're just going to have coffee,' he said to Oliver. 'Will you join us when you're ready? Have a brandy, perhaps?'

'We've arranged to go back to Locksley Green for coffee,' Oliver said. 'Simone has a mass of papers to collect from Annis's house. Nice to have seen you.'

When she and Jerry were settled in the 'lounge' Tina remarked, 'What I would really have liked to ask Oliver was whether, since he's talking to a designer, there's any chance of his second opera being performed in the near future.'

'Not for a year or two, I think,' Jerry said. 'These things have to be scheduled so far ahead. I'd like to see it staged. He's a talented composer.'

He seemed to think that disposed of Oliver, because he made a very deliberate break in the conversation, turning it to a business trip he was due to take to the United States.

'It looks as if it will coincide, at least partly, with your own commitment to rehearsals for *La Traviata*,' he said. 'Which is just as well, because otherwise I might find myself kicking my heels at the stage door.'

'I'm sure you'd find other company,' Tina said.

'Not company I want,' Jerry said deliberately.

He was looking at her steadily, forcing her to understand what he was saying. She was going to have to start taking him seriously. This was more than an evening's diversion. If she understood him correctly then he was prepared to wait until after his business trip and until her strenuous rehearsals were over, not to mention her opening night. And then ... Jerry Bilchester wanted her and she was going to have to make up her mind just how much she wanted him.

For the second time he let her go at the end of the evening with no more than a long kiss. Tina stirred in his arms, liking

175

it, liking him, excited by the practised ease with which he held her. She was not in love with him, but it would not be difficult to fall. It was a heady experience and she felt out of her depth. At least she would have time to get herself sorted out before he started pressing her for a real commitment.

'I'll see you once more before I go,' Jerry said. 'And after that ... keep me in your mind, sweet singer. I have a perch where I would very much like you to alight.'

He was laughing, but Tina was serious as she replied, 'A perch? Or a cage?'

Jerry raised her hand to his lips. 'Never a cage, I promise you that.'

If Rosamund's notices had been good for *The Huguenots*, Tina had a real triumph in *La Traviata*. This was a very elegant Violetta. From the moment she first appeared in a swirl of pale lilac silk she was seen to have more refinement than her companions in the demi-monde. Here was a young woman who might have graced any table, if it had not been for her lapse in morals, but behind her high spirits and ability to please lay an intense vulnerability. This Violetta was really not quite sure how it had come about that she had risen to the top of her dubious profession, and at the back of her mind there was a fear of what would happen when she was no longer as young and beautiful as she was when the opera opened. She saw Alfredo's love as the answer and responded not only with passion but with a wonderful feeling of release from her former life.

Tina had been well served by her dress designer for this role, from the elegant and dashing evening gown in the first act, to her simple grey and white organza in the second when she was living in the country with Alfredo, and the dramatic black lace over red silk she wore after she had given him up in response to his father's pleading and returned to take up her life in Paris.

The third act was heart-rending. None of the usual gibes about a soprano allegedly dying of tuberculosis, but still singing at the top of her voice, applied to Tina's handling of her sad adieu to the past, nor could anyone doubt her miraculous revival of strength when her lover returned. It

176

was, for once, quite true that there was scarcely a dry eye in the house as that strength ebbed away and Violetta fell back dead.

Tina was surprised by the degree of exhaustion she felt afterwards. After all, it was not the first full-length operatic role she had sung.

'I could lie down and die, just like poor old Violetta,' she said. 'And I always thought I was so strong!'

'You gave out more of yourself tonight than you ever have before,' Annis said. 'What can I say? I've seen more Violettas than I can remember. I was one of the great ones myself. I thought I knew all the nuances of the role. And look! My handkerchief is quite wet. Dear Tina, you were not just good, but truly great.'

They were crammed into Tina's dressing room — Annis, Oliver, Rosamund, Will and Elsie — and there was a throng of people outside trying to get to the new young soprano to congratulate her. Tina felt dazed. What she wanted more than anything else was for all of them to go away and leave her time to come to terms with what she seemed to have achieved.

Jerry put in only the briefest of appearances. Just like him, Tina thought; he was not one to compete with the crowd. He took her hand and pressed it, saying 'Congratulations' and Tina just had time to say hurriedly, 'Jerry, your lovely present ...'

He smiled and pressed her hand again. 'I'm glad you liked it. We'll talk another time.'

Tina watched him as he moved through the throng to the door. He turned, touched his fingers briefly to his lips, raised his hand in salute and was gone.

She had opened the jeweller's box before the performance, slightly dreading that it would be something she would feel unable to accept. Inside there was a small globe intended to be worn as a pendant, a perfect representation of the world, with all the continents in gold and all the seas in deep blue enamel, suspended on a delicate gold chain. With it was a card on which was written, 'Dear Tina, the world is yours — Jerry'.

A very pretty toy and beautifully judged, just right for

the present stage of their relationship. Certainly it was not a thing she could think of refusing. Holding it in her hand, Tina realised that there was a small indentation in the line which marked the equator. She put her thumbnail under it and the globe snapped open to reveal a watch face. Tina was enchanted by its smallness, by the exquisite craftsmanship and by the thought that had gone into the choice of a bauble which was useful as well as lovely.

Perhaps only Oliver appreciated the generosity of Annis's response to Tina's performance. When it came to her music Annis could not lie. She had seen greatness and she acknowledged it. Only later when she was alone did she shed a few sad tears because she had been supplanted. Tina was the future, Annis was the past. Annis was profoundly thankful that she had already had the sense to acknowledge it and announce her retirement to Australia.

She held a party on the eve of her departure and it was a scintillating occasion, with all the great names in the operatic world who could get to London coming together to pay homage to a dearly loved singer.

'Not that I believe in this retirement,' Ransu Prokopi remarked. 'You are a young woman, dear Annis. We shall be hearing of triumphant concerts on the other side of the world and grinding our teeth because your fellow countrymen are luckier than we are.'

'I don't know about that,' Annis laughed. 'But, of course, I do mean to go on singing and I've already been approached about giving master classes for some of the young singers in Sydney.'

She looked across the room to where Tina was talking to Benno Neroni. 'Perhaps I'll discover another Valentina Burford,' she said quietly. 'I suspect that if I had done nothing else I would be remembered for having encouraged young Tina to take up singing.'

'She's something of a phenomenon,' Ransu agreed. 'I'm a little afraid for her. She understands all about the technique of singing, but she hasn't come to terms with her tremendous dramatic impact. She doesn't know *how* she does it.'

'Does anyone?' Annis asked. 'Rosamund, who is in every

way Tina's equal in musical terms, makes a conscious effort to act — and does very well — but Tina's instinct will always take her that one step further. Better, I think, not to tamper with that instinct.'

'As long as she doesn't come to rely on it and fail to work at her roles.'

'Not work? Tina? She's that rare thing, an instinctive artist who's also intelligent. Tina knows very well that her survival depends on hard work. I wish she had a suitable companion.'

'Lord Bilchester?'

Annis grimaced. 'They've been seen together a lot lately, but I don't quite see that as a long-term relationship.'

Ransu's gaze wandered round the room and settled thoughtfully on Oliver, who was leaning against the wall with a drink in his hand, looking abstracted, but watching Tina's animated discussion with Benno.

'Someone who shares her musical interests, naturally,' he said.

'A husband who is also her business manager, that would be ideal. A pity her young baritone went back to Australia. It's Tom Walden who's approached me about master classes. He seems to have a genius for organisation and he was devoted to Tina.'

They were interrupted by a crash on a gong. Annis had insisted that there were to be no speeches, but she could not be allowed to depart without at least a toast, and when that had been proposed and drunk a small parcel was brought forward on a silver salver and presented to her.

'But this is very naughty!' she exclaimed. 'I said this was to be a quiet goodbye.' She tore off the wrappings and exclaimed in surprise and pleasure. It was an exquisite antique diamond brooch.

'What can I say?' Annis demanded. 'Thank you, my dear, dear friends.'

Tina and Rosamund went home together afterwards, refusing the many offers of escorts they both received.

'At least we can afford to have a taxi without feeling

guilty about it,' Tina remarked. 'I say, Ros, isn't it nice to have money?'

'Wonderful! It was a good party, wasn't it?'

'Yes, but do you remember when the one object of going to a party was to look for a new boyfriend? And here we are, two ageing spinsters, sedately taking one another home.'

'I know, but I'm still trying to steer clear of Benno and your beau wasn't there.'

'I'm seeing him tomorrow night,' Tina said.

'How's it going.'

'I feel as if I'm being stalked by a very experienced hunter. Every time we meet he advances a bit nearer and yet . . . nothing much happens. I'm not sure I don't prefer the quick pounce; at least you know where you are.'

'Would you give him up?'

'Only reluctantly,' Tina admitted. 'I'm quite keen, actually. I spend all my time wondering what his next move will be. He's invaded my mind and part of me resents that.'

'Just like Benno and me,' Rosamund said sadly.

She would have been hard pushed to explain to Tina the mixture of fear and fascination she felt for Benno. She knew that he wanted her in his next operatic production, after he had finished his stint with the Welsh National Opera, but that was to be a French production of *Pelléas et Melisande* in Paris and Rosamund was by no means sure of being offered the role, nor was she entirely convinced that she wanted it. She had heard a recording of Debussy's strange, otherworldly music, but it was not a part she had ever thought of studying. Benno insisted that she had a quality that was exactly suited to Mélisande. The idea was hanging in the air, unsettling Rosamund and making her unsure of what she might be doing in the future.

When Jerry Bilchester remarked quite casually, over dinner the following evening, 'I'm in love with you, you know,' Tina jumped with the suddenness of it.

'You can't say things like that between one mouthful of sole bonne femme and the next,' she protested.

'Why not? Eating and loving are both important parts of my life.'

Tina looked round the crowded, discreetly lit restaurant. 'All these people.'

'Yes, that could be improved on,' Jerry agreed. 'When we've finished our dinner we'll go back to my flat and discuss it properly.'

'You've completely destroyed my appetite,' she complained.

'I'd like to think that's because you're longing to be alone with me, but I'm afraid it's more likely that I've made you feel anxious, which I regret.'

'What you've made me feel is unsophisticated.'

'Well ... I have to agree with you there. Drink your wine, darling, and try to look less like a startled deer. It's quite appealing, but it makes me feel predatory and I'm trying very hard to rein in my baser instincts.'

He was laughing and, in spite of her shock and, of course he was quite right, her anxiety, Tina could not suppress an answering gleam. Baser instincts, indeed! What Jerry wanted was to get her into bed and the wretched man had got her to the point where she could hardly wait to find out what it would be like.

Jerry's flat was like Jerry, exceedingly well appointed. There was a lot of plain polished wood and soft black leather furniture. All the colours were subdued with an occasional gleam of metal in the fittings. It had a small entrance hall, a kitchen and two bedrooms, each with its own shower room, but the main part of the flat was taken up by an enormous open space with a dining table at one end and a grand piano at the other, floor to ceiling windows with a view over the lights of London, and a terrace outside.

'It's all very opulent,' Tina commented, prowling round. 'Do you ever make it untidy?'

Jerry laughed. 'I do, but someone comes in and tidies up after me. Do you like my pictures?'

'Very much,' Tina said, coming to rest in front of a riot of colour which gradually resolved itself into a flower market.

181

'I've got three in the flat, all by the same man, a British artist called Hugo Wood – dead, unfortunately. He's just coming into his own and I was lucky to pick up these paintings before the prices went through the roof.'

'I think they're wonderful,' Tina said. 'Apart from them ... it's very impersonal, Jerry.'

'An extension of my office,' he agreed. 'My real home is in Somerset. You must see that one day soon. This room is wonderful for parties, which is what it was designed for. When I'm on my own I just use one bedroom and have breakfast in the kitchen. But it's the one place where we can be completely private, that's why I brought you here. Tina, my darling ...'

'Suppose I say no?' Tina asked.

'I'll put you in a taxi and send you home, but I'm damned if I'll come with you. You can't refuse me now – can you?'

She could no more turn him down than she could fly to the moon. The touch of his hand was magic, the pressure of his lips on the curve of her breast made her moan with pleasure. They moved from the enormous cold living room to the bedroom, undoing one another's buttons as they went. Jerry laughed as Tina's fingers fumbled with his cufflinks.

'We'll arrive where we want to be more quickly if we undress ourselves,' he said.

They stood one on either side of the bed flinging off their clothes. Tina was ready first. She lay down and held out her arms. When Jerry joined her she shuddered from head to foot at the feel of his body pressed against hers.

He was a sophisticated lover, but his care for her pleasure could not disguise that he was desperate for her, and Tina liked that. When Jerry forgot his careful calculation of her readiness to receive him and took her with a passion that was almost rough she cried out and clutched him to her with an eagerness that equalled his own.

They lay together quietly for a long time afterwards, exchanging small, sweet kisses. At last Jerry raised himself on his elbow and looked down at her.

'You're a fine and generous lover, my darling,' he said.

182

He sounded rueful as he added, 'I don't know when I've been so carried away.'

'It was wonderful,' Tina said. 'Tell me *now* that you love me.'

'I do, indeed I do. Funny, I didn't allow for that magnificent temperament of yours. In everyday life you seem so . . .'

'Ordinary.'

'Not ordinary, never that. Matter of fact, perhaps. But when you're aroused, either by your music or here, in my fortunate bed, you're like a raging forest fire.'

They resumed their gentle caresses, until their hands became more urgent and Jerry asked in a low voice, 'Again? May I?'

'Don't ask,' Tina said. 'What you want, I want. Now and always.'

She was deliciously tired the next day and not sorry that their many engagements made it impossible for her and Jerry to meet again that week. Nights of love were all very well, but she was dazed by the completeness of her surrender. It had been so long . . . She had almost forgotten what it was like to love and be loved in return, to give everything she had for the pleasure of her lover and to receive that pleasure back a thousandfold.

'Not much doubt about what's been happening to you,' Rosamund said. 'Quite apart from the fact that you've been out all night, you look as if you've discovered fairyland.'

'Paradise,' Tina corrected her. 'Oh, Ros, he's marvellous! I'm so happy I could fly.'

'Don't tell me, I don't want to know,' Rosamund said. 'What happens next?'

'I've no idea. All I can think about is that I'll see him again on Monday.'

'Fitting you in between appointments, is he?'

'Don't be like that. We're both busy people and anyway I can do with a respite. I've got *Traviata* tomorrow night and Saturday. I simply must put Jerry out of my mind.'

Tina had made up for her previous oversight when she appeared in *Carmen* by making sure that her Aunt Daphne was sent a couple of tickets for *La Traviata*. She was prepared for Daphne to come round to see her after the performance, but she was irritated when her aunt appeared between the second and third acts, and still more annoyed when she saw that Daphne had brought a young man with her.

'I don't usually see people in the intervals,' Tina said. 'How did you manage to get in?'

'Oh, trust me!' Daphne said airily. 'I know my way backstage too well to be kept away. Well, ducky, you've made quite a hit.'

'Are you enjoying it?'

'It's terrific. And you're stunning. Look, I've brought my Nicky round to meet you.'

Nicky — whoever he might be — was in his early twenties, a very good-looking young man with the classical features and physique of a Greek god. His eyes were blue and his hair was a cap of burnished gold — a little too suspiciously bright in Tina's opinion, but the effect was undoubtedly striking. He wore a dark suit, a silk shirt and a dashing tie and he carried off his expensive clothes with nonchalant grace. An actor, Tina thought, and my word doesn't he like himself!

Nicky smiled, revealing an entrancing dimple in one cheek, and held out his hand. Tina had no choice but to take it, but it was difficult to get her hand away once Nicky had enclosed it in his warm, strong fingers.

'I certainly am pleased to meet you,' he said. He had a faint trace of American accent, more cultivated than native, Tina suspected. 'You're the first one of Daphne's family I've met,' he went on. 'Daphne, you're right, she's the living image of you.'

Automatically, Tina glanced into the large, brightly lit looking glass on her dressing table. Her aunt's face was reflected in it, too, and there was no denying the resemblance. They had the same broad, high cheekbones, the same straight nose, the same rounded chin. Daphne was skilfully made up and looked younger than her years, while Tina's stage make-up aged her.

'You could be sisters,' Nicky said. There was something

sly in the glance he cast at Daphne as he added, 'Except that, of course, you're not.'

Tina thought her aunt looked slightly put out.

'Never mind about that,' she said impatiently. 'Let's tell Tina our news.'

She held out her left hand, on which a new ring glittered.

'Nicky and I are engaged. We're getting married in a couple of weeks' time.'

Tina felt her mouth gaping open. For a moment she was incapable of saying anything. She glanced at Nicky. He was smiling his dimpled smile, but his eyes were watching for Tina's reaction. Complacent young puppy, she thought furiously. He couldn't be much more than twenty-three and Daphne must be – what? – forty-five or six.

'What can I say?' she managed to bring out. 'You've taken me completely by surprise. Congratulations.'

She spoke that last word to Nicky. As far as she could see, there was no reason to congratulate Daphne.

'The wedding's to be at Caxton Hall and, of course, you must come,' Daphne was saying.

'I don't know ...' Tina began.

'You must come,' Nicky said. 'I'm counting on you being there. And Elsie and Will. I've not yet met them. I can't tell you how much I look forward to it.'

Tina tried to imagine that meeting and failed.

'I must start thinking about changing for the third act,' she said. 'Nicky, it's been ... most interesting, meeting you, but I'll have to ask you to leave. No, don't you go, Aunt Daphne; stay and tell me a little more about your wedding arrangements.'

She thought she had contrived that rather well. Nicky saw through it, of course, but when Daphne blew him an airy kiss and said, 'See you back in the stalls, darling', he went off with a good grace.

'What does he do for a living?' Tina asked as soon as the door had closed. She only hoped she could be sure that Nicky did not have his ear glued to the other side.

'He's an actor, of course. What else could he be with those looks? Isn't he divine?'

185

'Very handsome,' Tina agreed. 'Aunt Daphne . . .'

'Do drop the "aunt", darling. As Nicky said, we might easily be sisters. Now, I know exactly what you're going to say. You think the age difference between us is too big, but honestly, darling, we never think about it. Nicky adores me − silly, isn't it? We're fantastically happy and we're both, I hope, going to get parts in a new musical that's coming over from America soon.'

'Which means you won't have to keep him?'

'I'm not keeping him now! That's a most offensive thing to say. True, he lives with me and I pay for all expenses of the flat, but that costs no more than if I lived there alone, and a damned great barn of a place it is to live in without company.'

'Must you marry him?'

'Nicky wants it and I must say I think it's lovely of him. He's utterly devoted to me.'

Tina did not respond. A toy boy, she thought scornfully, but she managed not to speak those words out loud.

'Don't sit there with that disapproving look on your face,' Daphne said. 'In what way am I different from your precious Annis Gilroy? Didn't she live with a man umpteen years younger than her?'

'That was a special case,' Tina said unwisely, stung by the comparison.

'How? You can't answer me, can you?'

Tina struggled to explain to herself the difference between two people who, out of profound affection, had consoled one another for a deep loss, and this union between her aunt and the pretty young man with the watchful eyes.

'It's like comparing gold with glitter dust,' she said.

'That's not a nice thing to say. I keep telling you, this is a real love match.'

'Even Annis and Oliver split up,' Tina said wearily. 'Where will you and Nicky be in ten years' time?'

'Who cares? Time enough to worry about that when it comes. I want him now and he wants me. You can't imagine what boost that's given me. I look better, I feel better. I'm ready to take on the world, just so long as Nicky and I can be together.'

'Then there's really no more to be said. I can't talk about it any more. I simply must change and prepare myself for the last act. It's quite taxing and I need a rest.'

'Oh, come off it! What do you have to do but lie on a couch and sing? You should try having a third act with three big numbers and a dance routine.'

'Yes, of course, that must be hard work. What I have to do is a bit of mental preparation, so please leave me now.'

'I won't get in your way. Are these your togs for the last act? Very pretty. Go on, strip off, it won't worry me.'

Tina lost her patience. 'Aunt Daphne, please go. I've tried to be tactful, but the truth is I don't welcome visitors until after the performance and particularly not visitors who give me such ... such startling news. I want to be left alone. Surely you can understand that?'

'All right, all right! I never thought you'd turn into a temperamental prima donna, young Tina, but if that's the way you want it then I'll go. I was thinking of coming out in the open and telling you something else, but if the simple news of a wedding can upset you so much then I'd better keep it to myself.'

'Yes, yes,' Tina said, not attending as she preparing to slip the silk and lace of her third act peignoir over her head.

As Daphne opened the door she said, 'You will come to my wedding, won't you? And bring Will and Elsie along? Nicky's dead set on having all my family there, I can't think why, considering how little they're likely to approve.'

'I don't know,' Tina said. 'Yes ... I'll try.'

Daphne went at last, hustled out in the end by Tina's dresser, who was seriously worried by this prolonged visit.

Fortuntely, it was an easy change and Tina still had a few minutes to clear her mind of her aunt and her tiresome fiancé. She sat back in her chair with her eyes closed. Never mind about family matters, never mind about the world outside. She was Valentina Burford, leading soprano in an acclaimed production of a popular opera. She was Violetta Valéry, the courtesan, who had given up everything for love and then renounced that love for the sake of her young lover and his family; she was alone, she was sick, she was dying, and the only thing that kept her going was the hope of seeing Alfredo once more. Daphne and her affairs receded. Tina was back in the nineteenth century, her wasted body sagged, her breath caught in her throat. When the call came she was right back in the part and ready to go on and sing as if nothing had happened.

'I couldn't be more irritated by my aunt,' Tina told Jerry. 'Have you seen the papers? Whacking great pictures all over the place of her and pretty Nicky, and the things she's supposed to have said about their engagement! Quite nauseating.'

'The *Financial Times* seems to have missed the story,' Jerry said, with a hint of a smile.

Tina grinned. 'Of course, it must all seem quite remote and unimportant to you. Sorry, darling, I'm letting it get out of proportion.'

'Nothing to do with you is unimportant to me,' Jerry said. 'But we do have other things to discuss. When are you going to move into my flat so that we can be together more often?'

He had suggested this before and Tina had put him off with a vague answer. Now she said slowly, 'I don't think I can do that, darling.'

'Why not?'

'Lots of reasons, none of them very well defined. I need a life of my own ...'

'You'll always have that as long as you go on singing. I'm not asking you to give up your career.'

'Of course not. I need a place ... somewhere of my own.' Tina looked round with a smile and said. 'This flat, it isn't really *me*, you know.'

'And that shabby old house in Kensington *is* you? Surely not. You're an international star ...'

'You sound like Auntie Daphne.'

'Don't put me off with a joke. I'm serious. You deserve a better setting than the student digs you've had for the last few years. I think you fit in perfectly here.'

'My family is the other obstacle. If I let them know I've moved in with you Mum will say she always knew it would come to that if I went on the stage.'

'And that matters to you?'

'Very much. Don't you have any family, Jerry?'

'I believe I have a couple of cousins somewhere, but I was an only child and my parents are dead. I just can't imagine being put off from living with the woman I love because my mother might object.'

'It won't stop me loving you, but I don't feel I can move in with you.'

Jerry looked dissatisfied, but he said in his equable way, which had won more arguments than anyone else's bluster, 'I won't press you for now. I believe you'll come to see how much more convenient an arrangement it will be.'

'One thing I must do is move some clothes in here,' Tina said. 'You won't mind?'

'The thin end of the wedge,' Jerry said with a smile. 'Now, are you coming to Somerset with me this weekend?'

'Oh, darling, I can't! It's Aunt Daphne's wedding and, tiresome though it is, I simply must put in an appearance.'

'That family of yours is a bloody nuisance.'

'I know. I often swear, too, but I still love them, you see.'

'More than you love me?'

'Don't be silly,' Tina said, going to him. 'I love you more than anything in the world, but you mustn't try to stop me doing what I think is right.'

Daphne's wedding was a trying occasion. The ceremony was attended only by the bride and groom, the bride's family, her agent and a friend of Nicky's with a large camera, who took an inordinate number of photographs. Nicky insisted on shot after shot of himself and Daphne with Elsie, Will and Tina. It became very boring and seemed unnecessary considering that Press photographers were also covering the event.

They went on to a reception at a nearby hotel to which a number of theatrical personalities had been invited. Nicky was in his element, flitting from group to group, laughing and chatting and being charming. Daphne, who looked, as Tina was forced to admit, as radiant as if this were her first venture into matrimony, and certainly not a slightly damaged forty-five, watched him with adoring eyes.

189

'She's daft about him,' Will said disbelievingly.

'She'll live to regret it,' Elsie prophesied. 'Half her age and looking like a film star, how long is he going to put up with a middle-aged wife? I give it five years at the outside.'

She stopped abruptly as Nicky came skimming up to them, his face alight with goodwill.

'You haven't got a drink,' he said reproachfully. 'And we're just about to cut the cake and have a toast. Will, I suppose you wouldn't like to propose it? No? Then I'll get Daphne's agent man to do it. After all, she looks on him as a sort of father figure. How I wish I could have known her *real* father, not to mention her mother, who must have been a really strong woman, a tower of strength, wasn't she, Elsie?'

'She was a good sort,' Elsie said stiffly, but Nicky had sped away without waiting for her answer.

The toast was given, the party continued and finally the happy pair departed for a short honeymoon and Tina felt she could suggest leaving.

'Yes, let's get away,' Elsie said. 'It's not the first time I've seen Daphne making a fool of herself, but it doesn't get any easier to watch. Is there anywhere we can get a decent cup of tea, Tina?'

'Come back to the flat,' Tina said – and that, she told herself, was not something she could have suggested if 'the flat' had been Jerry's luxurious penthouse.

She called a taxi, an extravagance which made Elsie shake her head, but they all felt relief at leaving behind them the overheated atmosphere of a show business wedding. Will was very quiet, as if he had something on his mind, and when Tina left them alone while she went to put on the kettle, she caught a scrap of conversation which puzzled her.

'She's told him,' she heard Will say.

'No!' Elsie exclaimed. 'Whatever makes you think that?'

'He was throwing out hints. Else, don't you think it's time for Tina to know?'

Tina hesitated with her hand on the kitchen door, then she went in, saying, 'Tina to know what?'

She had the distinct impression that Elsie rushed into speech to stop Will saying anything.

'Your dad's worried he might be made redundant.'

That was not what they had been talking about, Tina was sure of it, but it was sufficiently worrying for her to exclaim, 'Surely not, Dad, not after all these years?'

'They think you're ready for the rubbish dump once you reach fifty these days,' Will said. 'It's all talk at the moment, but I wouldn't be surprised to be given the push.'

'I can't imagine you not working,' Tina said.

'Neither can I,' her father agreed. 'And your mum won't want me round her feet all day. I'll have to find *something* to do.'

Chapter Ten

The time when the advertisement for a new musical said 'Daphne Durrell in ...' had passed. There were fresh names at the top of the bill. Daphne complained that she had sunk to being a 'with' and Nicky consoled her by telling her that she was still the best thing in the show.

Tina, Elsie and Will were invited to the first night and went along with a feeling of doing their duty, not altogether willingly. It was rather better than they had expected and Tina was relieved to hear her father laugh. If the evening took his mind off his worries about his job then it had more than justified itself.

Daphne had a cameo role with two good songs. Tina, with her critical ear, thought that her aunt was singing better than she had in the last full role she had carried. Nicky was merely one of three friends of the hero. He had a few speaking lines and joined in a comic quartet which had a catchy tune and was appreciated by the audience. He had a pleasant, light baritone voice. Too light, Tina thought. A good drawing-room voice, but he'd never reach the top unless he improved its carrying power. However, he looked good, he moved well and he danced with verve in a routine with the other 'friends'. The three of them took a curtain call together at the end and received a round of applause.

It all looked very promising and yet, unaccountably, the show never really caught on. After the first month they never played to full houses. Tina gathered that the show was staggering on from week to week with the possibility of closure in the air. She could spare very little thought for it, being far more taken up with her own career, her involvement with Jerry and, just to make everything even more difficult, her father's problems. Will's fears had proved justified and he was out of work.

Tina racked her brains to think of some job he could do. The trouble was, he had specialised for far too long.

'Thirty-five years,' Will said, still not quite able to believe it. 'After thirty-five years they've got no more use for me. I've been round the Job Centre, of course, but there's not much hope for a man of my age. I just can't reconcile myself to sitting around and doing nothing.'

'The terms were quite good,' Elsie said, twisting her hands. 'We can pay our way, but that's not the point ...'

'I'll make enquiries at the theatre,' Tina promised, knowing that it would be useless.

'Daphne said the same,' Will said.

'You've seen her?' Tina asked in surprise.

She herself had gone home for the weekend, more to show sympathy than because she thought there was anything she could do to help, but she had not expected to hear that Daphne had been visiting.

'She and Nicky came. Nicky's got some idea of writing up Daphne's early life. Trying to make a bit of money, if you ask me, because that show of theirs doesn't look like running. He wanted old photographs of Daphne and Elsie as children.'

'Poking into things that don't concern him,' Elsie muttered.

Will looked harassed. 'I suppose Daphne's got as much right to your mum's old photograph album as you have,' he said doubtfully. 'And she did promise to let you have it back.'

'I hope she does,' Tina said. 'I love those old photographs.'

She went back to London and kept her promise to make enquiries about a suitable opening for her father, but as she had expected, there were no jobs to be had. She toyed with the idea of mentioning it to Jerry, but only for a moment. He had already shown mild exasperation over her preoccupation with her family and even Tina could see that it was not reasonable to ask the chairman of a vast international company to look for work for a redundant telephone installer.

She wished she could rid herself of the feeling that there was something wrong with her parents, something more than the loss of Will's job, and because she linked this uneasiness with Daphne and her over-charming young husband, she went round to call on them unannounced.

As it happened, she found Daphne alone and not particularly pleased by her visit.

'This is unexpected!' she exclaimed. 'I can't remember you coming to my place before. Nicky's out. Our show's a bit rocky and he's gone to audition for a spot in a night club.'

'I hope he gets it,' Tina said politely.

'Well, I don't! He'll be out till all hours.'

'I suppose you haven't managed to find a job for Dad?'

'Of course I haven't. I only said I'd ask to satisfy Elsie. If my show closes the theatre will be dark. I think that's the only reason they're keeping it staggering on. God, I do have the lousiest luck! I thought we were all set for a long run when I took on that mingy little part. I might just as well not have demeaned myself.'

She was wearing a cream satin negligée over scanty underwear. Her hair was tousled and she looked as if she had just woken up from sleep although it was the middle of the afternoon.

'Do you want a drink?' she asked, fiddling with a bottle and the thick cut-glass tumblers which stood on a tray near the sofa table.

'I'd rather have tea,' Tina said.

'I doubt if there's any milk. Have a look in the fridge, and bring me some ice. I'm having a gin.'

Tina went into the kitchen. It had a strangely pristine look, as if it were rarely used for cooking. As Daphne had suspected, there was no milk, but Tina did find a tin of Coke.

'Mum tells me you've got our old photograph album,' she remarked as she carried her drink and Daphne's ice back into the sitting room.

'Oh, that! Yes, we brought it away so that Nicky could browse through it.'

Daphne took a pull at her drink and added abruptly, 'He was going to write an article about me, but now he thinks it should be a full biography.'

'Do you have a publisher?'

'One or two have said they might be interested. My agent's keen on the idea and he's trying to promote it. If we do it, it'll appear under my name, but Nicky will have to help me.'

'Can Nicky write?'

'He can put down the story if I tell it to him, can't he? Anyone could do that.'

Tina doubted whether that was quite the case, but she was diplomatically silent.

'Did Elsie ask you to come and see me?' Daphne asked.

'No, she doesn't know. It was just a sudden impulse, quite my own idea. If you've finished with the photographs, can I take the album away with me?'

'No, you can't. It's mine as much as Elsie's and I'll hold on to it as long as I like. You may as well know, Tina, that if the full story's told there'll be things come out that it won't suit some people to have said.'

'Things that affect Mum and Dad?'

'If I choose to tell what went wrong in my life when I was a kid then that's my business. Nicky says that's what'll sell the book.'

'Scandal always sells,' Tina said, but she was at a loss to know how the spicy details of Daphne's youth could affect her mother and father, except perhaps to embarrass them.

She was hoping to learn more, but Nicky's return put paid to Daphne's confidences.

'Did you get the job?' she demanded.

'No! Pipped at the post by a revolting Wop pretending to be South American. Tina, darling, how nice to see you! You've been getting yourself into the tabloids, haven't you? "Close friend of Lord Bilchester" − and we all know what *that* means!'

'In my dictionary friend means friend,' Tina said.

'Ah, but *close* friend ... but I won't tease you. What brings you round to visit us?'

195

'I really came to find out whether Aunt ... whether Daphne had managed to find anyone willing to give Dad a job, but it seems she's had as little success as I have.'

'Times are hard,' Nicky said lightly.

'Yes, indeed. I must go. Do let me know how you get on with your autobiography, Aunt Daphne.'

'She's told you!' Nicky exclaimed. 'I meant it to be a surprise. I promise you, it'll be *riveting*.'

Tina felt thoroughly ruffled when she left Daphne's apartment block. She had laid herself open to Nicky's insinuations, she had achieved nothing and there was still that undercurrent that troubled her. Nicky was amused, hugging some secret which pleased him, and Daphne was on the defensive, as if she knew she was about to do something that would cause mischief.

Tina looked round, considering whether to take a taxi back to her Kensington flat, or a bus, or even to walk, and then it occurred to her that Oliver also lived in Daphne's neighbourhood. He had always been kind to her parents and there was just a possibility that he might have an idea about an opening for Will. She retraced her steps and went in search of his flat.

Oliver's minute flat was nothing like Daphne's palatial premises. There was no lift and Tina had to walk up three flights of stairs to get to Oliver's floor. Good for the breath control and the figure, she told herself.

'This is my afternoon for surprising people,' she said when Oliver answered her ring on the bell. 'I've just been to see Aunt Daphne – she only lives round the corner – and I thought I'd drop in on you, too. Am I being a nuisance?'

'Of course not. I can do with a break.'

'If you were thinking of a break with tea it'd be very welcome. I could do with something to buck me up.'

'Something stronger?'

'No, tea will be fine.'

Tina looked round with interest as Oliver disappeared into the kitchen to fill a kettle. The room was small, dark and cluttered, most of the space being taken up by Oliver's piano. Sheets of music manuscript littered the floor. When

Oliver had said he could do with a break he obviously meant he had been composing. Tina looked with respect at the scribbled lines of music.

'It's a mystery to me, how you can conjure up music out of your head,' she said when Oliver manoeuvred himself round the door with a tray in his hands.

'I had a long and arduous training, just as you did.'

'But I interpret and you create. What are you working on?'

'A film score. My bread and butter work.'

Oliver waited patiently while Tina sipped her tea, but after a long uninterrupted silence he asked, 'Did you actually call in for anything besides the pleasure of my company?'

Tina grinned at him. 'I did just wonder whether you might know of a job for my dad? He's been made redundant.'

'I'm sorry to hear that. All those years of experience, can they really afford to throw them away?'

'Dad doesn't think so, that's what makes him sick.'

'There's one possibility,' Oliver said slowly. 'Your father's always been a keen gardener, hasn't he?'

'Mad about it. He keeps our little garden beautiful and has an allotment as well.'

'I've just bought Annis's house . . .'

'No! Isn't it rather big for you?'

'It's a house I like and this flat is far too small. I had to haggle with Annis − not for the usual reason, but to force her to take a proper market price for the property. We've got it all settled now and the house is mine. The only reason I haven't moved in is that Annis took most of the furniture with her and I've not yet found time to buy even the bare essentials. The old gardener she employed has given up and the garden's got into a bit of a mess. Do you think your father would bring it back into order for me?'

'He'd enjoy it.'

'And we could make it a regular arrangement if nothing else turns up for him. Say two days a week. Not much, but . . .'

'Better than nothing. He needs an interest more than anything else. Oliver, I can't thank you enough.'

Impulsively, she reached up and kissed him on the cheek.

197

To her surprise, Oliver took hold of her chin and held it firmly.

'If you're going to kiss me, Valentina Burford, then do it properly,' he said.

The kiss prolonged itself to the point where Tina felt obliged to push herself away from him.

'Oi!' she said. 'We're not on those sort of terms and, besides, I'm spoken for.'

'Jerry?'

'Mm, we're sort of living together.'

'Only sort of?'

'I'm jibbing at actually moving in with him, but it's a full-fledged affair and I'm divinely happy.'

'How nice.'

'Don't be sarcastic about it. I must go. I'll be in touch when I've spoken to Dad about the gardening job.'

Oliver saw her to the door. When Tina ran down the first half-flight of stairs and looked back he was still standing there watching her.

'I hear the new gardener at Rigby House is Tina's father,' Monica Drew said. 'I must say it seems strange. You'd think she'd have more pride, particularly since he's been hawking vegetables round the village like a costermonger.'

'"When Adam delved and Eve span, Who was then the gentleman?"' Rosamund quoted lightly.

'Don't be flippant, Rosamund. Must you go on sharing a flat with her?'

'I'd like to keep a foothold in London, but I'll be in Paris in the near future. I've accepted an offer to play Mélisande in Debussy's opera.'

'It's wonderful that you're becoming internationally famous, but I can't help wondering whether you're not overdoing it. You're as thin as a rake.'

'I've had a trying few weeks. I'll be all right once I start working on the new role.'

Rosamund closed her eyes briefly. She was exhausted. A brief trip to Paris ought not to have had this effect on her. Of course, the real trouble was the tussle of wills with Benno. She had given in and allowed herself to be auditioned for the part and once it was offered to her she had been too flattered and excited to refuse. All the same, she was dreading it. With Benno there were no compromises. Everything went the way he wanted or he would rehearse her until she dropped, even though he was fiercely and reluctantly in love with her.

As for herself, Rosamund was drawn to him by an overwhelming attraction which was nothing like the curiously innocent love she had felt for Carlo. Then she had been a girl, eager for what at the time had seemed like the ultimate experience, now she felt herself to be a mature woman, who ought not to allow herself to be entangled in an affair which could only end unhappily.

She had no doubt that she would suffer if she entered into a liaison with Benno. She told herself that as long as she admitted in the beginning that there was no future for them together then she would be armoured against the inevitable parting, especially if she was strong enough to be the one who ended it, but she suspected that the breakup would still be painful when it happened.

Tina was sympathetic, but a little impatient with her.

'I quite see that Mélisande is a super role for you,' she said. 'On the other hand, if you turned it down then Benno would be safely tied up on the other side of the Channel for months on end and you'd have time to get over this extraordinary weakness you have for him.'

'Is it so extraordinary?'

'No,' Tina admitted. 'He's got a personality that bowls you over and a terrific talent. As a producer I'd put him just this side of genius. I've felt that hypnotic pull, too. If he'd made up to me, I might have found it difficult to resist, just as I couldn't hold out against Jerry.'

'Not much to choose between us,' Rosamund said. 'I say, I was riveted to hear that Oliver has bought Annis's house. Mum told me this weekend.'

'And my dad is his gardener,' Tina said evenly. 'Did she tell you that, too?'

'Of course. I got told off for quoting the Peasant's Revolt at her.'

'I take it she doesn't know about you and Benno?'

'Lord, no! She thinks I'm going to Paris to further my career — as I am, of course.'

'If it were any other producer I might think it was a good move for you. Ros, can't you withdraw?'

Rosamund shook her head and Tina realised she was wasting her breath. Rosamund was determined to throw herself over the precipice, eyes open and afraid, but unable to stop herself taking the last fatal step.

'When you took my dad on as a gardener I didn't expect you to set him up as a greengrocer,' Tina informed Oliver.

'He's so keen on growing vegetables and I've got so much spare ground that one idea grew out of another.'

She had called in on Oliver at his London flat and found it in chaos.

'I'm packing up and moving permanently to Rigby House,' he explained.

'Did you finish your film score?'

'I did, and it's been approved, I'm glad to say.'

'Do you have to bother with things like that?'

'I have to eat. Don't be so patronising, young Tina. The film music was a sound bit of craftsmanship and I'm not ashamed of it.'

'What about your opera?'

'*Crown of Glass*? One or two people have seen it and the reaction's been favourable. However, saying nice things about music on the page and actually putting on a completely unknown opera are two different things.'

'Surely someone will want to do it? After all, *The Partisans* was a success.'

'The ultimate verdict on *The Partisans* is much the same as Ransu Prokopi's — an immature work with flashes of brilliance. It's a curiosity, not a part of the permanent repertoire.'

'You speak so dispassionately,' Tina exclaimed. 'Don't you care?'

'Looking back, what do you think now of, say, your performance in *Die Fledermaus* before you went to the Guildhall?'

'For goodness sake! I had the voice, even then, but I

had precious little else — no training in movement, nor in drama, and I had no idea how to pace myself over an entire performance. It was fun, but I wouldn't want to be remembered for my Rosalinda.'

'Precisely. We can both take a professional view of our past achievements. I shan't grieve if *The Partisans* isn't performed again in its entirety, but just between ourselves I must admit that I do ache to see *Crown of Glass* on the stage.'

'Of course you do.'

'What plans do you have for the future? What roles are being talked about for you after Violetta?'

'I wish I knew,' Tina said ruefully. 'I must talk to my agent. He's an old dear and it was he who got me my audition at Covent Garden, but sometimes I think he's a bit past it. The trouble is, if I made a change I wouldn't know where else to go.'

There was a long, long silence and then Oliver said, 'I've been wondering whether to tell you. I had a letter from Annis yesterday. She says Tom Walden has decided to give up his singing career in favour of the business side.'

'No! But Tom has a really fine voice. How could he bear to waste it?'

'I don't know about that, but apparently Tom doesn't think there's enough scope for him in Australia. He's returning to London and, according to Annis, his ambition is to be a sort of super agent-cum-impresario.'

'Oh, Jerusalem!' Tina said blankly.

'Quite. It's either an answer to your prayers or the realisation of your worst nightmare, depending on how you feel about him these days.'

'That's all over. I mean, there's Jerry now. The last time I saw Tom was at Wexford. He was still keen then, but I held out against him. He might make a marvellous agent, but only if he can accept that we're nothing more than friends.'

'I've got musical training, I've got contacts and I've got money,' Tom said. 'I'm buying out dear old Herbert Kohl, who's at last going into retirement. He must be seventy if he's a day.'

'Herbert's my agent,' Tina said.

'I know. Are you going to let me take care of your career or do you want to move elsewhere?'

Tom had got in touch with Tina as soon as he arrived in London and she had agreed to meet him on the neutral ground of a restaurant near Covent Garden. She had turned up, a little worried in case Tom still resented the way she had fobbed him off at the Wexford Festival, to find that he had apparently put that behind him. It was Tina who was ill at ease, toying with her food and finding it difficult to keep up her end of the conversation.

'I don't know how you can bear to give up singing,' she said, not answering Tom's question.

'It's been a surprise to me, too, especially after all the work I put into becoming a top-flight baritone. But when I look back at my time at the Guildhall, the high point was when I was arranging that tour of Germany − and not only because the girl I loved was in love with me then.'

He was looking very prosperous, in a way that Tina found off-putting. Who would ever have expected to see Tom in a navy blue pinstriped suit? He had turned into a businessman and that was hard to accept.

'I enjoyed the organisation, making the bookings, keeping everything under control,' Tom went on. 'I never got the same buzz out of singing after that. I thought I'd revive the excitement when I went to Sydney, but it never quite worked for me. It wasn't until Annis arrived and I started working out a schedule of master classes for her and selling the package to a TV station that I realised what I'd been missing. I was born to be a wheeler-dealer, like it or lump it.'

'But that fine voice! It's such a waste!'

'I won't give up singing altogether. There'll be no harm in booking myself for an occasional engagement.'

'You'll lose the edge ... you know what I mean, the fine honing you get from making use of your voice all the time.'

'I dare say I will. It's no longer important to me. You, on the other hand, are obviously destined to go on getting better and better. Take time to think it over if you must, but I hope you'll agree to commit yourself to me. And Rosamund, too, I hope.'

'Oh, Rosamund ... she's put herself into hock with Benno Neroni for the next few months. He's her snake charmer.'

'Mélisande, isn't it? I can see her in that part. Come on, Tina, stop messing about. Are you joining me or not?'

'Strictly on a business footing,' Tina said carefully.

'Of course. I'm only in it for the money.'

'If I thought that I certainly wouldn't come to you,' Tina retorted. 'I know you better than that. You love opera, really love it, even though you're turning your back on it as a performer. Yes, of course I'll transfer to you when you've concluded your deal with Herbert. I suspect I'm lucky to have the chance. It's true you've always been a good organiser. I wouldn't have hesitated if it hadn't been for ... for our personal involvement.'

'Our love affair,' Tom said cheerfully. 'That's in the past. I still think you're ragingly attractive and I dare say I'll still make the occasional pass at you, but if you give me the cold shoulder then I'll shrug and accept it.'

'Will you? I was afraid I'd hurt you at Wexford.'

'I was a bit put out,' Tom admitted. 'Since then I've discovered how true it is that there are other fish in the sea — and there's an awful lot of ocean between here and Australia, honey girl.'

He was laughing at her and Tina resented that. She told herself it was a relief to know that Tom accepted that it was all over between them, and tried to believe that she meant it.

'I only hope you can do something to sort out my career,' she said, resolutely abandoning emotional difficulties. 'I seem to be stuck with singing three minor roles and one major one. Tom, I had a real success with my Violetta and yet I haven't had any other offers. I've got concert engagements, but I want to get my teeth into something really demanding. I can do it now, I know I can.'

'I know it, too,' Tom said. 'Annis brought out your notices for *Traviata* and I was really impressed.'

He looked at her thoughtfully, taking in the beautiful unkempt hair, the dash of eyeshadow which was all Tina wore by way of make-up, the unremarkable dress Elsie had run up for her, her bare legs and sandals.

'The time has come for you to move up a notch,' he said.

'That's just what I think,' Tina agreed.

'Ah, but are we thinking along the same lines? You, my dear, are going to become an international star and for that you need grooming.'

'You sound just like Jerry!' She paused and added uncertainly, 'I don't know if you know there's another man in my life.'

'Lord Bilchester, that well-known connoisseur of singers,' Tom said calmly, which was not the way Tina liked to hear Jerry described. 'I know, of course, as anyone might who can read between the lines in the gossip colums. I'm surprised, I must admit, to see you still looking like our old Tina, the pride of the Guildhall Grubs. I would have expected him to have put a bit of polish on you.'

'He tries, and I do make an effort when we go out together, but the truth is I'm afraid if I start changing it will get out of perspective. It's my voice that's important, Tom, not the length of my fingernails.'

'Of course, but you won't be given the status you deserve while you still look like a penny-pinching teenager.'

'I'm not going to let myself be packaged and presented like another Callas,' Tina muttered resentfully.

'I can't make you take my advice, but now that I'm your agent I can insist on you listening to it. I'd like you to get your hair cut and styled — I'll tell you which hairdresser to go to ...'

'How can you possibly know?'

'I've studied the women's magazines with just this in view. You should get some advice about make-up — no, I don't mean you should plaster your face an inch thick, that's not your style at all — but you could be improved. How much exercise do you get, apart from walking round the stage?'

'Not a lot,' Tina admitted.

'I'll make you a member of a health club where you can swim and work out in the gym. You look fit enough, but you know how important it is to keep the muscles toned up.'

Tina was looking at him in fascination. 'Tom, how long has it taken you to think all this up?'

'I worked it out on the plane coming over. Having seen your notices and the photographs that went with them, I could see just what you needed, assuming you agreed to come to me.'

'Are you going to do the same for Rosamund?'

'I'll talk about that with Ros.'

'I think I've been snubbed,' Tina murmured.

'I can't discuss one client with another.'

'Cor! Haven't we got pompous!'

'You're annoyed because you think I'm criticising your appearance.'

'Well ... it's a bit unexpected, from you. And Jerry's been going on at me, too. Am I really such a mess?'

'Yes.' Tom smiled at her warmly. 'A beautiful, untidy mess, with a wonderful voice and a talent for acting through it that I've never seen surpassed. A few couture gowns and a bit of glamour and you'll be kicking the world around like a football.'

'And all I want to do is sing,' Tina said gloomily. 'The trimmings don't seem important to me, but I suppose in the end I'll take your advice.'

The final rehearsals of *Pelléas et Mélisande* were being held at the Paris Opera House. Benno was glowering at his Pelléas, who had displeased him by a clumsiness of movement in a part Benno thought should be all lightness and grace. Rosamund dug her hands into the deep pockets of the loose black velvet jacket she was wearing and shivered, glad that for once it was not she who had called down Benno's scathing criticism. Why did they work with him? Why did they forgive him for the tongue which could raise blisters in four fluent languages? Because he was the best. Even in her worst moments, when he had reduced her to silent tears, Rosamund knew that Benno could get a performance out of her that no one else would have forced her to give.

A note was handed to her and she opened it, one ear perpetually waiting for her next cue as she read the few brief lines. Lord Bilchester was in Paris and wanted to know whether she would dine with him that evening. Rosamund took no more than a moment to consider. Benno would have to let them go soon and it would be a relief to spend an evening away from him. A relief for him, too, perhaps. They were sharing a hotel suite and on a physical level their relationship was an intense and exciting experience, but when they were not making love they frequently disagreed, and Rosamund had the unsettling suspicion that in some way she did not understand Benno was disappointed in her. At least with Jerry Bilchester she could relax, and all the more so because of knowing that he was Tina's property.

He called for her in a chauffeur-driven car, on loan from the Paris office of his international company. It was a real luxury to sink into the well-upholstered seat without even having to wait for a taxi to be called. She was glad she had had time for a decent bath rather than a quick splash under the shower, that she had taken trouble over her hair and face and was wearing her most becoming dress.

'Do I detect a Mélisande influence?' Jerry asked with an amused glance at the floating chiffon shaded from dark blue to black as they seated themselves in the restaurant he had chosen.

'Quite right,' Rosamund admitted. 'My costumes are so becoming that when I saw this dress in a shop window looking very similar I couldn't resist it.'

'You were right. You look beautiful.'

He refrained from commenting on her pallor and her thinness, and it would have taken someone who knew him exceptionally well to recognise that under his urbane manner he was angry that this lovely, sensitive girl had been reduced to a shadow of what she should have been. And all in the name of art, Jerry thought sardonically. Damn and blast Benno Neroni.

He smiled at Rosamund and began to discuss the menu and Rosamund, who had thought that she was not particularly hungry, suddenly discovered that she had an appetite after all and could enjoy the delicious food in his undemanding company.

They only touched on the opera once, when Jerry said

that he was planning to bring a party over to Paris for the first night.

'I'll fly them over in the company's private jet,' he said.

'Lavish!' Rosamund exclaimed.

'I'll have to pay for anyone who isn't strictly a business connection. Would your parents like to come?'

'They would, I'm sure. How very kind of you.'

Jerry shrugged off her thanks. 'Tina will come, of course,' he said. 'I almost forgot, I was supposed to give you her love and tell you she's thrilled your first night comes in a week when she'll be able to attend.'

'We do try to support one another. She's on top of the world as usual, I suppose?'

'When was Tina anything but blooming? Her new agent has cracked the whip and made her pay some attention to her appearance, something I'd quite failed to do.'

Rosamund thought she detected a trace of annoyance in the way Jerry spoke.

'Tom is an old friend,' she said diplomatically.

'Is he going to be your agent, too?'

'It depends what I decide to do. Benno is going back to the States when his work on *Pelléas et Mélisande* is completed. He doesn't believe in hanging around once the work is staged. I shall have to stay in Paris, of course, for the performances I've been contracted to do. Then he wants me to join him in New York.'

'Is that what you want?'

She shook her head. 'I'm afraid of America. It's hard for a European singer to break into the operatic scene there. If I'm to be a success I shall be dependent on Benno's support. He'll push for me to be in any production he takes on. It means becoming totally identified with him.'

'Your own personality will be swamped.'

'It might. I can't stand out against him, he's much too strong for me.'

'The wise thing to do is to let his return to the States be a natural break between you.'

'Yes, I know.' She raised her head and looked at him with haunted eyes. 'It's not that simple.'

'No, my dear, I realise that,' Jerry said gently. 'I'm going to say something that will shock you,' he went on. 'I'm by no means convinced that you're a natural born opera singer. Have you ever thought that you might be happier singing oratorio?'

Rosamund gave a gasp. 'What a question, when I'm on the eve of opening in the leading role at an opera house famous all over the world! Singing in opera has always been my ambition.'

'Because you had Annis Gilroy as a role model?'

'Perhaps. Annis always took it for granted that anyone with a voice naturally gravitated towards opera. I never questioned it. More than that, none of my teachers ever questioned it.'

'I'm quite sure you're going to be outstandingly good as Mélisande, but is it really worth what it's taking out of you?'

'I sometimes doubt it,' Rosamund said in a whisper. 'There are days when I'm afraid of collapsing. I can't sleep ... it helps to have Benno there. He does understand what it means to be an artist.'

'If you follow him to America will he always be as supportive?'

'I don't know. Sometimes he gets impatient ... if he stopped giving me the reassurance I need then it would be difficult to go on.'

She gave him a painful smile. 'It's as bad as being a drug addict,' she said. 'Without my fix of Benno I might not be able to appear on the stage.'

'Keep my suggestion in mind. Now, would you like some coffee?'

Benno was asleep when Rosamund got back to their hotel, the impenetrable sleep of complete exhaustion. She slid into bed without disturbing him, but then lay awake for a long time, her eyes open, staring into the darkness and thinking over what Jerry had said.

When Benno woke early and turned to her she held him in her arms, responding sleepily to his lovemaking, and for the first time she felt that his need of her was greater than hers for him. It made her feel protective towards him. How would Benno react if she decided not to join him in the United States? Badly. He wanted her, and she understood that he believed that if he wanted anything hard enough then the object of his desire was bound to be his.

As he was dressing, Benno asked, without any great interest, 'Did you have a good evening with your lord?'

'Very good. Jerry is an interesting man.'

'Pots of money, too. Worth cultivating. I doubt whether his company would put any cash into a production outside Britain, but keep him sweet for me, just in case I need him.'

'You must do your own bargaining,' Rosamund said with careful restraint. 'Jerry is my friend.'

Jerry kept his word about airlifting a party over to Paris for Rosamund's first night. The Drews came, with Monica, to Tina's inner amusement, trying to look blasé about the VIP treatment they were being given, and the rest of the party consisted of Tina and Tom Walden, two business associates and their wives and Jerry's secretary, a pleasant, sensible woman in her fifties, who confessed to Tina that she was a complete opera buff and had seen her *Traviata* three times.

'A fan!' Tina said approvingly. 'Do be sure to tell Tom how wonderful you think I am. He's my agent and I'm trying to stir him up to find another good role for me.'

In accordance with Tom's wishes, she had made a special effort for the Paris trip. Her hair had been cut into a thick waving bob, her eyebrows had been shaped and her eyelashes dyed and she wore discreet make-up. She had, and always would have, the well-developed chest of an opera singer, but her new, beautifully cut clothes hung from the shoulders and emphasised all the good points of her figure. Her visits to the health club had trimmed away a couple of unwanted inches from her waist and hips and improved her posture. She looked alert and healthy and very happy.

The staging of *Pelléas et Mélisande* was everything that was expected of a Benno Neroni production. The singing was marvellous, the characterisation was meticulous, the scenery was clever and the costumes were lovely. Above all, he had managed to capture the atmosphere of the strange, melancholy tale.

Rosamund as Mélisande was heartbreaking. She seemed to float across the stage, otherworldly and innocent with the terrible innocence of a child who does not understand evil. It was not a difficult role to sing in that there were no set pieces, no great arias, no high notes to sustain, but what had to be retained was the musical line of Debussy's score and it had taken months of rehearsal for the singers to learn their roles satisfactorily.

The reception was ecstatic. This was an opera the Parisians felt to be peculiarly their own and they responded rapturously to a new production which did it more than justice.

Lord Bilchester's party joined the cast afterwards for a congratulatory reception. Tina made a determined effort and pushed through the crowd surrounding Rosamund and hugged her.

'You were superb,' she said, but secretly she was dismayed by the brittle bundle of bones she was holding in her arms.

Rosamund smiled at her, but her eyes were bright with unshed tears.

'It was good, wasn't it?' she said. 'I felt it. Oh, Tina, I'm so *tired*.'

She was claimed by Benno and she turned away to receive more congratulations.

'Really, one would have thought she would have had time for a word with her own parents,' Monica said in an aggrieved voice. 'Of course, Tina *would* push her way in.'

She was soothed by a glass of champagne handed to her by Lord Bilchester. Such a delightful man, and he must be interested in Rosamund to have arranged the visit to Paris. If only Rosamund played her cards right ... a title, a house in the country, a real position ... of course, she was famous now, but stage fame meant nothing to Monica Drew compared to the solid achievement of a good marriage. It was true that he was rumoured to be involved with Tina, but Monica did not consider that a great impediment. She looked with disfavour at the new, unexpectedly glamourous

Tina, who was talking to Tom Walden.

'If you try to nobble Ros to talk about future plans now, I'll strangle you,' Tina said to him.

In spite of what she had said to Jerry's secretary, Tina knew that Tom had a lot of work lined up for her in the near future, but he was intent on linking her career with Rosamund's.

'The two of you together,' he said. 'What a package! Fiordiligi and Dorabella, Donna Elvira and Donna Anna.'

'It's an interesting idea,' Tina admitted. 'I've always wanted to do *Così Fan Tutte* with myself as Fiordiligi, but if Ros did Dorabella it would mean it wouldn't be a mezzo role.'

'No problem. It's often been done by a soprano. I suppose you see yourself as Elvira rather than Anna in *Don Giovanni*?'

'That's what I'd prefer. After singing Zerlina for so long I've had a chance to compare the roles and I think I'm better suited to Elvira, which isn't to say that I wouldn't like to tackle Anna as well.'

Tina was immensely excited by the idea of playing these important roles, but this was not the occasion to talk about such matters, not when Ros had just come off the stage after giving a demanding performance, not when she was so obviously worn out. When it looked as if Tom was about to open the subject that occupied most of his waking thoughts, Tina took him firmly by the arm and led him away.

Tina called to see Rosamund at a reasonable hour the next day and was relieved to see that she looked rested.

'You were really, really good, Ros,' she said. 'It's a perfect role for you. I doubt whether I could do it — my feet are too obviously on the ground. Your singing was superb, and the love scene with Pelléas went beautifully.'

'It cost me a lot of trouble. Endless rehearsals. But I think you're right, it did come off in the end.'

'I know Tom has written to you. Have you decided to let him be your agent?'

'Yes,' Rosamund said, but she spoke in a curiously hesitant way.

'He's got some wonderful offers for both of us, but I won't let him put any pressure on you until you feel ready to talk about the next step.'

'I'm not sure ... Benno goes back to America at the end of next week.'

'I can't say I'm sorry. He drains you, Ros.'

'I know, but I need him and I've come to realise that he needs me, too.'

'Please, please don't let him persuade you to join him in New York. You're an intensely European performer, Ros, very much in the French tradition. You might do well as an occasional visitor, but I'm not at all sure there's a suitable niche for you in the United States, not as a permanent fixture.'

'We've neither of us been there,' Rosamund pointed out. 'It might work out ... I don't know. I've got a lot of thinking to do.'

Chapter Eleven

'*Così Fan Tutte* and *Don Giovanni* are certain,' Tom said. 'And I might allow you to do an occasional Violetta, but two new roles in a year will be enough for you at this stage of your career, young Tina.'

Tina grimaced, but she knew that Tom was right. The last thing she needed now, when she was approaching the height of her powers, was to overstrain her voice.

'Rosamund, too,' Tom said with satisfaction. 'I can't tell you how pleased I am that she's refused to go to America. Not that I rule it out in the future, for both of you, but not yet.'

'What about Oliver's opera?' Tina asked. 'You know how keen I am to do that.'

'I've got hopes,' Tom said. 'I might put a bit of cash into it myself, though I know it'll be money down the drain.'

'Not necessarily,' Tina protested.

'A new opera, by an almost unknown British composer? Come on, Tina, you know as well as I do, it's not a recipe for profitability. On the other hand, Oliver deserves support. One of our few really distinctive musicians. You ought to get Jerry involved.'

'Oh, Jerry ... he's being a bit difficult at the moment because I'm going off to Stuttgart when he wanted me here in London to be hostess at some big party he's giving.'

'Stuttgart is important,' Tom said immediately. 'You're not yet sufficiently well known on the Continent.'

'I'll do what you say, sir, but just remember you're to move

213

heaven and earth to make sure I'm available if Oliver's opera is put on.'

'It won't do you any harm to be associated with new music,' Tom agreed. 'But I'm not committing you without seeing the score. Will our arrogant friend allow me to see it, do you think?'

'Arrogant? Oliver? He's not,' Tina said in disbelief.

'Not with you perhaps. He's very take-it-or-leave-it with the rest of the world.'

'It's that scar on his eyebrow that makes him look sort of supercilious. I used to think so, too, but now it's a side of him I never see. He's wonderful with my mum and dad, for instance. He and Dad have gone into business together, growing and selling vegetables. Oliver has provided the land and Dad is doing the work. It's beginning to show a profit and it's done marvels for Dad's morale.'

'Oliver's got an ulterior motive, if you ask me,' Tom said in a disgruntled way.

'Because he wants me to sing in his opera? Don't be daft, Tom. He knows I'm crazy to do it.'

'That wasn't what I had in mind,' Tom said drily. 'But if you can't see it then I'll say no more.'

'You're jealous,' Tina accused him. 'And of Oliver, of all people!'

'I still fancy you something rotten,' Tom said with a smile.

'What a lovely way of putting it! Nothing doing, Tom, as you very well know. I've got my hands full with Jerry, I don't need any more complications.'

Speaking of her parents had jogged Tina's conscience. It was weeks since she had last been home and now that she came to think of it, she had been worried then at how tired and nervous her mother had seemed.

Elsie looked no better when Tina made a determined effort and managed to get to Woodington for the day the following Sunday. Will, on the other hand, had never been fitter. The open-air life he was leading suited him and he was enthralled by his success in growing and marketing vegetables locally. If Elsie was still upset by his redundancy then she was quite off the mark because, to Tina, it seemed as if her father had taken on a new lease of life.

'Are you feeling all right?' she asked her mother, speaking tentatively because Elsie had never welcomed enquiries about her health.

True to form, she almost snapped her reply. 'Of course I am. A bit tired, as is only natural for a woman at my time of life, but there's nothing wrong with me.'

From that oblique remark Tina guessed that her mother was going through the menopause. It was the nearest she was ever likely to come to admitting it, and there was certainly no point in suggesting she might benefit from a visit to the doctor. Elsie believed in letting nature take its course. Tina felt at once relieved at this simple explanation of her mother's jitteriness and impatient because she would not seek help. With so many other things pressing in on her, it was not difficult for Tina to put it out of her mind.

What did surprise her was the discovery that Nicky had been visiting Woodington. It would not have been mentioned if she had not seen the old photograph album back in its accustomed place and exclaimed in pleasure that Daphne had returned it.

'Has Aunt Daphne been down?' she asked.

'Not her. Nicky brought it back,' Will said. 'He's been down two or three times. Getting background information for that book she's writing, he says.'

'Aunt Daphne's still going on with that?'

'So he says. She's not doing so well since that musical closed. To tell you the truth, I wonder how long Nicky will stick to her.'

Elsie had been sitting silently by, her nervous hands busy with some knitting.

'He'll stick,' she said. 'As long as he can see a profit in it.'

'I suppose if the book sells ...' Tina said doubtfully. 'It ought to be quite a good story, but I would have thought the really interesting part would be in the United States rather than Woodington.'

Will glanced at his wife in a worried way. 'We've told him we don't want to be dragged into it,' he said. 'And, according to what Elsie tells me, he's agreed not to play up the family connection.'

That might be so, but Tina doubted whether Nicky would be able to resist a few references to Daphne's niece, the famous young soprano. It gave her a momentary stab of surprise that she should so naturally think of herself in those terms, but of course it was true. She was one of the most promising young singers in Europe, not just in Great Britain, and her forthcoming appearance in Stuttgart would confirm it.

The European trip was more than a success, it was a triumph. By the time Tina returned to London, Tom was able to tell her that he had had enquiries about her availability from New York, Sydney, Venice, Milan and Paris.

'You sort it out,' Tina said. 'God, I'm tired! Is there any news about Oliver's opera?'

'I was afraid you'd ask about that,' Tom said. 'Yes, English National Opera have got sponsorship for it and it's being scheduled for eighteen months' time, which is exactly when I was hoping to launch you in the United States.'

'I told you *Crown of Glass* was a top priority. New York can wait.'

'They're not used to being pushed into second place at the Met. They want you to do *Tosca*.'

For a moment Tina wavered, then she said firmly, '*Crown of Glass* first, *Tosca* next.'

With her usual resilience, Tina bounced back to life after a couple of days doing nothing but sleep and eat. Conscientiously, she went down to Woodington as soon as she had recovered. Elsie and Will, she knew, would not regard what she had been doing as real work and it would be difficult for them to understand the depths of fatigue from which she had suffered.

She had a surprise for her parents. She had bought a car. To Jerry's annoyance she had resisted his attempt to make it a present and had insisted on paying for it herself. She had kept it a secret until she had passed her driving test, and this would be the first time she had gone to Woodington by road instead of by train.

216

She drew up outside the little house and rang the doorbell to bring them out so that she could show off her new acquisition. It was Will who came to the door.

'Look what I've got!' Tina said.

'Very nice,' Will said. 'When did you learn to drive?'

'Before I went away. And I passed my driving test at the first attempt. Call Mum so that she can see it, too.'

She had expected them to be excited about it, far more than they were about her overseas triumphs, because it was a visible sign of affluence, something tangible that everyone could see, and she was slightly disappointed when her surprise fell flat. It was not until they went inside that she realised how worn they both looked. Whatever had been wrong with her mother on Tina's last visit was now affecting her father, and nothing would persuade Tina that he was suffering from the menopause.

They both said they were well and Will brightened noticeably when she asked about his market gardening venture, which was apparently flourishing, so presumably they had no money worries.

'Is Oliver at home, do you happen to know?' Tina asked. 'I particularly want to see him. Perhaps we could go for a run in my car and pick him up for a drink somewhere.'

She saw the look her parents exchanged and then Will said deliberately, 'He's definitely at home. And I think you ought to see him.'

Elsie made an agitated noise and her husband took her hand in his. 'Go now,' he said. 'I'll give him a ring and tell him to expect you.'

'I've only just arrived,' Tina said, startled.

'All the same ... we want you to talk to him,' Will said.

'There's something going on' Tina said suspiciously. 'I've known for a long time that something was wrong. Mum, are you *sure* you're not ill? And why should Oliver know and not me?'

'Your mother's all right, though she's had a lot on her mind,' Will said. 'Oliver tried to deal with it. I don't know he went the right way about it, but he meant well. It'll be easier if he explains. Easier for us. We'll talk when you come back.'

Nothing would induce him to say more and to Tina's dismay her mother began to cry in a weak, miserable way, so that she felt she had no choice but to allow herself to be bundled out of the house and into her car she had expected to display with such pride.

At least that car made the journey to Locksley Green quick and easy. Tina could scarcely contain her impatience as she turned into the drive and parked.

The door was opened by Oliver, as if he had been waiting for her arrival. His face was bruised and he had a magnificent black eye.

'My word, what a shiner!' Tina exclaimed. 'How on earth did you get that?'

'I tried to murder the bright-haired Nicky,' Oliver said grimly. 'Come in, Tina. Will telephoned and I've got his permission to tell you the whole story. I'm not sure whether to offer you a strong drink or a nice cup of tea.'

'I'll settle for the tea,' Tina said. 'Come on, I'll make it and you can talk while the kettle's boiling.'

In the kitchen she filled the kettle and put it on to boil. 'Don't keep me waiting,' she begged. 'I can't bear it. Nicky? What's he been up to?'

'Blackmailing Elsie,' Oliver said.

'Mum? Oh, come on, Oliver! What has Mum ever done in the whole of her blameless life that would be worth blackmailing her for?'

'You'd better let me make the tea,' Oliver said. 'I don't want you spilling boiling water over yourself. She falsified the entry of a birth.'

'But ... I'm the only child she ever had,' Tina said. 'Aren't I?'

Oliver was swilling hot water round in the teapot and ladling tea leaves into it. Tina had the impression that he was giving himself time to think.

'Oliver ...' she said.

'My dear, you are not her child. Your mother is Daphne Durrell.'

He had spoken slowly and deliberately and yet for a moment Tina was convinced she had misheard him.

'Aunt Daphne ... no, Oliver, no!'

'I'm afraid there's no doubt about it. Elsie not only never had a child, she is incapable of bearing one. It was something she only discovered after she and your father were married and it was a great grief to her. Then Daphne became pregnant.'

'And Mum took the child,' Tina said, her voice no more than a dry whisper.

'I gather it was your grandmother who thought up the scheme. She had recently moved to the south coast where no one knew the family. Elsie told everyone she was pregnant and was going to stay with her mother on the grounds that she needed special care if she was to carry the baby, and after eight years of marriage everyone knew how anxious she was to have a child. Daphne joined them and the two sisters switched identities. As far as the south coast nursing home knew, the child was born to Mrs William Burford.'

'All that elaborate deception! Did keeping it quiet matter so much?'

'We're talking about twenty-six years ago,' Oliver reminded her. 'The attitude to illegitimacy was more liberal than it had been, but not so easy-going as it's since become and, yes, it did matter to Daphne, nineteen years old and just at the beginning of a promising career. Of course, there could have been a simple adoption ...'

'No,' Tina said wearily. 'I can quite see that deception would appeal to Mum more than having to go through an adoption procedure. I still keep calling her "Mum". I can't take it in.'

'I don't see why you should call her anything else. She's the one who brought you up. In my eyes, she's your true mother.'

A memory was struggling to be recalled in Tina's mind. Something that had happened when she had first wanted to embark on her singing career. Daphne being willing to pay for her training and threatening to make some revelation which had almost sent Elsie into hysterics. Tina had been sent upstairs out of the way and had resented being discussed behind her back, then when she had come down her father had told her of the compromise they had reached. Her father ...

'Oliver! If Daphne is my mother then who was my father?'

'That's the thing Elsie and Will found it impossible to tell you,' he said.

'They must know?'

'Yes, of course. Will is your true father.'

'Dad? You mean, *Dad* and Aunt Daphne ...?'

'I gather it was a very brief fling. Poor old Will, even to this day he's bitterly ashamed of it.'

'As well he might be! Mum's own *sister* ...!'

'They were in some amateur musical comedy together. Will had a useful tenor voice in those days. Elsie stayed at home and sewed the costumes. Tina, these things happen. A sort of madness. And if the woman is willing ... God knows, I can't bring myself to point the finger at Will. There was something he said when he was telling me about it – "she was like a creature made of light", he said. Can't you see the temptation and forgive it?'

'I don't understand why he told you,' Tina said, shying away from that question.

'Because of Nicky. Daphne told him and he couldn't resist twisting the knife in the wound, nasty little beast. He started visiting Woodington, ostensibly poking around for details for the book he's helping Daphne to write. He promised Elsie he'd keep the story of your birth out of the biography provided she made it worth his while.'

'How much?'

'Five pounds a week.'

'Good God!'

'I know. Pitiful, isn't it? All the same, there were weeks when she found it difficult to lay her hands on the extra cash.'

'No wonder she looked so worn out and nervous.'

'Eventually Will put two and two together and challenged her and she told him. Will and I have grown quite close and he felt able to talk it over with me, which was when I made my rather stupid attempt to knock some decency into Nicky.'

'I could kill him.'

'I did my best,' Oliver said regretfully. 'I might have

succeeded if Daphne hadn't attacked me. I suppose his death at my hands would only have made a worse scandal. If it's any consolation, he looks much worse than me.'

'Oh, Oliver!'

Tina felt frantically for her handkerchief and blew her nose vigorously.

'Drink your tea, darling, and take stock. After all, does it really matter all that much? A mere biological accident. If Elsie hadn't been willing to take you, you might not have been born at all. I can't bear to think of it. All that beauty and artistry wasted. As it is, you've had a good life, you've achieved miracles, you've given delight to thousands. Be thankful, Tina, that Elsie was able to forgive her husband and bring up his child without ever for one moment showing bitterness towards that child.'

'Yes, of course.' Tina wiped her eyes and then took his advice and drank her tea. 'I don't know how I'm going to face them.'

'Once you're made your entrance it won't be difficult. Just tell them you still love them, that's all they want to hear. I'm afraid there are some difficult days ahead. Daphne's made up her mind to publish all the lurid details.'

'We must stop her!'

'It's too late. The book's been read by the publishers and they've arranged a serialisation in a Sunday newspaper. You're in for some very uncomfortable publicity, my dear.'

Of course, Oliver was right: once Tina had let herself into the house there was no need for much to be said. No ring at the doorbell this time. She used her key and walked straight through to the kitchen. Her mother and father (how could she ever think of them in any other way?) were sitting in attitudes of such frozen stillness that she had the feeling they had not moved since she left them.

Tina stretched out her arms. With one hand on Will's shoulder she bent down to kiss Elsie, then she turned to him and gave him a kiss and a hug.

'As far as I'm concerned, nothing's changed,' she said. 'You're still my mum and dad, the two people who brought

221

me up. I've only got one reproach to make — you should have told me.'

'I wanted to,' Will said wretchedly. He could not bring himself to look her in the eye. Tina felt for him, this grey-haired man shamed by an old sin. 'But Elsie said ...'

'It had to be kept quiet,' Elsie intervened. 'After what we did ... Tina, will I go to prison?'

'Of course not,' Tina exclaimed, speaking out of complete ignorance of the law, but desperate to reassure her. 'After all this time ... no one's going to be particularly bothered. Look, I know it means taking one more person into our confidence, but it'll all be out in the open soon anyway; I think I ought to talk to Tom. He's my agent, he's supposed to help me out of difficulties and he's got a terribly good grasp of legal things.'

She would have to tell Jerry, too. He would be livid if the news broke in the newspapers and he had been kept in ignorance, but there was no need to mention that.

She was relieved to see Elsie relax. 'I always liked Tom,' she said, which Tina took as permission to discuss the problem with him.

'You agree, Dad?'

'We need advice from someone and your mum ... Elsie was against going to a lawyer.'

'Say mum, for goodness sake. That's what she is to me and always will be.'

There was no need for Will to spell out the difficulties Elsie had caused with her nervous fears. Of course she would not consult a solicitor, she was afraid of what he might say. Better, in her eyes, to go on from day to day, always afraid of exposure, always worrying about the penalties that exposure might bring. Better, even, to pay Nicky to keep silent, rather than face bringing an old scandal out into the open.

'Oliver thinks there's no hope of suppressing the story,' Tina said. 'I don't know how much of a stir it will cause. Quite a bit, I'm afraid, because Daphne is an international star, even if she is past her prime, and I'm quite well known myself.'

'She'll exploit you if she can see any advantage in it,' Will said.

'I know, but I don't mean to play that game with her.'

By the time Tina left, Will and Elsie were behaving almost normally. Elsie, in particular, was relieved that a man was going to take charge. Oliver's outburst of temper had obviously frightened her. She saw Tom as more level-headed, more the sort of person who knew how to handle difficult questions of law.

'So there it is,' Tina said. 'Daphne had an affair with my poor old dad and I'm the result. What really worries me is not the publicity when Daphne's book comes out, but Mum's situation.'

'I've no idea how her unofficial adoption of you may be regarded, but I can't imagine anyone is going to send her to the Tower,' Tom said. 'After all, it must be Daphne who's committed an offence, surely? She was the one who bore the child; it was her responsibility to see the birth properly registered.'

Tina stared at him open-mouthed. 'Not one of us thought of that,' she said. 'Mum is so burdened by a sense of guilt she made everyone think she was to blame. Tom, you're so practical.'

'Nice to have my good qualities appreciated,' Tom said with a grin. 'I think the important thing is for your mother – by which I mean Elsie – to make a written statement about it before the book appears. I'll get my solicitor to draw up something suitable. A full confession and an act of contrition will probably meet the case.'

'I hope so. She's lived all her life with this hanging over her, it's about time she was let off the hook. What are we going to do about the publicity?'

'There are two ways we can handle it. The first way is to milk it for all it's worth – Press conference, photographs, interviews ... would you like to appear on the Wogan programme?'

'No, thank you! Not for this story. Tom, you can't be serious?'

'Not really, not for an artist of your stature. The other way is a prepared statement followed by dignified silence.'

'That's more like it. And I'd like to get Mum and Dad

223

out of the way before the story breaks.'

'They'd do better to stay and face the music. It'll only be a nine days' wonder, you know.'

'An awful lot of suffering can be packed into nine days. I'd rather they went away for a holiday. Somewhere secluded, perhaps even abroad.'

'I'll give my mind to that, too.'

'One thing I'll have to do,' Tina said slowly. 'And that's see Daphne. Funny, I can't bring myself to call her "aunt" any more, even though I still find it natural to call Mum what I've always called her.'

'Don't go alone,' Tom said. 'I'll come with you.'

If Tina could have been sure of seeing Daphne on her own she would have preferred not to have had Tom's company, but when she remembered that Nicky would probably be there she decided to let Tom go with her.

As Tina had feared, Nicky was reclining on a sofa when she and Tom followed Daphne into the living room of her flat. He was wearing a black silk dressing gown and not much else, as far as Tina could make out. His right wrist was supported in a sling and the face he turned towards them was even more battered than Oliver's had been.

'What's this? Another of your bully boys?' he asked, looking Tom over. 'I really can't be expected to fight all of them, darling.'

'Very wise,' Tina said. 'You seem to have got the worst of the last encounter and Tom is bigger than Oliver.'

'You can tell your friend Oliver that I'm taking advice about sueing him for assault.'

'Oh, do! Please do! I'd love to go to court and tell everyone how you blackmailed a nervous woman. Screwing five pounds a week out of the wife of a redundant telephone engineer! Do you really want to be known for such a mean, petty crime?'

'She pressed the money on Nicky,' Daphne said quickly. 'You know what Elsie's like, frightened of her own shadow. And, anyway, that's not what Oliver and Nicky fought about. He made some most unnecessary remarks about our marriage and Nicky told him a few home truths about living with an opera singer years old than himself.'

Tina was silenced. She could believe that Oliver would see red if Nicky disparaged Annis, but she thought he might have told her that this had been his reason for hitting out.

'Let's not get into an argument,' Tom said. 'My client and I are here to try to limit the damage, not to add to it.'

'Your client! That sounds very official,' Nicky exclaimed.

'Tom's my agent and I've asked him to help me live through what is obviously going to be a very trying time,' Tina said.

'Is it so difficult to accept me as your mother?' Daphne asked.

She caught Tina's eye and looked away again hurriedly.

'My difficulty lies in believing that my mother rejected me even before I was born,' Tina said evenly. 'I'm prepared to acknowledge publicly that you *are* my mother. That's as far as it goes.'

'Look, we could make a good thing of this,' Daphne burst out. 'The book's going to be a success. My publishers are really excited about it. You're in show business, just as much as I am. Let me line up a photo call, give a party, arrange interviews ...'

'No way! I don't need that kind of publicity. Tom agrees with me. I'm not going to be exploited just so that you can sell a few more copies of your tatty book.'

'Then why are you here?'

'I need to talk to you. Can I see you alone for a few minutes?'

'Come into my bedroom. Nicky, stir yourself to fix us all a drink.'

It was like going into the bedroom of a thirties film star, all oyster satin and white fur rugs. Strangely, something about the absurdity of it made Tina more tolerant. Daphne lived in a dream world and nothing she did had much relation to real life.

'Mum and Dad told me hardly anything,' Tina said abruptly. 'I just don't understand how it could have *happened*.'

'Me and Will? Looking back, I can hardly believe it myself. He wasn't bad-looking in those days. Lively, too, and full of fun. Something went out of him after Elsie made him give up amateur theatricals. He had quite a nice voice and, of course, I always sang like a lark. We were in *The Student Prince* together and it was a terrific success. We took it on a little tour. Elsie stayed at home. I suppose being thrown together, making love on the stage ... I got carried away and Will did, too. From first kiss to last it only went on for about three weeks. No hard feelings as far as I was concerned, though I could see he was beginning to feel bad about it when it was time to go home. Then I discovered I was pregnant. If you want the truth, I'd just as soon have put an end to it, but I wasn't too sure how to go about it. The only sensible thing I did was to go to Mum − your Gran − for help. She was a tough old bird. She thought up the whole scheme and made me go through with it.'

'Poor Mum, what a terrible time she must have had.'

'Oh, Elsie ... If she hadn't been so determined to stay at home and be a housewife she could have come on tour with us and played the piano. But, no, she didn't think it was suitable for a married woman. She was always flaunting her married status at me. Of course she was married! She was eight years older than me. I was only nineteen. Just starting out and mad to have a career on the stage. She wanted you ...'

'And you didn't.'

'Not then. That's not to say I haven't been proud of what you've done since. I helped you, didn't I? And I'd have done more if I'd been allowed.'

She went over to the elaborate dressing table and looked at her reflection.

'We're alike, you know, and in more than just looks. You're as determined as I ever was. You inherited more from me than a decent voice and a good figure.'

'Perhaps,' Tina said. 'I've told you, I'll acknowledge the relationship and I'll be as kind as I can, but I won't do anything that will hurt Mum and Dad; that's got to be my first consideration. When will the book be out?'

'On the fifteenth of next month. But the first instalment of the serial will be in the paper on the previous Sunday. And there's already a bit of gossip circulating. These things always leak out.'

226

'Or are leaked,' Tina said. 'I'd better go now, while we're still on reasonably friendly terms.'

'Stay and have a drink. Nicky'll take it badly if he's mixed them and you don't accept it.'

'I'm tempted to say damn Nicky. He's a nasty bit of work. Why on earth did you marry him?'

'Because he's bloody good in bed, darling, and it happens to be something I need, that's why. Why are you having an affair with Jerry Bilchester? For the money?'

'Of course not. We'd better change the subject.'

Tina took the proffered drink and she and Tom stayed another ten minutes, but she could find little more to say. She had, she thought, some slight inkling of how Daphne and Will had come to embark on their ill-fated affair. She realised that she had thought of her father as always being middle-aged but, of course, he had once been a young man and as open to temptation as the next one. She could only forgive him and try to put it out of her mind.

The statement she and Tom hammered out more or less satisfied Tina.

'It was only recently that I learnt that Daphne Durrell is my mother,' it read. 'I have always been immensely proud of being closely related to such a scintillating star of the stage and screen ...'

'Do I have to say that?' Tina asked mutinously.

'It's diplomatic,' Tom replied.

' ... of the stage and screen, but I still look upon the mother and father who brought me up with devoted care as my true parents and I suppose I always will.'

'It's not bad,' she admitted. 'Do you think it will satisfy the Press?'

'No, but if you keep your head down and say nothing more they'll soon get tired of chasing you. Any hint of a family feud will only feed the bonfire.'

'I'm singing three nights out of six during the week the story will come out. I only hope it doesn't distract me.'

Tom looked at her with a tolerant smile. 'Ducky, if we had an earth tremor, a hurricane and a lightning strike, the only thing you'd be likely to notice is that the conductor took the tempo of your second act aria too fast.'

'True,' Tina admitted. 'Tom, you've been great. I'm grateful. I only wish you could help me over my next hurdle.'

'What's that?'

'Telling Jerry.'

'Will it be so difficult?'

'Yes,' said Tina. 'It will.'

'What a tangle,' Jerry said.

He spoke lightly, but Tina looked at him with anxiety, distrusting that cool manner.

'The thing is,' she persisted doggedly, 'that I'll need a refuge during the weekend when the serial starts. Could I come down to Somerset?'

She had several times joined him at his country house and she thought of its seclusion now with real longing.

'Your connection with me is one of the things the Press will seize on,' Jerry said. 'I'm inured to speculation about my love life, but I don't particularly want it splashed all over the Sunday papers.'

'No,' said Tina. 'Of course not.'

Jerry smiled. 'Don't go all stiff on me, darling. I'm not going to desert you. I'm just trying to work out the best way of playing down what is, after all, an entirely private matter between you and me.'

Tina was looking down at her ringless hands. It struck her rather forcibly that Jerry had never once suggested formalising what he called their connection. Did it occur to him that if they were married, or even engaged, the sting would be taken out of any speculation about their relations? Not that she was sure she would accept if he asked her to marry him, but it would be nice to be asked.

'I could find you a more secure bolthole,' Jerry said, thinking aloud. 'Let me look at my diary.'

Tina waited with resignation while he consulted the book that dominated his life.

'I'm in Scotland on the Friday,' Jerry said. 'I meant to come back to London, but I'll arrange to stay there over the weekend. I dare say I can fix some rather public engagement which will make it clear that I'm on my own.

In the meantime, I'm afraid Chadd Manor is definitely not the best place for you to be; too many easy ways of getting into the grounds. Every time you pop out of doors there'll be a telephoto lens focused on you.'

'I'm not royalty,' Tina said in irritation.

'I know, darling, but you are a celebrity. And so, unfortunately, am I, for rather different reasons. Would you like to go over to Paris and stay with Rosamund?'

'Not particularly.'

'I doubt whether you could trust the staff at any hotel not to talk. A private house would be best. You've met most of my closest colleagues and I'm sure any of them would be delighted to put you up for a day or two. How about Don and Alice? They've got a lovely secluded house and you liked them, didn't you?'

'I don't want to stay with strangers,' Tina said. 'Don't worry, I've thought of somewhere I can go. No, I'm not going to tell you where it is. If you don't know, you can't give it away, can you?'

'Are you cross with me?'

'I think you might have been more helpful. And more welcoming. I don't often ask for favours.'

'Not often enough,' Jerry said quietly. 'You're the most independent woman I've ever known.'

'"Known" in what sense?'

'Stop trying to quarrel with me.' Jerry reached out a long arm and pulled her closer to him. 'I still love you and I'd like to be around to support you when this story breaks, but common sense tells me that it would do more harm than good. I'm in the middle of some very delicate negotiations concerning a Government contract — and that's something you must keep to yourself — and the last thing I need is a searchlight turned on my private life.'

'I'm in the middle of a fairly gruelling operatic season and I could do without the added pressure, too,' Tina said.

'I know, darling, but believe me, the pressure won't be eased by fuzzy pictures of the pair of us at Chadd Manor with accompanying suggestive headlines. When this has blown over and when we both have some free time, will you come away for a holiday with me? I'm thinking of hiring a yacht and cruising round the Greek islands.'

'It sounds wonderful,' Tina said, but the flatness of her voice betrayed her lack of interest.

Jerry's arm tightened round her. 'You're really upset about this book, aren't you?'

'It's not the book, it's the fact that it's *true*,' Tina said. Her face crumpled and she buried her head against his shoulder, scowling fiercely. 'I hate it, I just hate it. You know, better than anyone, how I've bent over backwards not to hurt Mum's feelings. And all the time she *wasn't* ... and it was really Daphne, who wouldn't have given a damn if I was living with you or not. She says I'm like her and that's true, too, and I can't bear it. All the things I've been certain about, all my life, have been turned upside down. Dad ... a real old stick-in-the-mud ... he can't look me in the eye and we've always been so fond of one another. I've tried to be extra nice to them, but it's not the same. We all know it's not the same. I've lost something I'll never get back again.'

'Gently, darling, gently. I didn't realise you were so hard hit. Look, cancel your engagements and I'll take you away. I won't be able to stay with you all the time, it simply isn't possible, but I'll work out some way of being with you as much as I can. I'll put my secretary to work on it in the morning.'

Tina sat up and found a handkerchief to wipe her eyes.

'Bless you, but no,' she said. 'I can't cancel my stage appearances any more than you can call off a board meeting. I'll slog it out and go away for the crucial weekend as we planned just now. Look, I'm better. All I wanted was a short wallow in self-pity and a bit of sympathy.'

'Sympathy and my love,' Jerry said. 'I wonder, would it help you to see a psychiatrist? To get the hang-up over the family aspect sorted out?'

Tina put away her handkerchief and began to smile. 'No, thank you,' she said. 'It's a very practical suggestion − oh, Jerry you are *funny*! − but I'll get by without the help of a shrink, thank you.'

Chapter Twelve

'Do you want to be sheltered from the headlines or would you rather see the Sunday papers?' Oliver asked.

'I'd rather know the worst,' Tina said.

'I'll walk down to the village and pick up an armful. More toast?'

'Mm, please. Oliver, it is angelic of you to take me in this weekend.'

'Isn't it? And not a question asked about why you're with me and not with Jerry.'

'He did offer to take me away,' Tina said quickly. 'But it was all so complicated.'

'Why the hell doesn't he marry you?'

'I think if Jerry marries he'll want a wife who'll devote herself to him. I couldn't do that.'

'It's difficult to believe you're really in love with the man.'

'I am, of course I am. When I'm with him it's great. I need him, Oliver. Without Jerry I could lead quite a lonely life, especially when Ros is away.'

'If Jerry weren't around you might be surprised by the rush there'd be to fill the void,' Oliver said drily. 'However ... I'd better go to the newsagents before you tell me it's none of my business.'

The headlines were every bit as trying as Tina had expected. 'My Secret Valentine,' 'I gave my voice to the child I could not acknowledge', 'We are proud of one another say Daphne and Tina.'

'I think my favourite is "A Love Nest of Singing Birds",'

Oliver remarked. 'There's a touch of poetry about that. Cheer up, Tina. On the whole it's a sympathic treatment and there are one or two very favourable comments about your singing.'

'From people who've never heard me,' Tina retorted. 'All right, it could be worse. I suppose I'll survive.'

She went back to London and gave three radiant performances. Every evening there were reporters at the stage door trying to get her to say something about herself and Daphne, especially on the Thursday, which was the day the autobiography came out in book form. Tina had refused to go to the publication party, even though Tom had thought it might be advisable to put in an appearance, nor could she be tricked into making any comment.

The book was in all the bookshop windows with the unmistakeable face of Daphne Durrell 'television personality, star of stage and screen' smiling on the cover. Tina received a copy with the inscription 'To my darling daughter' scrawled inside. She put it on one side, feeling slightly sick. She would have to read it one day, she knew that, but for the moment she had had enough of her mother's revelations.

The following Sunday the serialisation revealed details of Daphne's two American marriages and her adventures in Hollywood and New York, and the relationship with Tina faded into the background.

'I told you so, a nine days' wonder,' Tom said.

'That's what you think!' Tina retorted. 'Daphne rang me up last night, very excited. Apparently a film company is interested in making a film of her life and, guess what, she suggested I should play her when young!'

'Good Lord deliver us! Is the woman completely insensitive?'

'A hide like a rhinoceros. I said no, of course, but if she takes the idea any further you must deal with it.'

'You can trust me to fend off any attempts to put you into a second-rate film, especially with rehearsals for *Così Fan Tutte* starting shortly. When is Ros due back?'

'On Wednesday. I'll be glad to see her.'

Almost as soon as Rosamund was back in the Kensington

flat it was borne in on Tina that Jerry had been right in saying that they had outgrown their student digs. Tina had become used to having the flat to herself. On that basis it was adequate, but now she and Rosamund seemed to get in one another's way in a manner they had never done in the past.

'What's happened to us?' Tina demanded. 'Did we always both want to use the bathroom at the same time? And where has all the hanging space gone?'

'I've got used to having a hotel suite with maid service,' Rosamund said. 'That was Benno's doing. Your wardrobe has expanded, too. I must say you've got some gorgeous clothes. I suppose you need them for your dates with Jerry. He's not a T-shirt and jeans kind of person is he?'

'Not in London,' Tina agreed. 'Yes, I have rather overflowed into your space. Ros, is it going to work, us being back together again?'

'I'm not sure that it is. Do you want me to look round for somewhere else?'

'The flat's in your name. And I do have the offer to move in with Jerry any time I want. I think I might be ready to do that now.'

Tina would not say so to Rosamund, she would not quite bring it out into the open and admit it to herself, but she was conscious at the back of her mind of a subtle shift in her relations with Jerry. She had been disappointed by his response to her need of him at the time of the unfortunate publicity over Daphne's biography and she knew that he was aware of it. She felt him slipping away from her. He was as loving as ever when they met, but they did not meet quite as often as they had in the first heady days of their affair. The thought of losing him disturbed Tina. She had grown used to having him around, not only because of their exciting sexual relationship, but as a willing and attentive escort, the provider of flowers and compliments and small, delightful presents. She had come to enjoy the prestige his company gave her. She was not only Valentina Burford, the well-known soprano, she was also Lord Bilchester's chosen companion, the woman he preferred above all others, and goodness knows there

233

was plenty of competition for the situation if Tina ever vacated it.

Tina sang that evening for the last time before going into rehearsals for the Mozart opera in which she and Rosamund were to be together for the first time since Wexford. She received the ovation to which she had become almost accustomed. Almost, but not quite; it still gave her a thrill to know that all those people were clapping and shouting and showering the stage with flowers for her, Tina Burford from Woodington, who might have been a secretary and an amateur singer if it had not been for a chance meeting with one of the great sopranos of the day.

She was excited and restless after the performance, and she changed quickly, wanting to get away with Jerry. She had a new outfit, rich blue satin trousers and jacket over a filmy blouse, which she thought he would like. She was almost ready when he arrived in her dressing room.

'You look delightful,' he said, bending over to kiss her. 'And your performance tonight was superb.'

'Thank you for the flowers, darling,' Tina said, lifting up her face for his kiss. 'I don't know how you manage to send such wonderful bouquets when you're out of the country. Italy this week, wasn't it?'

'I have a standing order with the florist,' Jerry said, amused. 'And yes, I've just got back from Milan.'

'Did you get to La Scala?'

'I did, and it was magnificent, but not as good as your own performance tonight.'

'Oh, you're just saying that!'

'I mean it, I assure you. I've bought you a little present — within the acceptable limits, I think.'

There was a touch of dryness in his voice which Tina chose to ignore as she tore the wrappings off a pair of black suede gloves, as fine and supple as silk.

'Lovely!' she said. 'As for acceptable limits, I have a surprise for you, but I'll explain later.'

They went to one of the restaurants where they were known. It was a place where celebrities gathered, but even though the other diners might have been expected to be blasé about fame, heads turned as Tina and Jerry walked to their table. Tina was conscious of it, but had learned to pretend that the stir of interest did not exist for her. With a flash of insight she realised that Jerry liked it. He cared little for his own standing in a world that was hardly capable of assessing his achievements except in terms of money, but he enjoyed being with a woman who merited that passing tribute.

'So what's this surprise you have for me?' he asked as they studied the menu.

'I think I'll have fish,' Tina decided. 'Scallops to start and then salmon escalopes in sorrel with wild rice and a small salad. About the surprise, I don't think Ros and I are going to fit into our little flat as well as we used to.'

'That was what I predicted, so I'm afraid I'm *not* surprised, not so far,' Jerry said. He chose his own meal and the wine and turned back to her.

'Would you still have me as a fixture in your own flat?' Tina asked.

She hoped she imagined the almost imperceptible pause before Jerry said, 'Of course. It's what I always wanted.'

'Before the Daphne scandal. Does that make any difference?'

'It seems to have blown over.'

Tina thought about the possible film and decided against mentioning it. She studied Jerry carefully, willing him to be frank with her. 'Jerry, you don't have to have me. I'm perfectly prepared to go flat-hunting for a place on my own. I just thought I'd give you first refusal.'

The diners at the next table turned their heads curiously, wondering what his companion could have said to make Lord Bilchester break into helpless laughter.

'Tina, you're irresistible,' Jerry said. 'Of course you must come to me. As from tonight?'

'I'll move my clothes in the morning,' Tina said in relief. 'When did you last have your piano tuned?'

'I'm not sure,' Jerry admitted.

'Better get it done. I'll be doing a lot of practising. That won't matter, will it? You'll be out all day and the flat is much too high for the neighbours to be bothered.'

'What about Rosamund? Will she stay on in Kensington?'

'I think she'd like a change, too.'

'She deserves a better setting. I'll get our property department to make some enquiries. I'm sure we can help her. Ask her round for a drink tomorrow evening so that we can have a chat about it.'

'Tina, this is a stunning flat,' Rosamund said, looking round her friend's new home. 'Especially this room. The view! Why on earth haven't you moved in before?'

'Oh ... you know me − independent. And a bit of a hang-up over shocking the parents. Now, that hardly seems to matter. Do you really like it? I find it overwhelming. Everything looks as new as it did the day I met Jerry. I don't think it gets cleaned, I think they just change the furniture once a week.'

'Idiot! Where is Jerry?'

'He'll be along shortly. He works a frightfully long day, but he's looking forward to seeing you. In the meantime, what would you like to drink?'

She opened a cupboard to reveal an impressive array of bottles. 'Everything from rice wine to white port,' she said. 'What'll you have?'

'A dry sherry.'

'Unadventurous! All right, I'll join you. That sounds like Jerry coming in.'

Rosamund turned as Jerry came towards her with his hand outstretched. I like him, I really like him, she thought. Lucky Tina.

'Rosamund, you look stunning,' Jerry said. 'It's very good to see you again.'

He took her hand and looked down at her with a smile. She was wearing a very plain black dress which she had bought in Paris. Her hair, which she had grown long for the part of Mélisande, was twisted up into a smooth chignon, skewered by a big gold and pearl pin. She looked very fine-drawn and elegant by the side of Tina's golden magnificence.

'I'm glad to have Mélisande behind me,' Rosamund said. 'I'll be singing it again in the future, of course, but for the time being I'm settled in London and looking forward to doing *Così* with Tina.'

236

'I was slightly surprised when I heard you were to sing Dorabella. I would have thought that role might have been better suited to Tina, with you playing the more serious Fiordiligi.'

'It's a question of the balance of the voices,' Tina said. 'Fiordiligi requires the sort of spinto voice I've developed, while Dorabella is more lyrical. Even when Dorabella is sung by a mezzo-soprano the voice has to be light and agile. Besides, I prefer Fiordiligi.'

'You think it's the better part,' Rosamund said gently.

Jerry glanced at her sharply, sensing a hint of criticism, but it passed Tina by.

'It requires a bit more acting,' she said. 'She holds out longest against the blandishments of the men they think are strangers and there's that hint of regret at the end ... You know acting has never been your strong point, Ros.'

'It didn't use to be,' Rosamund agreed.

'Did I ask for a gin and tonic?' Jerry said, looking at the drink in his hand.

'No, but it's what you usually have,' Tina said. 'I was anticipating the requirements of my lord and master. Do you want something different?'

'No, this will do. Now, Rosamund, I've brought home with me some details of flats that might be suitable for you.'

'Not too expensive, I hope,' Tina said.

'That's for Rosamund to decide, but I think I've pitched it about right. Do you want to look through the details now or would you prefer to take them away?'

'Oh, do let's look at them, Ros,' Tina exclaimed.

She knew she had a shrewder eye for practical details than Rosamund was likely to show and, sure enough, it was Tina who foresaw difficulties about getting a piano up stairs and criticised the size of the kitchen.

'I'm not a great cook, like you,' Rosamund protested. 'Did you make these delicious cheese biscuits?'

'I did, as a matter of fact,' Tina admitted.

'Isn't that rather a waste of your time, darling?' Jerry said.

'Cooking relaxes me. And I'd like to point out that you've just helped yourself to your third biscuit.'

'They're very good,' Jerry said. 'Any decisions, Rosamund?'

'I think we can narrow it down to three. I'd like to see all of them.'

'I'll send one of my young men round tomorrow to escort you, if that's convenient?'

'Yes, but ...'

'They'll be fighting one another for the honour. Have you any plans for this evening? Would you like to join Tina and me for dinner?'

'We're eating in,' Tina said. 'As well as cheese biscuits I've made fresh tomato soup, chicken casserole and a pineapple cheesecake. The kitchen is beautifully equipped, but strangely lacking in utensils. I must buy some sharp knives. I think the caterers you usually call in must bring their own with them.'

'They'll have to start billing you as "the domesticated diva",' Jerry said. 'Will this meal of yours stretch to three?'

'I think so,' Tina said, but Rosamund intervened.

'I'm meeting Oliver.'

'Oh, Ros, why didn't you say? He could have come round for a drink, too. I haven't seen him for weeks. Give him my love. He was angelic to me the weekend Daphne's book was serialised.'

She did not notice Jerry's silence, especially when Rosamund went on, 'Oliver's got some news about his opera. The ENO have persuaded Ransu Prokopi to do a season with them and one of his conditions is that they let him conduct *The Crown of Glass*.'

'When?' Tina demanded. 'I've made all my plans on the basis of being free for *Crown of Glass* in eighteen months' time. You tell Oliver that if he lets them do it with any other singer than me I'll slaughter him.'

'I'll give him that message,' Rosamund said, picking up her handbag. 'Though quite honestly, if it comes to a choice between putting on the opera and disappointing you, Tina, I think the opera will win.'

'I know,' Tina said. 'Of course any composer would feel the same, especially with Ransu Prokopi conducting. Find

238

out everything you can and telephone me tomorrow.'

'What shall I do if Oliver offers me the lead?' Rosamund enquired demurely.

'Leave town! Your life won't be safe. Don't be daft, Ros, you're as much committed as I am for the next year and a half. Besides, *Crown* isn't at all your cup of tea, far too much heavy drama. When shall I see you again? Would you like me to come with you to view your flats?'

'I'll see them on my own first,' Rosamund said. 'As soon as I've made a decision you shall be my first visitor.'

'It's a very, very nice flat,' Tina said, looking round approvingly. 'To be honest, I like it better than Jerry's modern place. I know our view from the terrace is splendid, but I think you're just as lucky, being on a level with the treetops, and this is a very pleasant little square.'

'Do you regret moving in with Jerry?' Rosamund enquired.

'In some ways it's great, but there are difficulties, just as I thought there would be. Jerry's knowledgeable about music, but he doesn't know a lot about the life of an artist. He doesn't understand about having beans on toast and putting your feet up after a hard day's work. His idea of relaxation is a quick shower, a drink and a meal out. I love my food, as you know, but I'm getting tired of dining in restaurants.'

'Surely that's what you were doing before?'

'We met three, or even four, nights a week,' Tina agreed. 'I could cope with that, especially at the beginning when I was mad to be with him.'

Looking back, she realised that she had scarcely noticed what she was eating in those early days. All that had really mattered was getting back to the flat and going to bed. Now, they were still in love, but their lovemaking had become more routine. Without the stimulus of constantly parting and meeting again, Jerry had become less demanding. They were almost like a settled married couple, except that marriage was one thing they never discussed.

'Jerry doesn't like me to be domesticated,' Tina said. 'He wears me like a decoration and takes me out so that his

239

glittering star can be admired. The funny thing is, I'm sure if he had a wife he'd want her to be completely different.'

'I suspect you're right,' Rosamund agreed. 'If he had a wife he'd like her to stay in the country and make a home for him there.'

'While he was unfaithful to her in town,' Tina said.

'Not necessarily. I think Jerry might settle down into a delightful husband and father, provided his wife put a bit of effort into keeping him interested.'

'The harem mentality,' Tina said in disgust.

'That's rich, coming from someone who's peeved because her lover doesn't like her slaving over a hot stove for him.'

'I know, I'm being completely inconsistent. There's one good thing about the flat though, Ros. That big room may not be my idea of a comfortable living space, but it's got stunning acoustics. Let's make some plans to get together for some individual rehearsals there.'

If Jerry had not known very much about the life of an opera singer in the throes of rehearsals he was soon to learn. Both Tina and Rosamund had been studying the score of *Così Fan Tutte* and they had both had private coaching. Now they were committed to singing the version their producer had in mind. Line by line, almost note by note, they assembled the roles allotted to them.

In rehearsal rooms, in Jerry's flat and, finally, on the stage of the opera house, they walked through their movements and began to put in the characterisation that would bring the roles alive. This was what Tina throve on, but Rosamund began to wilt. She lost the weight she had put on after her return from Paris and the dark circles under her eyes betrayed her restless nights.

'Why don't we take Rosamund down to Somerset for the weekend?' Jerry suggested one evening after he had met Rosamund just leaving the flat after an extra session with Tina to refine their scenes together.

'Darling, what a lovely idea!' Tina exclaimed. 'We could get away Friday afternoon and we're not called again until the middle of Monday morning. It would be a real rest for her. She does look tired, doesn't she?'

'Whereas you're bursting with energy,' Jerry said with a smile.

'It's partly because I'm buoyed up by excitement,' Tina admitted.

'I'm making one condition — no music, not even a mention of Mozart.'

'That's not possible,' Tina said. 'We must do some work every day, even if it's no more than routine vocalising. Yes, Jerry, it's essential. You wouldn't ask an athlete in training for the Olympics to put his feet up and rest, would you? Our muscles have to be exercised in just the same way. The role of Fiordiligi spans a range of two and a half octaves; it's the equivalent of running a marathon with hurdles.'

'And Dorabella?'

'Equally demanding.'

'No wonder poor Rosamund looks exhausted.'

Perhaps because of this conversation Jerry was particularly attentive to Rosamund that weekend. The house had never looked more beautiful. The trees were heavy with autumn leaves just turning colour, the crops were harvested and ploughing had started, and the hedgerows were full of blackberries and wild rosehips.

'Lovely, lovely place,' Rosamund said. 'What a tranquil atmosphere! Jerry, how can you bear to stay in London?'

'I have to make the money to maintain the place. The farm is self-sustaining, but there are no profits to divert into keeping up the house and grounds. I come down whenever I can, but less often than I used to because ...'

'Because I keep him tied to London,' Tina said cheerfully. They were walking across the paddock towards the house and she took his arm and hugged it to her. 'That's true, isn't it?'

'It's got something to do with it,' Jerry admitted. He whistled softly and a big black horse cantered towards them, pausing and tossing its head uncertainly when it got near. Jerry felt in his pocket and held out a small apple and the horse allowed itself to be persuaded to take it from him.

'You don't ride, do you, Rosamund?' Jerry asked.

'I had a pony when I was a little girl, dappled grey like

241

a rocking horse, but once I grew out of him I had to give it up,' Rosamund said.

'Would you like to try again?'

'No!' Tina exclaimed in horror. 'Suppose she fell off and broke an arm or something? It doesn't bear thinking about.'

'She means because I'd have to be replaced in *Così*,' Rosamund informed Jerry solemnly.

'I realise that!'

'It's all very well to laugh, but you must admit it would be a calamity,' Tina protested. 'Ros, we'd better go and get rid of this mud. Jerry's invited the neighbours in for drinks before lunch.'

There were eight people who looked in for an hour or so before dispersing to eat, all local, all country people, some old enough to be retired, and all slightly out of their depth in dealing with two young women from a world they hardly knew. Rosamund exerted herself and made conversation; Tina smiled and looked beautiful and privately thought them dull.

Perhaps it was because she was keeping rather quiet that Tina caught the murmured comment of one red-faced man to another, '*Two* opera singers? Old Jerry's going it a bit, isn't he?'

The other man snorted with laughter and turned his laugh into an embarrassed cough when he saw Tina looking at him.

He began talking about the iniquities of the latest edict from Brussels and the effect it would have on farming and she stopped listening. There was music running in her head and nothing Jerry might say could stop her listening to her aria '*Come Scoglio*' and thinking about the big jump in the score which worried many sopranos, but which Tina knew she could handle.

She came to with a start and realised that people were beginning to leave. She had a guilty feeling of not having played her part, but her position was difficult. What was she? An acknowledged mistress, but that was not likely to weigh with these people. Jerry had not suggested that she should play the hostess, not in the way he expected her to do when he invited people to the flat in London. Lacking guidance, she had stayed in the background and she had the irritated feeling that Rosamund had appeared to advantage while she had seemed awkward and lacking in social sense.

'"An enchanting production, exquisitely sung",' Tina read out of the newspaper she had spread out on the floor. '"Two of the best young operatic singers on the stage today – both British" they would have to put that in " ... gave performances which were as near to perfection as anything we are likely to see or hear ..." and then he goes on to praise the rest of the cast. Very glowing. Are the rest of the reviews as good?'

'Without exception,' Jerry assured her. 'One thought the sets and costumes too pastel ...'

'He's got a point, all those blues and pinks, but the actual set was a joy to move about in.'

'And one suggests that you overacted.'

'I didn't, did I?' Tina asked in alarm. 'I tried terribly hard not to make the characterisation too emphatic.'

'I thought you got it right. Just enough contrast with Rosamund's delicate comedy. And the idea of having Despina as an older woman instead of a pert young maid worked very well.'

'Yes, we all liked that for a change. We brought it off. You've no idea what a relief that is. However hard you rehearse, you never really believe you can sing the role until you come to performance.'

'You must have been fairly sure,' Jerry protested. 'When I think of the hours you spent in front of the mirror perfecting every movement, and that after a day in the rehearsal room ...'

'It's not the same. Nothing comes alive until you have an audience. Oh, Jerry, there's nothing like it when things go right. It's like stroking a great furry purring animal. And at the same time knowing that the beast can turn and savage you if you don't give it what it wants.'

Jerry was looking at her curiously. 'You couldn't live without it, could you?' he asked.

'Not now that I've come to think of it as my due,' Tina said with blinding honesty.

'What about Rosamund?'

'She's still terrified of her audience, poor dear. She suffers tortures of stage fright before every performance. I have about ten minutes of pure terror before a first night, but once the music starts I forget it. There's always a certain tension, of course, and I feel it as much as anyone, but once I've proved I can sing a role then I just go on and sing it.'

'And enjoy it.'

'Every minute, though no performance is as effortless as it looks. You have to *think* all the time, you see. I may seem to be swooning with love, but actually I'm keeping in mind that the music's approaching a phrase that ends in a high C and saving myself a little to make sure that I take it successfully.'

'Don't give away all your secrets,' Jerry said, bending over to kiss her. 'Last night was as near to a miracle as I'm ever likely to hear. My only regret is that I now know too much about the sweat and tears that go into making it happen.'

The production of *Così Fan Tutte* established Valentina Burford and Rosamund Drew in the front rank of operatic sopranos. Tom found himself in the happy position of pencilling in projects for them three or four years ahead. Tina was thrilled, but Rosamund, he noticed, was oddly noncommittal about the prospect of singing at La Fenice in Venice or even the Metropolitan Opera House in New York; and whereas Tina was openly looking forward to the production of *Don Giovanni* in which she was to sing Donna Elvira and Rosamund was booked for Donna Anna, Rosamund admitted that she was dreading it.

'But Anna's a good role for you,' Tina pointed out. 'It's the contrast between us that everyone's going to pick on again. Me all passion and despair and you aristocratic and cool, demanding vengeance for your father's death before you'll get married. I must say, I've always thought that a bit hard on Don Ottavio.'

'I suppose I'll live through it,' Rosamund said. 'I don't mind learning the role, if only I didn't have to face the audience!'

'Opera behind closed doors,' Tina said flippantly. 'At least the pressure's off *Così Fan Tutte* now that *Carmen* has come back into the season. I'm rather sad about not doing Micaela any more, but just think, a whole week without a performance over Christmas. That reminds me, what are you doing for Christmas, Ros?'

As she expected, Rosamund looked uncomfortable as she replied, 'Jerry has asked me to join your skiing trip.'

'It's not *my* skiing trip,' Tina said sharply. 'I'm not going. For one thing, I don't want to break a leg and, for the other, I simply must spend Christmas with Mum and Dad.'

'Jerry said there was some doubt about it,' Rosamund admitted.

'There's not, there's no doubt at all. I'm not going to Switzerland and that's flat. What I wanted to say was, don't let it stop you. Jerry's taken a villa, complete with maids, and it'll be a lovely holiday for you, if you like that sort of thing and don't want to be with your parents.'

'They wouldn't mind. Neither would yours, Tina. We're not children any more.'

'It's my wretched conscience,' Tina said. 'I've been neglecting them, Ros. I said I loved them just the same and the story about Daphne hadn't made any difference, but of course it *did*. I don't feel the same, not quite the same, as I did before. I resent the deception and they sense it. They know I'm living with Jerry and they don't like it. He says they have no right to criticise and, of course, at my age it's absurd, but I still can't slap them in the face by going off to Switzerland with him, not over Christmas.'

'You really wouldn't mind if I went?'

'You'll be a party of eight,' Tina pointed out. 'Jerry's peeved because he wanted me to do the hostess thing, but you'll do that just as well as me, if not better. And you already know how to ski, don't you? I'd be floundering round on the nursery slopes, hating every minute of it.'

'You don't know what you're missing,' Rosamund assured

her. 'White snow, blue sky, fast motion — it's heaven.'

'You sound like an advertisement. I'll try to keep a straight face if you have grey skies and rain the whole time you're there, but it'll be an effort.'

Chapter Thirteen

'Oliver, you beast, you've been hiding from me,' Tina said. 'I haven't seen you for an age. I'm telephoning to wish you a happy Christmas. I'd come over and see you if it wasn't for this wretched snow. The laugh's on me, actually. I sent Rosamund off to Switzerland with Jerry because I didn't want to get involved with the stuff and now we've got more here than they have there.'

'If you'll pause for breath I'll wish you a happy Christmas, too,' Oliver said. 'I take it you're at Woodington?'

'Where else? Snowed up! Well, of course, it is possible to get out, but I wouldn't like to drive.'

'No, it wouldn't be wise. So, unless there's a rapid thaw I shan't see you on this visit. A pity, because I'd like to talk to you.'

'About *Crown of Glass*?' Tina demanded. 'What's the news?'

'It's scheduled for November.'

'Oh, bliss! That's my best Christmas present yet.'

She could hear Oliver laughing. 'You do wonders for my ego,' he said. 'Suppose it's a flop?'

'Valentina Burford doesn't appear in flops,' Tina assured him solemnly. 'Thank you for your lovely letter about *Così*. I really appreciated it, coming from someone who knows what he's talking about.'

'You were superb.'

'And *Giovanni* to come in April! I can't tell you how much I'm looking forward to that.'

'You're a glutton for work. Three new roles in eighteen

months, that's quite a programme.'

'It's not too much,' Tina assured him. 'Not the way I'm singing at the moment. I could conquer mountains – though not on skis.'

'So Rosamund's taken your place with Jerry?'

'I wouldn't put it quite like that. He organised a villa party, I declined to take part. And, yes, to anticipate your next question, he is annoyed about it.'

'But that doesn't worry you?'

'Well ... no, not really. Jerry knows I have to have my independence.'

They chatted for a few more minutes, but finally Tina had to ring off, reluctantly, because talking to Oliver felt like being in touch with the real world again. She was bored, and annoyed with herself for being bored. A quiet family Christmas was all very well, but during the past year she had grown away from Elsie and Will. Her very success had distanced her from their limited hopes; she had money, she had fame and she was living with a man whose name was rarely out of the newspapers. They were nervous of her and they went to far too much trouble to make her comfortable, especially Elsie. Being cooped up in snowbound Woodington was no one's idea of an exciting Christmas. Tina almost wished she had given in to Jerry and gone to Switzerland.

There was something bothering her parents, and before she went back to London Tina found out what it was.

'Daphne put a note in with her Christmas card,' Elsie said abruptly. 'That film of her life is going ahead.'

'Oh, hell!' Tina exclaimed.

'They're making it as a musical. Daphne's going to be in at the beginning and then they're doing it in what she calls flashback.'

'Is Nicky in it?'

'It makes me sick. He's acting the part of Will, only they're changing the name to Bill.'

Tina gave a gasp, trying not to laugh.

'It's ludicrous,' she said. 'Mum, it's got nothing to do with us any more. They'll change the story out of all recognition and no one will remember our connection with it at all.'

'No? You won't say that when you see Daphne up on

the screen mooning over her stage-struck daughter.'

The prospect was intensely distasteful, but Tina still thought that it was best to keep quiet and say nothing.

'I wish you'd talk to Tom,' Elsie said. 'He did more to help us than anyone.'

'All right. I want to see him anyway, to discuss Oliver's opera. I must go and pack my suitcase and get back to London.'

'You haven't enjoyed it, have you?' Elsie asked.

'I have! It's been the most marvellous rest. I didn't anticipate being cooped up indoors by all this snow, but apart from that it's been lovely. And I love this jumper you knitted for me. I shall wear it to all my rehearsals.'

'Blue's your colour,' Elsie said, slightly reassured. 'I've put a piece of Christmas cake and a few of my mince pies in a tin for you. Be sure to separate them as soon as you get back because the cake will make the pastry soggy.'

'Yes, Mum,' Tina said solemnly.

She telephoned Tom as soon as she got back to the flat, after a slow drive over the slushy roads.

'Jerry's not due back until tomorrow,' she said. 'I suppose you wouldn't like to cheer my solitude? I can offer you soup and an omelette and Mum's mince pies.'

'I'll be right over,' Tom said.

Tina was pleased to see him, looking big and solid, his face reddened by the cold. She held up her face and got an enthusiastic kiss.

'No need to make a meal of it,' she protested.

'I don't often get the chance,' Tom said. 'So, what's gone wrong in your life?'

'Why should there be anything wrong?'

'Would you have rung me otherwise? Don't tell me the lovely Rosamund has hijacked your Jerry?'

'Of course not. It's Daphne again. The film's going ahead.'

'I know. I was asked to put some money into it.'

'You refused, of course.'

'I wrestled with my conscience, because actually I think it might be a success, but in the end I decided it wasn't worth offending my favourite client.'

249

'So I should hope! I would never, never have spoken to you again if you'd financed that travesty of my poor old parents' life. Is there no hope of stopping it, Tom?'

'I doubt it. The book's out, the serial's been printed, it's a bit late to quibble at a film. Besides, I've seen the script and the story's very much altered. The main emphasis is on Daphne's successful musicals. It's nostalgia time and I think the old songs will sell it.'

He looked at Tina's downcast face and said softly, 'Be thankful, Tina. At least it means you probably won't have to support your errant Mama in her old age.'

'That's a point,' Tina said, cheering up. 'Now, Tom, about my schedule for the coming year ...'

'Ros, you look wonderful!' Tina exclaimed. 'The tan really suits you, but you're going to have to tone it down a bit for Dorabella. It's really going to stand out against those wishy-washy costumes.'

'I had the most marvellous time,' Rosamund admitted. 'You should have come.'

'Thank you, I saw quite enough snow where I was.'

'You might just as well have been where you could enjoy it. Jerry missed you, I think.'

'Was he faithful to me?'

'Tina! Of course he was. The other people were all married to one another and I hope you don't think I would ...'

'Of course not. I'm glad to hear he behaved himself. I wouldn't put a little quiet adultery beyond Jerry if he thought he could get away with it. That Felicia Hensen has definitely got her eye on him.'

'She sprained her ankle the first day.'

'Good!'

'Tina, don't be horrid. It completely spoiled her holiday. Oh, you should have been there. The skiing was superb!'

'I'll take your word for it. Listen, Oliver's opera is definitely on in November.'

'I'm very pleased for him.'

'And I've started learning Donna Elvira. How about you and Donna Anna?'

'Give me a chance. I've hardly had time to unpack. Tina, I do dread it.'

It was obvious that she meant it. Tina looked at her friend anxiously, seeing something of the lovely bloom beginning to fade from Rosamund's face as she contemplated the months of hard work in front of her.

'I'll help all I can,' she said, but she knew that was not the answer.

Donna Elvira, Giovanni's discarded mistress, was a role Tina relished as much for its dramatic content as for the fine music. She sailed through her coaching sessions, confident of her ability to sing the part, and began to tackle the characterisation with a ferocious determination to put her own mark on the production.

'I feel about Elvira as I did about Violetta,' she said to Jerry. 'That I can make it mine. Fiordiligi, no; I love the music, it's sublime, but the role is more static. It doesn't give me the same opportunity for ...'

'Blood and thunder?' Jerry asked.

'Don't say that! I'm so afraid of sinking into melodrama.'

'Your producer should prevent that.'

Tina grinned. 'He's not as strong-minded as he might be.'

'In other words, he allows you to bully him. What about Rosamund? Is she getting on all right?'

'Not relishing it as much as I do, but singing like an angel, as usual. That skiing holiday bucked her up no end, but that was three months ago and now that the tan has faded she looks a bit worn.'

'Ask her down to Somerset this weekend.'

'Good idea,' Tina agreed.

She was lounging on the floor, with her head against the sofa where Jerry was sitting. When the telephone rang she said lazily, 'You answer it. It's much more likely to be for you than for me.'

Jerry got up and went to the telephone, but then he held it out to Tina.

'You were wrong,' he said. 'It's Tom Walden for you.'

Tina scrambled off the floor and took the telephone.

'Tina, would you be interested in doing three performances of *La Traviata* in Vienna?' Tom enquired.

'Interested, yes, but when? You know how tied up I am with *Don Giovanni.*'

'I've checked your schedule and I think you could manage it. It would mean flying out tomorrow and performing Saturday, Monday and Tuesday, then coming back Wednesday.'

'Help! I didn't realise you meant would I go immediately. I don't think I can, Tom. I've got rehearsals on Monday and again on Wednesday.'

'The Wednesday call isn't until the afternoon. If I can get permission for you to miss Monday's rehearsal you ought to be able to manage it.'

'Missing Monday's session will be highly unpopular with Joel Messinger,' Tina pointed out.

'I'll twist his arm. Obviously it's an emergency. Marianna Petra has a throat infection.'

'Surely someone's covering for her?'

'They want you. You know how rarely any opera house lets the understudy perform. They want an international star. You should feel flattered.'

Tina did feel flattered. Behind the anxiety of taking on the task of singing a leading role in an unknown production at almost a moment's notice was a definite thrill of pride that her name should have been put forward in such a situation.

'Jerry's expecting me to go to Chadd Manor this weekend,' she said uncertainly.

Across the room she saw Jerry look up and the way he was starting to frown.

'That's a minor consideration, surely?' Tom said with some impatience.

'I suppose ... yes, I can get over it,' Tina said. 'What about costumes? Marianna Petra is five foot four with a size forty-two bust; nothing made for her is likely to fit me. Would the Garden lend out its costumes?'

'I doubt it, at such short notice. I'll bargain for you to go to a good theatrical costumier's here in London before

252

you leave and pick up a couple of gowns.'

'Three gowns,' Tina said. 'Two evening gowns and a nice-looking period day dress. I'll take my chance on the nightdress for the last act. I'll need a car to take me to the airport, of course, and one to meet me on arrival.'

'And a really first-class hotel,' Tom added. 'I may say that the fee they're offering tops anything you've received yet.'

Tina looked at Jerry warily as she put down the telephone.

'You gathered I've been asked to fly off to Vienna at a moment's notice?' she asked.

'This weekend?'

'Leaving tomorrow and coming back Wednesday.'

There was a brief pause and then Jerry said in the even way that meant he was displeased, 'I heard you tell Tom I was expecting you at Chadd Manor, but perhaps you forgot that I'd asked half a dozen guests for the weekend and that you'd promised to sing at a charity concert on Saturday evening?'

'No, I remembered. I'm sorry, but I can't pass up this Viennese trip. Be pleased for me, Jerry. It's an honour to be asked to take over from a well-known singer.'

'And the Hospice Appeal is of no importance?'

'Send them a donation,' Tina said. 'No, I tell you what, ask Rosamund to take my place. We were going to invite her to join us anyway. I'll give her a ring.'

'I'll do it,' Jerry said. 'It's my house, the guests are my friends and the Hospice is my particular local charity.'

'You're cross,' Tina said.

'I'm more than cross, I'm bloody angry. You've let me down. I only hope Rosamund will be kind enough to get me out of an embarrassing predicament.'

To Tina it was no more than a passing squall, though she did have a moment's qualm about allowing her name to be used as an attraction and then failing to appear at the charity concert. It was a relief when Rosamund readily agreed to take over. Rosamund, of course, understood the importance of an engagement at the Staatsoper, Vienna. Tina put the matter out of her mind and turned her attention to a quick mental revision of the role of Violetta. She knew the part well enough, goodness knows, but it was going to be something of an ordeal performing in a production she had not seen, with a strange conductor, orchestra and cast.

Tina flew off to Vienna and Rosamund drove down to Somerset with Jerry and was, just as Tina had predicted, a great success both with the house guests and with the concert audience.

For the concert she wore a long gown of deep blue velvet, very plain and sweeping. To the accompanist's relief she had uncomplainingly taken over the group of three songs Tina had agreed to sing in the first half of the concert, but had asked to substitute an aria from *Così Fan Tutte* in the second half and had met the pianist in the afternoon for a rehearsal.

She ate very little at dinner before the concert, quietly explaining to Jerry's housekeeper that a large meal would affect her singing and asking if something could be kept for her on her return to the house.

'You've quite won Mrs Turner's heart,' Jerry commented with a smile.

'I'm being a terrible nuisance,' Rosamund said ruefully.

'Not at all. I'm the one who's a nuisance, asking you for such a favour at short notice.'

'Tina knew I'd help if I could.'

'But I'm the one who's grateful. Will you allow me to show my gratitude? I happen to have something here which would look delightful with the dress you're wearing. I hope you'll accept it.'

Rosamund took the jeweller's case and opened it. Inside was a delicate pendant set with sapphires and diamonds and hanging from a fine gold chain. It would, as Jerry had said, look just right with her blue velvet. All the same, Rosamund looked up at him searchingly, the pretty pendant dangling from her hand.

'When you say you "happen" to have it,' she said, 'do you mean you were going to give it to Tina?'

'I hoped you wouldn't guess that,' Jerry admitted. 'Yes, it was to have been my "thank you" present to Tina.'

'Then I can't take it,' Rosamund said, putting the jewel back in its case. Without looking up from this task, she added, 'I can't take anything that belongs to Tina.'

She hoped he would understand her and that nothing more need be said, but Jerry persisted.

'Even if it's something that Tina has already lost?'

It had been a mistake to allow a situation of which they were both aware to be expressed in words. While Rosamund was still searching for the right response, Jerry said, 'You fit in here much better than Tina ever did.'

Rosamund stood up. 'I didn't hear you say that,' she said with determination.

'You fit into my life better than Tina does, or even wants to.'

'No, Jerry, no! You're out of humour with Tina at the moment, but you still love her and she still loves you.'

'Do I? Does she?'

'When she comes back from Vienna, covered in glory and bursting to tell you all about it, you won't have any doubts. You know how irresistible Tina is when she's on the crest of a wave.'

'Yes, I do,' Jerry admitted. 'But I'm less and less sure that the waves she rides are in my ocean.'

Vienna was, as Rosamund had predicted, a triumph for Tina. On the Wednesday she whirled into the flat at midday, dropped her suitcase, had a sandwich and a glass of milk and stormed out again to her rehearsal.

'You thought I wouldn't make it and here I am, five minutes early,' she pointed out.

'I hope you're not too tired to sing,' the producer said, but his voice was indulgent.

'No, I promise you. I had an excellent night's sleep, a good flight this morning and I'm raring to go. Ros, what was the weekend like?'

'Delightful, as always. You know I love Chadd Manor,' Rosamund said steadily.

'And the concert? Was it well attended? Was the accompanist reasonable? Did they love you? I know they did.'

'It all went off very well. The Hospice made a lot of money.'

'Oh, good! Perhaps that will make Jerry less miffed with

me. I hope he was suitably grateful to you?'

'He was.'

'He probably had a nice present up his sleeve, to thank me for singing at his concert, it would be just like him. I must see if I can wheedle it out of him and give it to you instead.'

'Please don't.' Rosamund spoke sharply and Tina looked at her in surprise.

'Not if you'd be offended,' she agreed. 'Right, let's plunge into the Don's dark deeds. What did I miss by not being here on Monday?'

The rehearsal was long and hard. Reluctantly, Tina had to admit that she was worn out by the time they broke up. Rosamund, too, looked at the end of her tether. The thought passed through Tina's mind that she would just as soon have gone back to their old flat with Rosamund and had a quiet evening in as go home to Jerry, especially since she guessed from Rosamund's muted replies to her questions that he was still in an unforgiving mood over her defection from the charity concert.

He was already in when she let herself into the flat, sitting in one of the big black leather armchairs with a drink and a book.

'What a nice, domesticated scene,' Tina commented, dropping a kiss lightly on the top of his head. 'We're not going out, are we? I'm dead on my feet.'

'I've ordered a meal to be sent in.'

'Oh, bless you! That was thoughtful. I'll go and have a shower and change into something comfortable. See you in a few minutes.'

Tina grimaced to herself as she went through to the bedroom. The atmosphere was decidedly chilly and she was going to have to work to get Jerry out of his disgruntled mood. She sat down on the edge of the bed, her face thoughtful. Damn it, why should she feel obliged to win him round? But the voice of honesty answered her − because his grievance was justified. She *had* let him down, and the fact that she thought it had been unavoidable was not an excuse she could expect anyone outside her professional circle to accept.

The meal was Chinese and very good. Tina, who had not eaten properly since the previous evening, devoured it with a hearty appetite, while at the same time trying to entertain Jerry with an account of her triumph in Vienna.

'I had six curtain calls on two nights and *seven* on the last,' she said. 'It really was a great success and everyone was tremendously grateful to me for stepping in at short notice.'

'How nice for you,' Jerry said.

'I can see I'm not forgiven,' Tina said, abandoning her attempt to pretend that all was well. 'Jerry, I've already seen Ros and I know that your weekend was a success, too.'

'Is that what she said?'

'She told me you made a lot of money for the Hospice. That was what you wanted, wasn't it?'

'What I wanted was a hostess for my friends, company for myself and a concert performance I'd been promised.'

'Tell me, Jerry, what would you have done if there'd been a financial crisis this weekend and you could have saved the day by flying to the continent?'

'That's rather different ...'

'Oh, yes, *that's* to be taken seriously. My point is that my work has to be taken seriously, too.'

There was a long silence while Jerry absent-mindedly chased a few grains of rice round his plate with a fork.

'All right,' he said at last. 'I don't equate singing on the stage with saving a company, but I understand that you do. We have different points of view. Given that, I can see that you believe you were justified. Yes, the weekend was a success, but it was thanks to Rosamund and not to you, and that rankles.'

'I warned you,' Tina said quietly. 'I told you right from the start that my work must come first.'

She stretched out her hand to him across the table. She was surprised when Jerry did not respond.

'It's not that simple,' he said heavily. 'This isn't the first time we've been at odds with one another.'

'And usually for the same reason,' Tina agreed. 'Because your expectations of me clash with my commitment to my career.'

257

'That's one way of putting it.'

'I do still love you,' Tina said. She spoke wistfully, willing him to believe her and to return to the easy-going relationship she thought they had achieved. This was not the moment when she wanted an upheaval in her life, not when she was about to embark on a major role and had to give her entire mind to it. She had had her moment of rebellion about winning Jerry round, but the truth was she needed him.

He remained obstinately silent, and she tried again. 'Vienna was a fantastic experience. I stepped into the role and sang it as if I'd been with the company for every rehearsal. It means something, Jerry, when not only the audience but the entire cast and the orchestra join in the applause for a singer.'

Her mind went back to the great gilded basket of red roses that had been brought on to the stage, the way the conductor had kissed her hand, the roars of applause.

'I would have given anything to have had you there to share it with me,' she said quietly.

It was true. She had really felt the lack of someone to whom she could have turned, someone who would have participated in that triumph. She shut her mind to the fact that it could just as well have been Tom or Rosamund or even neglectful Oliver, as long as it was someone who knew her and understood her achievement.

'I'm desperately tired,' she said. 'Singing last night, only having a few hours' sleep, flying back this morning and rehearsing this afternoon, it's been a gruelling schedule. I haven't got the energy to quarrel with you, quite apart from the fact that it's the last thing I want to do.'

'If you're that tired perhaps I'd better sleep in the spare room tonight,' Jerry said, getting up from the table.

Oh, no you don't! Tina thought in alarm. That's a sure recipe for disaster.

She went and leant against him, winding her arms round his neck. 'I want you with me.'

She was satisfied when Jerry appeared to yield, saying no more about separating for the night. She intended to cement their reconciliation by being particularly loving, but she had underestimated the depth of her fatigue. When she got into bed and settled down to wait for Jerry to join her she meant to do no more than close her eyes and rest for a moment, but when Jerry came into the bedroom she was sound asleep.

Jerry stood for a moment looking down at her total abandonment. Her bright hair was spread on the pillow, one bare shoulder was hunched and her other arm was flung out to his side of the bed, as if reaching over to him. His expression as he watched her was regretful and a little sad. He brushed back the hair from her face and the soft curls clung to his fingers, but Tina only sighed and buried her head deeper into the pillow. Very carefully, Jerry slid into bed without touching her again.

The new *Don Giovanni*, due to open in April, was to be a conventional production, set in the seventeenth century, with all the backgrounds and the costumes in rich, dark colours set off by gilding and embroidery. Apart from her first appearance, when Don Giovanni broke into her bed chamber, Rosamund wore plain black throughout, in keeping with her mourning for her murdered father. Tina had a wonderful gown of black and crimson shot silk, with a black lace shawl thrown over her head.

Tina had always known that they would be a good foil for one another and, sure enough, the contrast between Rosamund's anguish for her father's death and Tina's burning resentment at the way the Don had treated Donna Elvira added fresh layers of tragedy to the story. No one listening to this Donna Elvira could doubt that she had loved the man and, in spite of her knowledge of his nature, could love him still. Tina's rendering of Elvira's plea to Giovanni to reform before it was too late silenced even the muttering technicians at rehearsal and her despairing acceptance of his inability to change brought tears to Rosamund's eyes as she listened in the wings.

She waited while the conductor took the orchestra back over a phrase that needed refining, watching Tina in the middle of the stage, carelessly dressed in old slacks and a jumper her mother had knitted for her, her hair dragged back and tied with a piece of ribbon snatched up in the dressing room. Her concentration while she was singing was absolute and yet, at moments like this, Tina could relax

259

and even exchange a smiling grimace of impatience with her Giovanni. Rosamund, on the other hand, felt herself to be as taut as a wound up spring, and that was the way she would continue to be until the first night was behind her.

The rehearsal came to an end. The producer and the conductor held an inquest on some points that had come up during the run-through, there was a reminder about costume fittings the next day, a lighting rehearsal, and the dress rehearsal the following week, and then they were free to go.

'About time,' Tina grumbled. 'Ros, are you doing anything? Jerry's in the stalls, waiting for me.'

'I saw him arrive,' Rosamund said.

'He's flying over to Paris later tonight. I toyed with the idea of joining him after the costume fitting tomorrow, but in the end I decided not to. I asked him to pick me up and take me out to the airport for a meal before he goes. Come with us.'

'No ... I don't think so,' Rosamund said. 'Did Jerry ask you to go to Paris with him?'

'No, it was entirely my idea,' Tina said, mildly surprised by the question. 'Actually, I thought it might be a chance to mend a few fences. Jerry and I ... we're all right, but the affair's lost some of its zing, for me and for him. He's never quite forgiven me for that time I let him down over the charity concert. Sometimes I suspect him of having a bit on the side with someone else.'

'Tina, please don't talk like that.'

'I wouldn't with anyone but you. I could be wrong, but it would account for − what shall we call it? − a certain lack of enthusiasm.'

Tina was laughing, but Rosamund did not join in. Tina went off to wash her face, comb her hair and do a quick change into a more respectable pair of slacks and a clean blouse. She gave herself a dash of lipstick, snapped on a pair of earrings, caught up a brightly coloured jacket and her handbag and was ready.

When she returned to the front of the house Rosamund had joined Jerry. They were standing in the aisle of the darkened stalls, their heads bent, and Tina had the impression of a

260

conversation broken off as she joined them.

'I asked Ros to come to Heathrow, but she won't,' she said. 'Sorry, Jerry, the rehearsal went on a bit longer than I expected. I haven't made you late, have I?'

'We'll still have time for a meal before my flight,' Jerry said. 'Rosamund ...'

'I'll see you in the morning, Tina,' Rosamund said. She turned to go and gave a gasp as she bumped into the end of one of the seats.

'Careful,' Jerry said, his hand shooting out to save her from falling.

Rosamund shook off his hand and left without looking back.

'Poor Ros, she does get in a state,' Tina said. 'I thought we might get together this weekend while you're away, but she says she wants to rest, and perhaps it's a good idea. Now, let's zoom out to the airport. I could eat a horse, but I'll settle for a good plain steak.'

It was no use pretending that things were going well between her and Jerry, Tina finally admitted to herself. He had definitely not wanted her with him on his trip to Paris, whereas a year earlier he would have been pleading – no, not pleading, that wasn't Jerry's way – demanding her company.

She was going to have to have it out with him. Tina grimaced at the idea. Not until after the first night of *Don Giovanni*, she decided. The role of Donna Elvira was not so long as the Fiordiligi that was still in the repertoire, but it was sufficiently demanding to require all her attention. If she and Jerry were going to break up ... Tina contemplated the idea of life without Jerry and was astonished to realise how much it would matter to her. He was a fixture in her life. She was used to him. She needed him. It was painful to think of losing him to another woman, and yet she could see no other reason for his lack of interest in her.

On the other hand, Jerry was ruthlessly honest. If he wanted to get rid of her then she believed he would tell her. So, what was holding him back? Perhaps he, like Tina, still hoped that something could be saved from the strangely

261

lacklustre thing their passion had become. In which case, she was prepared to put her whole mind and body into renewing a love which had almost expired. When she had the time and energy to spare, that was. Which would be after the first night of *Don Giovanni*.

Don Giovanni, she had to admit, belonged to the men. The female roles, crucial though they were, were subsidiary to the Don and his manservant. All the more reason to put her mark on the dramatic interventions of Donna Elvira into the plot. Ros, thank goodness, had overcome the malaise that had made her droop about all over the place. She had new energy in the week leading up to the opening, so perhaps the weekend she said she had spent resting had been beneficial, but Tina was suspicious of the dreamy smile which haunted Rosamund's face. A dreamy Ros, in Tina's experience, meant a Ros falling in love. She ran through the cast, seeking for a possible lover, and failed to find the answer. The Don was a happily married man with a family, Leporello was fifty and fat, Ottavio was heavily involved with Zerlina and Masetto was gay. No one there to explain Rosamund's new lease of life.

The first night arrived and there was the usual bouquet from Jerry, a lovely arrangement of yellow roses. He had never once failed to provide flowers on an evening when she was singing. It had perhaps become a slightly mechanical gesture and Tina knew better now than to believe that he had gone to the shop and chosen the flowers himself, but it was still pleasant to receive them, and the scrawled card of good wishes that accompanied them.

The new production was well received. The Don had something of a triumph and Leporello was an old favourite. Tina and Rosamund, in their roles as Elvira and Anna, were cheered and showered with flowers. It was all very satisfactory, and yet Tina had a feeling of anticlimax. Perhaps that was because Jerry told her after the performance that he had to go away immediately for a few days.

'You'll go back to the flat?' he asked.

'Yes, of course,' Tina said.

It was a Friday night and they had intended going to Chadd Manor the following morning so that Tina could get a couple of days' rest before more performances during the coming week. She had been looking forward to the peace and quiet of the countryside after the hectic run-up to the first night, and the idea of spending the weekend on her own in London was distinctly unwelcome.

It occurred to Tina the next morning that there was really no reason why she should not go to Chadd Manor on her own. Jerry had never quite encouraged her to treat it as her home in the way that the London flat was her home, but she had been there often enough for the staff to be used to her and her arrival would certainly not disturb the well-organised Mrs Turner.

She would have liked to have slept late, but unaccountably she woke early. With sudden energy, she leaped out of bed, bathed, dressed, had her breakfast, packed the minimum clothes in a bag and set out in her car for Somerset. She could be there by late morning, and if Mrs Turner was put out then she would take herself off to the village pub for a meal.

The roads were clearer than she had anticipated and she arrived at the house well before midday. She drove round to the back of the house and parked in the courtyard. There seemed to be no one about. If Jerry had told the staff to take the weekend off and the house was locked up she would feel very let down. To her relief, when she tried the back door it was unlocked. She walked through the kitchen and was surprised not to meet Mrs Turner, although there were signs that some sort of meal had been prepared. She thought she heard the sound of voices coming from the front of the house and hesitated before going through. It would be embarrassing if she caught the staff using the house as their own while the master was away, and she was not sure how she would deal with it.

She opened the door of the small dining room which Jerry used when there was no extra company, and the two people still sitting over their belated breakfast looked up in surprise. More than surprise. They were horrified.

Rosamund and Jerry. Not even dressed, so there was not much doubt what they had been up to. Tina had been right in thinking Jerry had sent his staff away for the weekend.

263

He had wanted to be alone with his new mistress.

The silence prolonged itself to the point where the air seemed to quiver with tension. Tina could neither move nor speak, the shock had been so great. Rosamund and Jerry. Jerry and Rosamund.

It was Jerry who spoke at last. 'I wanted to tell you,' he said.

Tina looked at him, this stranger who was speaking to her. That was Jerry, her mind told her. Jerry, who had betrayed her with her best friend. It was still impossible to believe.

'Tina ...' Rosamund said in a whisper.

Tina turned her head. 'Rosamund?' she said, as if doubting the identity of the slender girl in a satin wrapper who still sat with one hand clutching a coffee cup.

'We couldn't help it,' Rosamund said in the same strained thread of voice. 'We tried not to fall in love ...'

'I doubt if Jerry tried very hard,' Tina said. 'And you ... you've always been a pushover for a man who told you he loved you.'

She released her hold on the door handle and found her hand numb from the force with which she had clutched the brass knob.

'Let's be civilised about this,' Jerry said.

'Civilised?' Tina found the words she wanted from the role she had sung the night before, '*Cor perfido!*'

Jerry winced and she was glad to see that she had hurt him.

'Rosamund and I have been attracted to one another for months,' he said steadily. 'At least since the skiing holiday.'

'How unwise I was to let you go away without me.'

'And I've known for certain since the weekend when you went to Vienna.'

'Leaving Rosamund to stand in for me. I didn't realise she meant to take over permanently.'

'I gave Rosamund a hint that weekend and she very decidedly turned me down, but it was no use ...'

'Truly we couldn't help ourselves,' Rosamund pleaded.

'My dear Ros, at Jerry's age a man can look at temptation and decide whether or not to give in to it.'

'That's not quite true,' Jerry said. 'I love Rosamund and I want to make her my wife.'

'I'm giving up the operatic stage,' Rosamund added.

'You can't do that!' Tina said, appalled.

'I can and I will. I shall go on singing — Jerry wants me to do that — but not in opera, not once the present season is over.'

'You've made all your plans and not said a word to me,' Tina said. 'I can't believe it. I just literally can't believe it.'

She sat down on the nearest chair, limp with the realisation of what these revelations meant for her. Jerry wanted to marry Rosamund. That hurt. Even though she had said she would not marry him if he asked her, Tina would still have liked to have been asked. Jerry had never thought of her as anything more than a mistress. More or less permanent, but replaceable if anything better came along. Tina closed her eyes and pressed her lips together, suppressing a primitive cry of pain.

'Rosamund made me promise to say nothing to you until after the first night,' Jerry said. 'I always disagreed with her and I think she'll see now that it was a mistake.'

'I was wrong,' Rosamund said. 'I thought ... it seemed better at the time.'

'No, you were probably right,' Tina said. She opened her eyes and looked at Rosamund in horror. 'We're going to have to go on working with one another, you realise that?'

'I know. That's why I've put it off ... Tina, I'm sorry, truly I am sorry.'

Very carefully, Tina got to her feet. 'I'd better go,' she said. 'Obviously I'll move out of the flat immediately.'

'There's no hurry,' Jerry began, but Tina turned on him fiercely.

'Yes, there is! she cried. 'I want nothing from you, nothing! Not even a night's lodging. I'll leave you now.' She glanced disparagingly at the cluttered table. 'Enjoy your breakfast!'

She went out to the courtyard and Jerry came after her.

'Tina, let me drive you to the station. You're not fit to drive back to London. Take the train.'

'I'll be all right,' Tina said. 'Do you expect me to hang about here while you get dressed? I'm perfectly capable of driving.'

She hoped it was true. Because she was aware of the need for caution, she found herself driving much more slowly than usual. At the first café she came to she stopped and had a cup of coffee, though she could not face eating anything. Inside her there was still that feeling of blank disbelief. Jerry and Rosamund. Rosamund and Jerry.

She sat so long over her coffee that the woman behind the counter came out and asked in a pointed way whether she wanted anything else. Tina came to with a start and shook her head. She got up to go, moving stiffly, but when she got into her car she sat still for a long time behind the wheel. The trouble was, she could not make up her mind what to do next. She had said she would move out of the flat, but the thought of going straight back there made her shudder. She did not think she could bear the sight of that vast empty room with its white walls, black leather furniture and glittering windows, nor could she face the bedroom with the king-sized bed.

Where else could she go? Always in the past when one of them had been in trouble she and Ros had turned to one another. That would never be possible again. She could not go home. Her parents were not likely to ask questions about Jerry, whose existence they preferred to ignore, but her mother was sure to ask after Rosamund, and what could she say? It was a wry joke that her real mother would understand the situation better than anyone, but Tina was not prepared to expose herself to Daphne's sympathy. She could book into a hotel, but the thought of a solitary, impersonal room and meals amongst strangers was as repulsive as anything else.

There was one person who had been a good friend in the past. Slowly, Tina allowed the possibility of taking refuge with Oliver to take root in her mind. He had been good to her at the time of the Daphne revelations. He would understand her pain and bewilderment and be kind in an impersonal way, whereas Tom, if she turned to him, would be demonstrative and affectionate, which Tina thought she would be unable to bear.

It was a bright April day. There were new leaves on the trees, very small and bright against the clear blue sky, and at Rigby House the short driveway was bordered by daffodils and the thick, stiff leaves of tulips not yet in flower.

As Tina waited for Oliver to answer the door after she had rung the bell she wondered what she would do if he were not at home. Before she had thought of any solution Oliver opened the door. He looked untidy and scruffy, in old clothes, with his hair on end, as if he had been running his hands through it. He was frowning and Tina had the impression that he had been concentrating so hard that he was having difficulty in refocusing his attention.

'Tina!' he exclaimed. 'This is a surprise. Come on in.'

He led her through into the music room. It was in a great muddle, with sheets of manuscript paper strewn on the floor.

'Sorry about this,' Oliver said, picking up loose pages. 'I've been commissioned to write a choral work to be performed at one of this summer's Albert Hall Promenade Concerts and I've been making an all-out effort to get it finished.'

Tina stood in the middle of the big drawing room, where she had had her first singing lesson from Annis, and said nothing.

'Are you staying at Woodington?' Oliver asked, still busy with his music. 'Will didn't say they were expecting you when he was here yesterday. Congratulations on your first night, by the way. Sorry I missed it, but I'm coming next week.'

Her continued silence made him look round enquiringly.

'Tina? My dear girl, whatever's the matter?'

'Jerry . . .' Tina said with difficulty. 'Jerry and Rosamund.' Even as she said it she was filled with profound disbelief. She forced herself to go on. 'I went to Chadd Manor. They were there together. Jerry and Rosamund.'

Oliver dumped his music on top of the piano and went to her. Without a word, he put his arms round her, holding her tightly against him. Tina, who had not thought she wanted any demonstration of affection, had a vague sensation of warmth and comfort.

'I didn't know where to go,' she said.

'This will do,' Oliver said. 'Come and sit down. You had no suspicion?'

'None at all. I knew Jerry had cooled off and I meant to have it out with him, but I never thought of Ros.' Her eyes were fixed on her cold, rigid hands. 'If it had been one of his society ladies I would have been angry, but this ... I hurt, Oliver, I hurt all over as if I'd been beaten.'

'I know.' Again he slipped an arm round her shoulders and with a little sigh Tina leaned against him.

'I've got to go back to the flat to clear out my things,' she said. 'But I couldn't face it today. Can I stay with you until tomorrow?'

'Of course.' Oliver glanced at his watch. 'For goodness sake, it's gone four o'clock. I've had no lunch and I was up at six. Are you hungry?'

Tina shook her head. 'I can't eat.'

'I'll make some tea.'

The hot tea was welcome. Tina had two cups and, in spite of what she had said, half of one of the sandwiches Oliver had made for himself.

'They're going to get married,' she said abruptly. 'Ros is giving up singing, at least in opera.'

'What a waste.'

'That's what I think. I suppose they'll have children. Lady Bilchester. Ros's mum will like that. It's been going on for months, Oliver, though I think they've only recently started sleeping together.'

A memory came back to Oliver. A crowded party after the first night of *The Huguenots*; Jerry talking to Rosamund with obvious admiration and Tina saying light-heartedly, 'Shall I go and cut her out?'

'I can see it working,' he said reluctantly.

'I suppose so. She'll do the social side much better than I ever did.'

'If you hadn't diverted his attention do you think Jerry might have taken up with Rosamund in the first place?'

'She was hypnotised by Benno,' Tina pointed out. 'I don't think Jerry could have taken her away from him, not at that time.'

268

'Are you still in love with him?'

Tina looked at him with a puzzled expression on her face. 'I don't seem to know. We've been together a long time. I'm used to having him around, having someone to love and to love me, all the little attentions, the usefulness of having a settled escort, even the luxury which I pretended to despise. Jerry himself, the man I loved, has disappeared.'

'That's not the real pain, is it?' Oliver asked gently.

Tina went on talking as if she had not heard him. 'I knew there was something wrong. I'd even faced the possibility of a break, though to tell the truth, I really thought that if I made a scene and we had a quarrel Jerry would be contrite and I would forgive him and we'd go on as before. But Ros ... when we were at school we said we'd be bridesmaids at one another's weddings, godmothers to one another's children, partners in our singing roles — well, we achieved that all right, but I don't think somehow I'll be invited to Ros and Jerry's wedding.'

For the first time her voice wavered and the tears she had not thought she would be able to shed gathered in her eyes.

'I've lost a slice of my life,' she said. 'My best friend. I helped her when she was in trouble and I always expected that if I needed her Ros would be there for me, too. I didn't know her, that's what hurts, Oliver, I never really knew her.'

'Yes, you did. Ros hasn't changed. Think, Tina. Ros was always the one at the mercy of her emotions. You've been exasperated before at the way she slipped in and out of love. This time she's fallen in love with the man you thought loved you. That's all that's different.'

'It's a big difference,' Tina said drily.

'Agreed. Now, let's be practical. Have you got a suitcase with you?'

'Yes. I meant to stay at Chadd Manor, you see, even though I thought Jerry was away.' Tina shook her head as if to clear it. 'It seems light years since I jumped out of bed and threw my things into a bag. It's in the back of my car.'

'Let's get it out and find you a room. At least I've got

plenty of spare beds. You'll stay here tonight and tomorrow we'll go up to that flat and clear out your things.'

'You don't have to come with me,' Tina said uncertainly.

'Yes, I do. I'll bring you back here to stay until you can make some more permanent arrangement.'

'I'm singing on Monday. Oliver, I'm singing with Ros!'

The horror in her voice was so extreme that once again Oliver put an arm round her. 'Steady, darling. If you're absolutely adamant on Monday morning that you can't do it I'll fix a medical certificate to get you off.'

He said it, but he was fairly sure in his own mind that Tina would not shirk giving a performance when she had had time to recover from the first shock of losing her lover to her friend. It was far more likely, in Oliver's opinion, that it would be Rosamund who would fail to appear, and he said so to Tina when they went to Jerry's flat the next day.

'Do you think so?' Tina considered. 'Yes, you're right. Jerry will want to shield her. But we can't put off a meeting indefinitely.'

She made a fairly methodical job of clearing out her clothes and belongings.

'All the music in the lounge belongs to me. Do you think you could put it together?' she asked Oliver.

She wanted him out of the bedroom while she did the most difficult thing of all, sorting out the jewellery Jerry had given her. None of it was of great value, but there were some pretty pieces. She had a moment's regret as she touched the globe watch that had been his first present. She had always loved it and she would miss it, but there was no way she could bring herself to keep any of his gifts.

She put all the pretty gewgaws into a box and added a brief note: 'Jerry, I'd rather not keep these. Perhaps they could be put into a charity sale or something.'

If she ever saw Rosamund wearing her little world with the watch inside she would tear it off her neck, but neither Ros nor Jerry would be as crass as that.

When the door of the flat closed behind her and Oliver, Tina put the keys through the letter box. That was that. The end of an era in her life, but not — as she had thought the day before — the end of her life. She would get over it. Pain knifed through her every time the memory of Jerry and Rosamund sitting at the breakfast table came back to her, but she had accepted that the situation was irrevocable.

'I shall sing tomorrow,' she said to Oliver.

'I knew you would.'

Oliver had been right in thinking that it would be Rosamund who would fail to put in an appearance. He took Tina to the theatre, but there was only one moment when she needed his support, and that was when a lovely bouquet of irises and carnations was brought to her dressing room. Tina looked in horror at the familiar oblong white envelope with her name on the outside, but she forced herself to open it.

She held it out to Oliver, unable to speak. 'All my love, Jerry' it said.

'He writes them up a dozen at a time,' Tina said in a dull voice. 'Then he gives them to his secretary. She looks up the dates when I'm singing and passes the order to the florist. He must have forgotten to cancel the arrangement. If they go on arriving until the supply of cards runs out I don't think I can bear it.'

Oliver tore the card into pieces. 'Leave it to me,' he said.

'Don't make a row.'

'As I did when Daphne and Nicky were so outrageous?' Oliver asked with a smile.

'That was because of something he said about Annis,' Tina remembered.

'Don't be silly. I was in a towering rage and itching for a reason to hit him. I shan't make the same mistake with Jerry.'

He left her and Tina began to change. She received the news that Rosamund was ill with a stomach upset with an equanimity that was a relief to the management. For once the replacement for the missing soprano was to come from within the company. Tina looked at the bouquet of irises and carnations, thrust into a corner, and then she carried it along the corridor to the petrified young singer who was torn between nerves and elation at her chance to sing an important role.

'I know you'll be wonderful,' Tina said steadily. 'Please take these with my best wishes. I'll do everything I can to help you tonight.'

By the end of the evening Tina had one comfort: her reputation had been enhanced. She had sung with all the emotional intensity for which she was famous, she had been generous to a beginner and she had satisfied herself that she would be able to go on, even after Rosamund returned. Only once had the thought of Jerry intruded and that was when she had turned on Don Giovanni in horror after he had rejected her plea to reform. '*Cor perfido!*' she sang. 'Treacherous heart!' She remembered how she had flung that accusation at Jerry and the way it had struck home.

Oliver drove her home, back to Locksley Green. He had spoken on the telephone to Jerry, a brief and hostile conversation.

'Your communications system seems to have broken down,' he said abruptly, after he had tracked Jerry down to the London flat. 'May I suggest that if you want to send flowers with all your love then you address them to the right woman?'

From the silence at the other end of the line he knew that Jerry was appalled.

'Tina sang tonight?' he asked at last.

'Of course. She's a strong woman, our Tina. As you're at the flat you'll have realised that she's cleared out of your life. Where's Rosamund?'

'Still in the country.'

'She'll have to come back, unless you stage a complete breakdown in health.'

'If she appears on Wednesday ...'

'Tina won't claw her eyes out, if that's what you're worried about. Jerry, for God's sake, whatever possessed you? Rosamund, of all the women in the world ... It nearly destroyed Tina.'

'I didn't realise ... I didn't think she'd care so much.'

'Loyalty is Tina's middle name,' Oliver said. 'I'd better not say any more. Tina wouldn't want it.'

He rang off without saying goodbye. The palms of his

hands were sweating. Oliver rubbed them against his legs, smiling ruefully. What was the point of getting so worked up? Jerry had not understood the big, generous heart of the girl he had taken so lightly into his life. He and Rosamund would marry and probably they would be happy, but always at the bottom of their happiness there would be the tiny corroding knowledge of the betrayal on which that happiness was founded, and Oliver was spiteful enough to hope that the memory would rankle.

Chapter Fourteen

'I came straight round as soon as I saw the news. At least, I did when I found out where you were living. You might have given your old mum your new address.'

'I did,' Tina said coldly, but Daphne appeared not to understand her.

She flourished the newspaper she was carrying.

'"Tycoon to marry opera star",' she read. '"Lord Bilchester, well known for his love of opera and until recently the constant companion of soprano Valentina Burford, has sent shock waves through the musical world by announcing his engagement to her fellow singer, Rosamund Drew. Even more astonishing, Miss Drew has announced her retirement from the operatic stage. Caught on her way into the Royal Opera House, Tina Burford: said "We are all good friends". Did you really say that?'

'It seemed as good a comment as any other.'

'Very diplomatic,' Daphne agreed. 'Well, ducky, you've got my sympathy, because I'm in the same boat. Nicky's taken off with the grovelling little brat who played me in the film and we're getting a divorce.'

'I'm sorry.'

'No, you're not. You never liked him. I'm sick about it, absolutely sick. He thinks he's made because he had one leading role, but the reviews weren't that good and he'll find parts aren't easy to come by, not without me behind him to give him a push.'

She blew her nose and Tina saw that she was deeply upset, but it was difficult to offer sympathy when, as Daphne had said, she was glad to see the back of Nicky.

'How are you coping?' Daphne asked.

'All right. I've known about Jerry and Ros for months. They put off making an announcement until the end of the opera season. They plan to get married in September.'

'Is she pregnant?'

'Not as far as I know.'

'You don't sound as if you cared very much. I came haring round thinking you'd need a shoulder to cry on.'

'I've done all the crying that's necessary. Now I mean to get on with my career.'

'Lucky to have a career to turn to,' Daphne said gloomily.

'You're not finished yet,' Tina said. She considered her mother carefully. Daphne was still not much more than fifty and admitted to forty-eight. Just now, sitting hunched up, her face sagging with dejection, she looked every day of her true age, but Tina had seen the way she could light up when she was fed with the admiration she believed to be her due.

'I'm auditioning for a part in a television play,' Daphne admitted. 'Someone's mother, of course. Still, it's not a bad part.' She straightened up. 'You're right, work's the only answer. Shows how much alike we are, doesn't it?'

It was not a particularly palatable thought, but there was something in what Daphne said. They both had a resilience that seemed built into their make-up. Tina had gone on and sung when her world had broken apart and she knew that Daphne would have done the same.

'I need to be seen in public,' Tina said. 'I'm tired of skulking away and pretending nothing's wrong. Now that the news is out I want everyone to know that I *don't care*! Get your face and hair done and come out to dinner with me.'

'Without an escort?' Daphne asked in distaste. 'I wouldn't go to a restaurant, not the sort of place where it's worth being seen, without a man in tow.'

'I doubt if anyone will molest us.'

'That's not the point. It's being seen to be wanted that counts.'

'I dare say Tom would oblige if I asked him.'

'Anyone so long as it's not that horrible Oliver.'

'Oliver's been good to me over the last three months,' Tina said.

She telephone Tom and he not only accepted the invitation, but volunteered to bring along a visiting Australian singer who was anxious to explore London's night life.

Tina sent Daphne off to an urgent beauty appointment and then hunted through her wardrobe for a striking outfit. She chose loose silk pants and a matching jacket in shifting shades of green and blue, with a camisole covered in metallic blue sequins. Her hair had been cut and styled for a concert performance the evening before and she needed to do no more than brush it and push the loose waves back into place. She had lost a little weight, which was not unwelcome. She had hollows in her cheeks which showed up the broad, high cheekbones she shared with Daphne. Viewing herself dispassionately in the mirror, Tina thought that she had never looked better. She had always been blessed with good looks, but now she had poise and maturity and the assurance that came from knowing that there was one thing she did supremely well and no one could take it away from her.

Daphne wore black lace, high-necked and long-sleeved over a strapless bodice, with a tight skirt that barely reached her knees. Why not? Her legs were still excellent and the visiting Australian was certainly not complaining. He was a heavy, smooth-skinned man close to Daphne's age, which made it all very suitable. Tina made up her mind to enjoy herself, though she could see she was going to have trouble with Tom afterwards.

They had drinks in the bar while they looked through the menu. Tina had a momentary qualm when Daphne asked for a second gin and tonic, but she stifled it. Her mother was an experienced drinker and presumably knew how much she could take. All the same, Tina regretted that Tom ordered champagne for them with their meal. Daphne, she knew, regarded that as something to be drunk like water.

Their little party was certainly convivial, but Tina was relieved to see that although Daphne was flirting outrageously with Tom's guest, she was well in control of herself, and he was obviously having a good time. Tina looked round the crowded restaurant and wished she could say the same. She was not exactly bored, she was too much on edge for that, but she felt herself to be at odds with this glittering, moneyed crowd.

'The trouble with me is I've got a scrambled-egg-on-toast mentality,' she said to Tom.

'Now you tell me, when you've finished eating my smoked salmon!'

'Not yours,' Tina protested. 'I invited you. We ought at least to share the bill.'

'Not on your life! It's a long time since you gave me the pleasure of taking you out.' He glanced at the other two, absorbed with one another. 'I could do without the company,' he said in a low voice. 'But judging by the way things are going, we can probably ditch them when we leave here.'

Tina had been right. She was going to have trouble with Tom. She smiled and turned the conversation to the engagements he had booked for her up to the time when she would be involved in Oliver's opera, but Tom was not paying attention. He looked past her and she saw an expression of dismay on his face. Tina turned her head. Jerry, Rosamund, and four other people were being shown to a table against the wall.

'Damn,' Tina said softly. 'The reason I suggested this restaurant was because I'd never been here with Jerry. What rotten bad luck that he should come here tonight.'

'They've probably been to a theatre. It's convenient for several round here. What do you want to do?'

'Give them a cool nod if they happen to glance in this direction. Otherwise, ignore them.'

The arrival of the party had attracted Daphne's attention. Her eyes widened and she turned to Tina.

'Isn't that ...?'

'Yes. Play it cool, Daphne.'

'Cool! How can you sit there and say that after the way you've been treated?'

'I don't want a scene in public.'

Daphne drained her glass of champagne and to Tina's annoyance a too-attentive waiter immediately refilled it.

277

Tina allowed him to fill her glass, too. She had no intention of drinking it, but at least it would be one glass less for Daphne.

They finished their main course and were waiting for the trolley of delicious puddings to be brought over to them. Once again Daphne had finished her wine. She touched Tina's glass.

'Aren't you going to drink this?'

Tina shook her head.

'Then I've got a use for it,' Daphne said. She picked up the glass, got to her feet and before Tina could stop her she was walking, none too steadily, towards Jerry and Rosamund's table.

Jerry looked up, startled, and made a half-hearted gesture towards getting to his feet.

'Don't move,' Daphne said. 'I suppose you think I've come to congratulate you. Well, you're wrong. No one gets away with treating Daphne Durrell's daughter the way you've treated my Tina. Here's what I think of your engagement.'

With a flick of her wrist she flung the contents of the champagne glass in Jerry's face. The level of conversation in the restaurant rose several decibels, and people were craning their necks to see what was going on. The head waiter was hurrying towards the table. Jerry was mopping at his face with his napkin. It was Ros at whom Tina looked. She was shrinking back in her chair, her face white.

'I'll deal with this,' Tom said.

'No, let me.'

Tina walked across the room, her head held high.

'What an unfortunate accident,' she said in the voice that could carry to the furthest reaches of the upper balcony. 'Jerry, I'm so sorry. Ros, I do hope your dress wasn't splashed. Daphne, I told you those heels were too high. I knew you'd trip up in them. Come back to our table before you do any more damage.'

With her arm firmly clamped through Daphne's, she guided her back to the table.

'Let's get out of here,' she said to Tom.

They left immediately and the buzz of excited comment followed them.

'I could kill you,' Tina said bitterly.

'I did it for you,' Daphne protested. 'No one treats my little girl like dirt.'

She was pleased with herself, even in the face of Tina's annoyance. She had made a dramatic gesture and she could see no harm in the fact that it would certainly get into the scandal sheets.

'In the best tradition of Hollywood,' Tom said after they had dropped off both Daphne and his visitor and were on their way back to Tina's flat.

'Tom, I'm so ashamed. I thought she could be trusted to behave herself. I'll never forgive her, never!'

'It was sheer bad luck that Jerry and Ros should have come in. And I have to say that the sight of him dripping with champagne did me a power of good. I've got two counts against him. He made you unhappy and he's robbed me of one of my best clients.'

In her agitation, Tina forgot that she had meant to make glib excuses about a headache to prevent Tom following her up to her flat. She got out her key and he took it from her and opened the door.

'Yes, please, I will come in for coffee,' he said. 'Seeing that I've been done out of it in the restaurant.'

'I wasn't going to ask you,' Tina said.

'But now that I'm here you'll be a kind girl and make me my coffee.'

'I suppose I will. Oh, hell's bells, this was meant to be my evening for showing the world that I'm back in circulation and not giving a damn.'

'I know. Never mind, love, there'll be other evenings. And I'll be your escort any time, you know that.'

He slipped an arm round her waist and stood close to her, big and kind and reassuring. For a moment Tina leaned against him, but when Tom's arm tightened and he tried to turn her so that he could kiss her, she broke away.

'Coffee!' she said.

'It could wait,' Tom grumbled.

She made the coffee and sat down in an armchair, although

Tom patently wanted her to join him on the sofa.

'I can see I'm being given the cold shoulder,' he remarked lightly. 'Still, I can forgive anything to a girl who makes a decent cup of coffee.'

'Idiot! Tom, I don't want to hurt you, but it's no good. I don't want to get involved.'

'You don't know what you're missing.'

'Actually, I do,' Tina said with a smile. 'I haven't forgotten, Tom. We were wonderful together, but that was long ago ...'

'And in another country,' he said. 'I know. We're two different people now. Tina, I wish you'd think very seriously about marrying me.'

'Tom!'

'Don't say "this is so sudden",' he begged.

'Marriage! I hadn't thought ...'

'I've mentioned it before.'

'Not for ages.'

'Not much use while you were wrapped up in Jerry. It makes a lot of sense, Tina. I love you and I believe I could win you over to love me again, too. Quite apart from that, I could look after your interests as no other man could. Your career certainly won't suffer by marriage to me. You've really taken off in the last year and there are plenty of people who know enough about what you've been through to admire the professional way you've carried on performing. You've got a tremendous reputation, not just for your voice — one of the best in the world today, in my opinion — but for being co-operative, responsive to guidance, decent to the rest of the cast ... a bit imperious at times ...'

'Tom, I'm not!'

'Yes, you are, darling. Do you remember the way Annis was before — and after — she went to Australia? You've got just her manner sometimes. And why not? You're the best, you know you're the best, and there's no reason why you should suffer fools gladly.'

'I'll have to watch it,' Tina said ruefully.

'We've wandered off the subject, which is when are you going to marry me?'

'I'm not.'

'Hard-hearted girl. I won't press you tonight because I can see that scene has upset you. Keep it in mind, though. I'll ring you about eleven o'clock tomorrow to see if you can give me a different answer.'

'Why then?'

'Just a time chosen at random. Would midday be more convenient? We may as well settle on a suitable hour, because I'm going to ask you every day until you say yes.'

The telephone rang and Tina hesitated. She had already fobbed off several curious journalists and a tearful Daphne, in addition to Tom's promised repeat proposal. She answered the call cautiously and an amused voice said, 'Oh, dear!'

Tina relaxed and began to smile. 'Oh dear, indeed! I take it you've seen the evening papers?'

'"Daphne Durrell appeared to have been celebrating, though one wonders what, considering the state of her own marital affairs ...".'

'Don't go on! Oliver, you've no idea how ghastly it was. I was tempted to hide under the table.'

'If I'd been there I might have joined you, though it would have done my heart good to see Jerry doused in champagne.'

'That was what Tom said,' Tina agreed.

'Oh ... it was Tom who was with you?'

'And a visiting Australian. It was supposed to be a signal that I was *not* going into a decline because of the engagement announcement, but it all went horribly wrong.'

'It'll blow over.'

'I suppose so.' Tina sighed and then said abruptly, 'Tom wants me to marry him.'

'From a career point of view that might be a good move,' Oliver said evenly.

Tina made a face at the unresponsive telephone. 'Tom manages my affairs perfectly well without being married to me.' After a moment she added uncertainly, 'That could have been better put.'

'It could.' Oliver was sounding amused again. 'Tom would be a great support in time of trouble, as you very well know. However, if you don't want to marry him, then don't.

281

'All right, then, I won't. Oliver, would you say I was imperious?'

'Certainly not. As long as your subjects do exactly what you want, you're perfectly gracious.'

'I can see you're not in the mood for a serious conversation,' Tina said crossly. 'Did you ring up for anything in particular, or just to have a laugh?'

'Are you coming to hear my choral work at the Proms? If so, I'll reserve you a seat.'

'Oliver! Yes, of course. I've got the date in my diary and it doesn't clash with anything else. Are you conducting it yourself?'

'Yes, I am, with some trepidation. I've been teaching it to the choir and taking preliminary rehearsals, and so far it's going quite well.'

'I was in such a state while I was staying with you I never even found out what it was called.'

'It's a setting of part of the *Song of Solomon*.'

'Very sexy! That was one bit of the Bible we all read at school.'

'Were you told that "the beloved" was a synonym for the church?'

'Yes! It took a bit of swallowing. I'm looking forward to hearing what you've made of it.'

'As I said, very gracious,' Oliver murmured.

'I didn't mean to sound condescending. If I've got to start watching every word I say to you ...'

'No, no! I was only teasing. A spot of supper afterwards?'

'Lovely.'

'And no champagne.'

He rang off, laughing, leaving Tina divided between crossness and amusement.

The Albert Hall was full. Tier upon tier of people filled the crimson seats that rose up towards the balcony and the domed ceiling. The promenade section in front of the orchestra was a shifting throng of people, mostly young, some outrageously dressed. They had had the opening overture and the choir had assembled, now they were waiting for Oliver to take

282

his place on the rostrum. There was a cheerful hubbub of conversation which gave way to a round of applause as Oliver threaded his way through the orchestra.

The promenaders broke into a prearranged chant, a quotation from the work they were about to hear: 'Who is this that cometh out of the wilderness?' Oliver had been looking serious and preoccupied, but that got through to him and he gave them a quick grin and a special bow. Tina, almost holding her breath in suspense, wondered whether he really welcomed that break in his concentration at such a moment.

In response to Oliver's gesture the choir rose with a soft whoosh of sound from the girls' long skirts. There was a brief introduction from the orchestra and then the women's voices began, very softly, 'I am the rose of Sharon and the lily of the valleys' and the men's voices answered 'As the lily among thorns, so is my love among the daughters'.

Tina had coaxed the information out of Oliver that he had set the second, third and fourth chapters of *The Song of Solomon*, using the King James' Bible version. Since then she had almost memorised the lovely, haunting words and the sensuous phrases had haunted her days.

In her own mind she had heard the work as a duet, but there were no solos in Oliver's setting, only the choir, male and female, singing separately and rarely coming together, as they did for the verses that began 'For, lo, the winter is past, the rain is over and gone.'

It was ravishing. Tina sat in stunned silence, the tears gathering in her eyes, and knew from the utter stillness of the audience that other people were as moved as she was.

The work moved on, through a strong passage for the male voices: 'Who is this that cometh out of the wilderness like pillars of smoke, perfumed with myrrh and frankincense, with all powders of the merchant?' to the striking imagery describing the beloved's attributes.

The whole choir came together for the final verse: 'Awake, O north wind; and come, thou south; blow upon my garden, that the spices thereof may blow out. Let my beloved come into his garden, and eat his pleasant fruits.'

With a swift, neat movement of his hands Oliver brought

the music to an end. There was a pause and then the applause began. Shouts, catcalls, whistles — they were an uninhibited lot in the promenade — and behind that the solid thunder of palm on palm. A success; an undoubted, popular success; and surely a work of real musical merit as well? Tina blew her nose and then went back to clapping until her hands tingled. Oliver went out and came back, he bowed, he made the choir stand and the orchestra, but when he tried to get them up a second time they refused to move and sat in their places applauding him. He shrugged and bowed once more. A group of promenaders who had held a hurried conference managed a new chant: 'Who is our beloved?' and back came the crashing answer: 'Oliver Leone!' This time Oliver shook his fist at them, laughing. Then he went out and refused to come back again.

It was the interval and there was still a Beethoven symphony to come. Tina doubted whether she could sit through it. She struggled out and found her way round the tortuous corridors to where Oliver was holding court. She managed to squeeze between two voluble men to reach a place in front of Oliver. He was wearing his deprecating smile, but she could see that he was pleased, shining all through with satisfaction. When he saw Tina he raised his eyebrows, mutely asking for her reaction.

'I cried buckets,' Tina said.

'Darling, it's meant to be a cheerful piece,' Oliver protested.

'It was so beautiful! I'm absolutely stunned!'

'You didn't think I'd got it in me,' Oliver suggested.

'Yes, I did! But you said so little about this work. How was I to know it was so ... so *stupendously* good?'

'I should have told you,' Oliver said gravely. 'Are you desperate to hear Beethoven's Fourth? Because, if not, we could make our escape. I'm famished. I dimly remember having a piece of toast about eight o'clock this morning, but I haven't been able to eat since.'

'Yes, let's get away,' Tina agreed. 'If we wait until the end you'll be mobbed by that crowd in the pit.'

'My claque,' Oliver said. 'If you knew what it cost me to get them to make that demonstration ...'

284

The warning bell went and the crowd began to thin. Tina moved closer to Oliver.

'You've done something wonderful,' she said. 'I know your attitude – if it matters, joke about it – but just this once couldn't you admit to being moved by a real success?'

Oliver took both her hands in his and held them so tightly that she thought the bones would crack.

'Just to you,' he said. 'When it was over and I realised I'd pulled it off, that it had been almost as good as when I heard it in my mind, I could have gone down on my knees. That was what mattered, my own satisfaction. All the rest, the applause and the kind words, even your tears, are trimmings. I know I've achieved what I set out to do. And for my next act I'll conquer the world or something simple like that.'

'Shall we have a good steak dinner first?'

'Let's do that.'

'I have to hand it to Oliver,' Tom said approvingly. 'He's made a success with his *Song of Solomon* at just the right time. He's got people talking and his name will be remembered when the publicity begins for *Crown of Glass*.'

'And if you knew Oliver better you'd realise that was the last thing on his mind,' Tina retorted. 'He was offered a commission, he accepted it and he sat down and wrote the piece of music that came to him. To Oliver it's as simple as that – or so he says.'

'You know him better than I do,' Tom agreed.

'I used to think I did. Now ... I'm not so sure. Of course no one could write anything as complex and complete as *The Song of Solomon* without enormous hard work. In fact, I know Oliver slaved over it because he was up to his ears when I went to him that ghastly weekend ...'

Her voice tailed away. Tom was watching her closely and after a moment he asked, 'I've often wondered, why did you go to Oliver?'

'He'd always been a friend and I knew he wouldn't make a fuss.'

'I see.' Tom glanced at his watch. 'It's coming up to proposal time. Tina, will you marry me?'

'Dear Tom, no.'

'I think perhaps I'll give up asking you.'

'I wish you would.'

'Very well. For the last time of asking, will you have me?'

'No.'

Tom was sitting behind the big desk in his office. He folded his arms and regarded her steadily.

'If I give up all hope of winning you I'll probably look around and find someone else. I'd like to have a proper family life – with children, you know.'

'Of course, that's what I want for you.'

'It's the end of a dream,' Tom said with an exaggerated sigh.

'Look on it as the beginning of a life based on reality,' Tina advised him. 'Now, having got that out of the way, tell me about the arrangements for doing *Tosca* at the Met next year. Am I ready for New York, do you think?'

'More than ready and they're clamouring to have you.'

To her surprise Tina felt sad that Tom had finally accepted her refusal to marry him. She searched around for the reason, sure that it was not regret at her decision, and finally came to the conclusion that it represented one more door closed behind her. His wish for a home and family had touched a chord in her. She, too, she realised, would like a settled base, and she thought about having a child with a hunger that startled her. She remembered – and would have preferred to have forgotten – Elsie's lament when she had heard disbelievingly that it was Rosamund who was going to marry Lord Bilchester: 'You could have had him if you'd wanted him, but no, you had to go your own way. I never agreed with you living with him, as you very well know, and it's no surprise to me that he's given you the go-by for a girl with a bit more respect for herself. You wait and see, Rosamund will be settled in a lovely home with her family round her and you'll end up a lonely old woman playing your old gramophone records in an empty flat.'

Tina had made an heroic effort and refrained from telling her mother how she had found out about Jerry and Rosamund's affair. Elsie had sounded dangerously overwrought and had required comfort and reassurance. Tina had tried to interest her in the forthcoming production of Oliver's opera and the American tour, but to Elsie they were second-rate options compared to a wedding and a fulfilled life. Tina wished that the picture she had painted of an ageing singer with nothing but past glories to keep her company had not stuck in her mind so clearly.

It was all nonsense, of course. Tina would find someone to share her life. The trouble was, looking round, she could think of remarkably few suitable candidates and, indeed, the thought of embarking on a new affair made her heart sink.

Perhaps because it was so much on her mind, she had a curiously vivid dream the night after Tom had at last brought himself to accept her decision as final. It was rare for Tina to remember her dreams, but this one surfaced just as she was waking and it stayed with her. She was in a garden, a garden that seemed familiar, with a wide lawn and trees. She was watching a little boy run across the grass and in the dream she knew that he was her son. He was about seven years old, just begining to lose his baby chubbiness and become a leggy, dark-haired child who moved well. She strained to see his face, but all she could get was a fleeting impression of clear-cut features and dark eyes. Not much of her in him, it seemed; as far as colouring went, at any rate. Somewhere in the background there was a man, but he was even more elusive than the child, and before she could fix him Tina was awake and the dream had gone.

She sat up, hugging her knees and frowning in an effort to retain that small, clear scene. It had been so real, almost as if it were something she had seen in the past, and yet she was quite sure that it was not.

She got out of bed, searching her memory for the garden which had been so familiar. A wide lawn, a boundary fence, fields beyond ... Tina stood still with one arm in her dressing gown. It was Rigby House. And the child ... those arching brows, that mobile laughing mouth ... was she giving them to him now or had she really seen them in her dream? The man in the background had been Oliver and the child was his son.

It was a most disconcerting idea. As she went into the bathroom she told herself firmly that it was just a trick of the imagination. Her stupid subconscious had latched on to the desire she had only just recognised to have a child. And, of course, Oliver had been very much on her mind because of *The Song of Solomon*. Considering the content of that work one might have expected the dream to be more esoteric. Tina grinned to herself as she stepped under the shower. That cosy domestic glimpse was hardly Oliver's scene – or hers either. And yet ... it had been strangely pleasant. She would have liked to have held on to the feeling of happiness that had suffused her. She regretted that it was beginning to fade.

Oliver, when she went to him for rehearsals of *The Crown of Glass*, was at his most businesslike. Positively impersonal, Tina thought gloomily. Not that she wanted him to be anything else. They were there to make music, not to indulge their emotions.

Much of the background to *The Crown of Glass* was already familiar to Tina, but she forced herself to concentrate as Oliver told the assembled cast the story of his great-great-grandfather, the master glassmaker from the island of Murano. Swiftly, Oliver described how the glassmaker had come to England to demonstrate his craft at the first Great Exhibition in 1851, and how he had also gone to the opera, where he had conceived a great admiration for a young Italian soprano, and had subsequently presented her with a crown of glass, a masterpiece of his craft.

'And what happened to it?' one of the cast enquired.

'If only I knew,' Oliver replied. 'She had a fine career and she kept the crown during her lifetime. In fact, it was around until the beginning of the First World War. After that, all trace of it disappeared and one presumes that it was broken and has long since been swept up and thrown away. I've given you the bare bones of the story but, of course, for the purpose of the opera my librettist and I have reworked it. In my version the young soprano is known to the glassmaker

288

and he is in love with her before they come to England. He makes the crown and she takes it, but she rejects him.'

'She chooses fame rather than an ordinary family life,' Tina said.

'She has a somewhat lurid career, becoming the morganatic wife of a Grand Duke who is assassinated, but I agree that the main theme is the conflict between the artistic life and the demands of every day. I hope I haven't laboured the point too hard. On one level the opera is a straightforward story of disappointed love, a magnificent career and an early death — quite a conventional operatic drama.'

'The scene at the end when she goes back to the glassmaking furnaces and hallucinates about the flames of hell is thrilling.' Tina shivered, remembering how she had felt when she had first sung over that aria.

'I'm having a little trouble with the designer over that scene,' Oliver said with a restraint that made Tina smile. He probably meant he was having a battle royal, and she would back Oliver to win. Suddenly she felt tremendously happy. The memory of that intrusive dream faded. This was where she and Oliver met on common ground. It was going to be an exciting project, bringing this new opera to life, and she looked forward to it with a zest that would carry her through all the trials of the rehearsals and the inevitable difficulties.

Ransu Prokopi did not join them until the *sitzprobe* when there was a full reading of the score, on the stage, with the orchestra, but without the staging planned by the producer. The cast stood, or even sat, giving their undivided attention to the music. It looked casual, but the concentration was intense. Ransu was hard on them, as Tina had known he would be. The only rest they got was when he turned to Oliver, who sat in the stalls, to discuss a point, but Ransu had already done hours of preparation and it was rare for Oliver to dispute his interpretation.

At last he put down his baton. 'So, we have completed the first act and the opening scene of the second act is, I think, satisfactory. We will take a break. Half an hour, ladies and gentlemen.'

He turned to speak to Oliver and Tina hesitated. She would have liked to join them, but she was reluctant to interrupt their discussion. The chorus was drifting away, the orchestra had disappeared with the astonishing speed orchestras always displayed when they were released from their confined space, and her baritone lover had made a beeline for the telephone to talk to his wife, who was expecting their first baby. Tina felt isolated. She ought to go backstage and eat the sandwiches and drink the coffee she had had the forethought to bring with her, while putting up her feet for the half hour Ransu had allowed them. Her most difficult scenes were still to come. Even in rehearsal she ought to prepare for them.

'Tina!'

She turned back to where Ransu shielded his eyes to look up at her.

'Oliver and I are going for a drink and a sandwich. You'll join us?'

Tina abandoned her coffee flask without a second thought. 'Gladly,' she said.

She tossed a black wool sarape round her shoulders and picked up her handbag. 'I was going to sit and brood about Gabriella's sad fate, but perhaps I'll do better to leave it alone.'

'I think so. So far, you have done well. It's a heavy role for you to carry.'

'I'm glad you realise it,' Tina said with feeling. 'Oliver seems to think I should take it in my stride.'

In the dim lighting she could just see that Oliver was smiling.

'I wrote the final version with you in mind,' he said. 'I know you can do it.'

As they made their way out of the theatre, Tina thought about this. She had not realised that Oliver had always meant the role of Gabriella to be hers. It made her performance an even heavier responsibility, but it was exhilarating, too. He had had her in his mind's eye while he was writing about the doomed, courageous rebel who had chosen fame rather than domesticity. It was not until they were comfortably settled with their drinks and sandwiches in front of them that Tina felt chilled by the idea that Oliver might see her career in that light.

'Do you believe in marriage for a singer?' she asked Ransu.

'Certainly! Marriage and children and a home. Of course, the babies are an interruption and sometimes the voice deepens after pregnancy, though no one has ever been able to explain why, but I do not agree with the choice Oliver has forced on his Gabriella.'

'A glassmaker, living in Murano ... and in the nineteenth century,' Oliver murmured. 'She had to abandon him. Of course, her subsequent career and her lover, the Duke, are pure invention.'

'It was her voice that destroyed her,' Tina said. She looked fiercely at the glass of red wine Oliver had ordered for himself and the outline dazzled and blurred. His fingers were playing with the stem, long, nervous fingers with a pianist's strength in them.

'I never intended you to see any similarity to your own life,' Oliver said.

'There's one line in the libretto that might have been written for me: "Happy? I'm only happy when I'm singing".'

'I think you are a little overwrought,' Ransu said quietly. 'Eat, drink, rest. You are always on such an even keel, dear Tina, that one forgets that you are an artist, with an artist's delicate balance. You have taken this role to heart, and that is good because you will give a magnificent performance, but to take it personally, that is nonsense. You are a twentieth-century woman with many choices before you.'

'Like Gabriella, I've tried the titled lover and that didn't work. What next?'

'You aren't likely to go home to die in the arms of your childhood sweetheart,' Oliver said with asperity. 'Pull yourself together, Tina. I won't have you breaking down on me at this point.'

Ransu looked startled, but after a moment Tina gave an uncertain laugh. 'Just a little fit of temperament,' she said. 'It won't happen again. I was shaken because you said you'd written Gabriella with me in mind.'

'I was thinking of your wonderful singing and your dramatic gift, not your misdirected love life.'

'Which, to you, is of no importance.'

'Which you can put behind you. Mark it down to experience.'

'Something that will add to the richness of my performance?'

'A stage in your adult life that should at least have taught you that you're not cut out to play the hostess at a rich man's table or be an ornament in his social life.'

'As Ros is?'

'Rosamund and you are completely different. Rosamund likes to be dominated, while you fight against it. Think about her love affairs. They were with men who lorded it over her. Jerry will do the same, but at least he has pretensions to being a gentleman. Ros will be happy with him – she *is* happy. She wrote me a very nice letter after she'd heard the broadcast of my *Song of Solomon* on the Proms.'

'You never told me.'

'You weren't very receptive to messages from Ros. She sent you her love.'

'Did she?' For a moment Tina was wistful. 'We were such friends.' She looked at Oliver resentfully. 'You rotter, you've completely diverted me from my worries about being another Gabriella.'

'So I should hope! Eat your sandwich. It's malnutrition you're suffering from. Ransu will resume the rehearsal without you if you don't get a move on.'

Ransu was leaning back in his chair and smiling. 'No one could accuse you of handling your prima donna with kid gloves,' he said.

'Boxing gloves are what you need to deal with Valentina Burford,' Oliver said, but the smile he turned on Tina was kinder and more understanding than his words and she began to eat her sandwich with sudden appetite.

As the first night drew near Tina settled into the role of Gabriella. It was not easy, partly because Oliver had chosen to write a work that was not 'modern', except in its psychological insight. He had taken a story that

292

Verdi or Puccini or Rossini might have handled, set in the nineteenth century and true to its period. Only the theme of the fight between love and artistic fame was new, that and the music, which was richly orchestrated and melodic, but very definitely of the twentieth century.

'The critics will think it old-fashioned,' he remarked to Ransu as the final dress rehearsal came to an end.

'Not if they listen with their ears open,' Ransu replied. 'Go home, Oliver. We've done all we can. Forget it until Thursday.'

'I must speak to Tina.'

'No last-minute instructions,' Ransu said sharply. 'The role is set and she is happy in it. Anything you add now will only confuse her.'

'I know. I'll say nothing but words of encouragement, I promise. Ransu, you've been magnificent ...'

'Go *home,* Oliver.'

Tina was in her dressing room. She had removed her last act gown and was sitting in front of the mirror cleaning off her make-up. She looked as tired as Oliver felt, but she managed a smile when he came in.

'All the usual dress rehearsal snags,' she said. 'I could have killed Andy when he stood on my skirt in the last scene.'

'Very maladroit,' Oliver agreed. 'Was there any damage?'

'A few torn stitches. It can easily be repaired. And I don't think Andy will make the same mistake again.'

'I was afraid the look you gave him would turn him into a pillar of salt. How are you feeling?'

'Oh ... you know ... as if the last thing in the world I ever want to do is to go on the stage and sing a whole new opera.'

'Yes, me too. Shall we flee the country and let the opera go hang?'

Tina laughed and began to look more cheerful. 'We can't do that, and by Thursday we'll both feel differently about it.'

'The next twenty-four hours will be grim, at least for me, and I just hate the thought of being alone. I suppose you wouldn't come down to Rigby House? We could spend a quiet day tomorrow, not talking about *Crown of Glass*,

293

which is obviously going to be a terrible flop and should never have been written, and I'll bring you up to London early on Thursday so that you can spend the day in your own flat preparing yourself for the evening.'

'For the performance when I'm going to be booed off the stage?'

'That's right, but it's the opera they'll be booing, not your fantastic performance — which just might lift the wretched work out of the trough.'

'The best music you've ever written is in *Crown of Glass*, and well you know it.'

'You're beginning to cheer me up already. Will you come and keep me company?'

Tina turned away to finish wiping off her stage make-up.

'How did you know I didn't want to be alone?' she asked.

'I was thinking entirely selfishly,' Oliver protested. 'I want someone to hold my hand and I'd rather it was you than anyone.'

'That's nice. All right, we'll give one another mutual support until the day of our ordeal. I'll need to call at the flat to pick up a change of clothes and so on.'

It was getting late as they drove out of London, but they found a roadside café for a meal which they both ate with a ravenous appetite.

'Bangers and mash,' Tina said. 'No one else gives me bangers and mash.'

'I'm noted for my lavish hospitality,' Oliver told her. 'You can have apple pie and custard to follow, if you like.'

'Actually, I'm having treacle tart.'

'What a good idea. And a pot of tea?'

'If it won't break the bank.'

'Perhaps you'd better check your purse, in case I need a loan.'

The cosy, unpretentious meal relaxed them. They lingered over their cups of tea, too exhausted to make conversation, but easy in one another's company.

As they walked across the dark forecourt towards Oliver's

car he took Tina's hand loosely in his. 'We'll be home in twenty minutes,' he said.

Home. The word struck Tina with sudden significance. It was what she needed, of course: a home. A place of sanctuary where she could just be herself. A flat where she lived alone was not the same at all. A home held more than one person. She stood waiting for Oliver to unlock the car and shivered in the chilly night air. Oliver had known that this was a time when she did not want to be alone. He always seemed to understand. And, finally, the knowledge that had lurked at the back of her mind for weeks swept over her and refused to be denied. Home was where Oliver was.

Tina was very quiet as they completed the journey to Locksley Green. She turned her head once for a surreptitious glance at Oliver's profile. If she told him she loved him, how would he react? It would be terrible if he repulsed her. He might be kind, damn him, and that sort of kindness was the last thing she wanted from Oliver. Despondently, she admitted to herself that if Oliver wanted her then he would make it abundantly clear. A few years ago he had had the reputation of being a light and easy lover. The rumours had died down and as far as Tina knew he was not involved with anyone at that time. But a passing affair was not what she wanted.

She had still not found an answer to her dilemma when the car made the difficult turn into the drive of Rigby House.

'That's odd,' Oliver said. 'All the lights are on.'

'Perhaps you've got burglars,' Tina suggested.

'I don't think burglars would advertise themselves quite so blatantly.'

'Well, do be careful,' Tina said as he parked the car and got out. She followed him as he unlocked the front door, not exactly nervous, but uneasy.

As they stepped into the hall the door of the music room was flung open.

'Darling! How fortunate that you haven't changed the locks and I've still got a key! I've come to support you on your first night.'

'Annis,' Oliver said. 'How ... splendid.' He moved forward and Tina followed him. 'Tina and I have both got the collywobbles, so we decided to keep one another company.'

Tina was seized in a warm, scented embrace. 'Dear Tina, how well I know the feeling! Did the dress rehearsal go well?'

'It was terrible,' Tina said.

'No, it wasn't,' Oliver contradicted her. 'There were a few snags and we all got over-tired. The singing was superb and Ransu's handling of the music couldn't be faulted.'

'We were planning to have a very quiet day tomorrow,' Tina said.

She felt as if she could have wept. Her whole body was sagging with fatigue and, if she had to admit the truth, with disappointment. Her time alone with Oliver was spoilt. Annis was a darling, but they could have done without her, just at that juncture.

'I have the most wonderful surprise for you,' Annis was saying, ebullient as ever. 'I thought of keeping it for the first night, but I simply can't wait to tell you what a wonderful discovery I've made. Come in here.'

On the table in the big drawing room which was always known as the music room there was a large box of rubbed green leather embellished with gilding. Annis opened the box and felt inside. Whatever she had in there, it was obviously heavy and not easy to handle. With infinite care she lifted it out.

'The crown of glass,' she said triumphantly. 'Your own original, authentic crown of glass, made by Ernesto Leone in 1851 and given to Eleanora Gabbata. And where did it end up? In Australia! Once I'd found it I had to have it and then I could think of nothing but rushing over here in time to give it to you, dearest Oliver, as a present for the production of your opera.'

Chapter Fifteen

The modern replica of the crown that Tina wore in Oliver's opera was made of acrylic, light and comfortable. The original glass crown was weightier and more ornate. Annis needed both hands to support it. She lifted it into the air so that the light caught the 'jewels' with which it was studded and Tina made an involuntary movement because she thought Annis was about to set it on her own head.

As if in response to her thought, Oliver stepped forward and took the crown from Annis's hands.

'I'm completely stunned,' he said. 'Annis, how on earth did you track it down? And why didn't you let me know?'

'I was so afraid I wouldn't succeed and you'd be disappointed. I first got word of it when I was talking about your new opera to one of the young singers at my master class and he said he was interested in the story because his grandmother had once had just such a relic. She and his grandfather had emigrated to Australia in the thirties. I asked him to make enquiries and he eventually told me that after Granny died his mother had sold the crown with a lot of other old rubbish. I went to see her and discovered that there had been a trunkful of theatrical props amongst her mother's belongings and they had gone to a waxworks exhibition. So I tried to tack that down . . .'

'You have been busy!'

'Indeed I have. The waxworks, of course, had long since closed, but there was an antiques shop in its place and the proprietor knew a man who collected Victoriana. He was a very old man, but to my amazement he remembered the

297

crown and he directed me to a fellow enthusiast ...'

'And he actually had it?'

'That's right. He was fascinated to hear about the connection and I persuaded him to part with the crown on the understanding that I would give it to you. And here it is!'

'Large as life and twice as natural,' Oliver murmured. 'I never for one moment thought I'd ever hold it in my hands. Annis, you're incredible!'

'Of course you must make use of it for publicity,' Annis said, her face glowing with pleasure at the success of her surprise.

'A bit late in the day for that.'

'It's only three days since I managed to get it and since then I've been travelling – and recuperating. I knew it was no use trying to get hold of you today with the dress rehearsal going on, so I've made some arrangements myself. Two or three newspapers are sending reporters in the morning and it's to be featured in a BBC arts programme on television. The cameras will be here by midday tomorrow.'

'We're supposed to be resting,' Tina said, aghast.

'Darling Tina, I didn't know you would be here. I meant to model the crown myself, but of course I'll resign it to you. Nothing could be better.'

She looked at them with such simple pleasure that Oliver's lips twitched in wry amusement. Very carefully, he replaced the glass crown in its box.

'Tina, you're dead on your feet,' he said. 'Go to bed. Have you allocated yourself a room, Annis?'

'My old room, of course. Is that all right?'

'I'll take one of the back rooms,' Tina said. 'Annis, forgive me; I'm too exhausted to show my excitement. And if the Press is descending on us tomorrow I'd better get some sleep.'

She stomped upstairs and threw her overnight bag on the bed in disgust. A Press conference. Television cameras. On the day when she had planned to get up late, lounge around in sloppy clothes, chat to Oliver, perhaps go for a walk, relax – above all, relax.

She undressed and washed. Downstairs she could still hear the murmur of voices. Damn Annis. Of course she could not have known that Tina would be at Rigby House, nor could she have known that she had managed to tilt the balance against a relationship that was just on the verge of moving on to a different level. If they could have had a slow, quiet day alone together the sympathy between Tina and Oliver might have flowered into something deeper, something Tina had at last come to see she wanted more than anything else in the world, more even than success in the forthcoming opera. With Annis around, not to mention the Press, they hadn't a chance.

The newspaper reporters were tiresome, the television crew even more so. Tina, wearing a bright silk shirt borrowed from Annis, at last, with some reluctance, took the glass crown and put it on. She shivered as the cold weight settled on her head. How right Oliver had been to take this as a symbol of fame — beautiful, brittle and heavy to wear. Her face grew thoughtful, remote. She forgot the watching cameras. Something that had previously eluded her in the character of Gabriella began to take shape in her mind. The wearing of the crown was something Gabriella had not been able to escape. She had as much of a duty to her talent as a king had to his people. She might be an acclaimed queen of song, but she was also its slave. Her dedication was the price she paid for perfection and neither her glassmaker lover nor her Duke had been able to break the spell that enthralled her.

Oliver had been watching her and after the cameras had left he said quietly, 'You didn't like wearing the crown, did you?'

'It's loaded with old memories.'

'The crown you'll wear tomorrow is modern, light and made especially for you. You'll wear it as your right.'

'My right to be called prima donna ... diva?'

'You're certainly that.'

'But I'm a woman, too,' Tina said helplessly.

Oliver's hand shot out and gripped her arm. 'Do you think I don't know that?'

'Darlings, it was superb,' Annis said, coming back from waving goodbye to the television crew. 'Tina, you looked like a Byzantine empress in that fantastic thing. The pictures will be wonderful.'

'I only hope the performance matches up,' Tina said.

Tina was at the Opera House by six o'clock, ready to begin a leisurely preparation for the first act of the opera. She liked this quiet time alone in her dressing room, it settled her and gave her an opportunity to think herself into the character she was to play. The previous day had not, after all, been so bad. At least the excitement of the glass crown's discovery had kept her mind off her nervous anticipation of the opening night.

As he had promised, Oliver had driven her back to her flat early in the day. Annis had come with them, with the crown in its leather box sitting on the back seat of the car beside her. It was now in Tina's dressing room and she rather wished it was not. She could not entirely rid herself of the memory of that cold weight resting on her head and the feeling of dread that had come over her.

It was well known that Tina did not like to be visited before a performance and she was irritated by a tap on the door only a quarter of an hour after her arrival. Her annoyance faded when she saw Oliver in the doorway, then she saw his look of shocked distress and got up quickly to move towards him.

'Oliver, what is it?'

'Ransu. He slipped on a patch of oil as he was getting into his car. He's hurt himself, quite badly. He's got a cracked rib and a broken arm.'

'He can't conduct?'

'It's out of the question.'

He looked so shaken that Tina pushed a chair towards him.

'Here, sit down. We're not going to cancel?'

'At a moment's notice? Hardly! The management's in a fine old state and, of course, they've come to the inevitable conclusion: that I ought to conduct my own work.'

For a moment Tina failed to react. She was aware of a crippling disappointment. She had come to rely on Ransu Prokopi. He knew every note of the score, every idiosyncrasy of the singers and, more than that, there was an empathy between him and Tina which gave her an almost mystical confidence in his ability to lift her over difficult passages.

Suddenly she realised that Oliver was watching her with something like despair and a great wave of indignation and affection rushed over her. This was Oliver's big night, far more than it was hers. He was a fine musician and what had he achieved? An opera that had been plagiarised, a handful of songs, some incidental music and film scores, the magical *Song of Solomn* and this, his finest work, and the one on which, she realised, he had pinned his hopes for recognition. She always thought of him as a young man, but he had reached his forties and unless musical success came to him soon he might end up a disappointed man. Nothing must spoil this evening for him and certainly not his prima donna throwing a tantrum because the conductor of her dreams was out of action.

'You can do it,' she said. 'Who could possibly know the music better than its composer? You've been in on rehearsals ...'

'True enough, but I've never conducted the theatre orchestra and I don't know how they'll take to me. I certainly haven't got Ransu Prokopi's charisma.'

'You're a perfectly competent conductor, as you proved at the promenade concert. The orchestra will back you; they're professionals and they'll adapt; they've got everything to lose if they give a bad performance.'

Oliver's expression had begun to lighten. 'It comes hardest on you,' he said. '*Crown of Glass* is very much the soprano's opera and you're hardly ever off the stage.'

'I have absolute confidence in you,' Tina said firmly. 'Tonight is going to be even more of a triumph than it would have been otherwise, and you have to admit that — leaving aside poor Ransu's suffering — it's another great publicity gimmick.' She looked with loathing at the green leather box on her dressing table. 'I blame it all on that crown,' she said. 'I knew it was bad luck the minute I put it on.'

'A bit arbitrary to cause the misfortune to fall on Ransu,' Oliver said, getting up. 'Tina, your visit to

301

Rigby House ... it wasn't the way I meant it to be.'

'Nor me,' Tina said ruefully.

She held out her hands and Oliver took them and drew her towards him. To Tina's relief, he was smiling. She slipped easily into his arms and raised her face. For a moment they were hesitant with one another and then Oliver's mouth was on hers.

There was a tap at the door. Tina and Oliver moved apart as Tina's dresser came in.

'Interruptions ... interruptions,' Oliver murmured.

'Go and talk to the leader of the orchestra,' Tina said, getting her breath back. 'I don't think I'll wish you good luck, because you don't need it. You can rely on your musicianship.'

'If I let you down I'll never forgive myself.'

'I feel the same, so between us we ought to produce a wonderful performance.'

One reason why it had been difficult to get Oliver's opera staged was that he had used a very large cast. The first scene was something of a *tour de force*, a representation of the Great Exhibition of 1851 in London, with the chorus forming a shifting crowd and an appearance by Queen Victoria, Prince Albert and their two eldest children. One of the things they stopped to admire was the glassmaking demonstration, which introduced the character of Ernesto. Gabriella appeared and sang a showpiece aria, to the applause of the crowd, and then there was a long and crucial scene in which Ernesto presented Gabriella, the girl from his own island of Murano, with the crown he had made for her and pleaded with her to give up the stage and marry him. This was followed by a fine quartet sung by the impresario who had brought her to London, the Grand Duke who was enamoured of her, Ernesto and Gabriella. It ended with Gabriella accepting the Grand Duke's offer to take her to his principality where he would build her an opera house in which she could sing anything she liked − 'like a bird in a cage' said Ernesto.

The second act was very dramatic. Driven to madness by their Grand Duke's extravagance, his people rose up against him. After a long confrontation with the rebel leader, in which Gabriella tried to defend her lover and failed to save him from the firing squad, she was accused of caring nothing for the suffering of the poor. In an impassioned aria she described her own improverished family, her home on a Venetian island and her inescapable fate — to sing. Moved by her sincerity, the rebels commuted her own sentence to banishment. She was turned out of the country, stripped of her jewels and fine clothes, and told to go and start earning her living again with the aid of nothing but her voice.

In failing health, and blaming herself not only for her lover's death but also for the suffering of his people in the fighting that had broken out in his country, Gabriella returned, sick and friendless, to the Venetian island from which she had come. This was the point in the scene that sent shivers down Tina's back, in which Gabriella had hallucinations and convinced herself that she was destined to descend into Hell.

It was all done with lighting effects, but the lighting would have been nothing without the music which described her tormented vision. She was rescued by Ernesto, who assured her that she would sing with the angels in Heaven. The lighting changed and there was a duet which could indeed be called celestial. Tina's voice was no more than a thread of sound, but the clarity at which she had worked unceasingly carried it to the far reaches of the theatre. There was a moment of heart-stopping silence and then the singer reared up in her lover's arms, her hands outstretched, her voice restored, and in a few bars of miraculous beauty proclaimed her own destiny — to go on singing for all eternity. She fell back, there were three plucked notes on the strings, like falling drops of water, and it was finished.

The opera house was utterly still. There was a sound like a great sigh, as if the entire audience had let out its breath at the same moment, then the curtains swept together and the applause began.

When Tina got up from the floor on to which she had sunk in her dying moments she was trembling all over. Her baritone lover took her hands and kissed them.

'Magnificent,' he said. 'Unbelievable.'

There were curtain calls and flowers, and more curtain calls. Loose blossoms floated down to the stage and Tina made the gracious gesture of bending to pick them up and present them to whoever happened to be near her at the time. The only moment that had any reality for her was when Oliver came up on to the stage and was greeted with a renewed roar of applause. He, too, took her hand and kissed it and she saw his eyes shining, almost as if he had tears in them. The principal singers went forward with their conductor. The audience were on their feet, still applauding. One more bow and then I'm going to collapse, Tina thought distractedly. My legs won't hold me.

Even after the final curtain there was still the hubbub on the stage to be gone through. Everyone seemed to be kissing everyone else. But Oliver didn't kiss her again. She would have noticed that.

She was followed to her dressing room and made her dresser shut the door in the face of the clamouring crowd.

'I must sit down,' she said. 'Just for a moment. I shall pass out if I stand up much longer.'

'Let me help you out of that gown,' her dresser suggested. 'And there's a bottle of champagne on ice.'

'I expect I'll have plenty of that before the night's out,' Tina said. 'But, yes, could you open it, Meg, and give me a nice loose wrapper.'

In her blue satin dressing gown, with a glass of wine to sip, Tina began to feel revived. She could hear the babble of voices in the corridor outside. There was no use trying to keep the crowd at bay. She nodded to her dresser and the door was opened.

Everyone she had ever known seemed to be there, even Will and Elsie, being looked after by Tom, bless him. Elsie looked bewildered. 'I didn't know,' she whispered. 'I didn't know.' What she didn't know was not explained, but Tina thought she understood. She kissed her and her father, promised to be in touch, and sent them home to their suburban house which they had finally come to realise had been the nest of a wonderful swan. Daphne was there, too, but she could look after herself. 'Atta girl,' she said, hugging Tina. 'I never had a greater triumph myself.'

Annis swept forward. Her face was streaked where her mascara had run. Being Annis, she made a magnificent gesture, dipping into a deep curtsey. 'Diva,' she said.

Tina leaned down to lift her up. 'Oh, no, Annis,' she protested. 'Not that, from you.'

'I thought one day you might be as good as me, but you are better and I acknowledge it.'

Tina shook her head, utterly confounded. She had been good, she knew she had been good, but this was all more than she had expected. She took a reviving sip of her champagne and looked round. No sign of Oliver.

By the door, hovering on the edge of the group of people who had pushed their way into the dressing room, was a slender, dark-haired girl in a loose tunic dress edged with lace. Tina squeezed through the throng.

'Ros,' she said.

'I didn't know whether to come ... but I had to. You were wonderful, Tina. Greater than I could ever have hoped to be.'

They looked at one another uncertainly and then Tina put her arms round Rosamund and hugged her. For a moment she wondered whether to tell her that she was going to marry Oliver, then she pulled herself up. He hadn't asked her yet. But he would. Surely he would?

She glanced down at Rosamund's expanding waistline.

'I say, Ros ...?'

Rosmund nodded. 'In about four months.'

'How lovely for you. It's what you wanted, isn't it? You're happy?'

'Very. And so are you, aren't you Tina? This is where you belong.'

But I want what you've got, too, Tina thought. Where had that wretched man got to?

A few more minutes and she began saying that she simply must dress. Everyone had been so kind ... yes, it was wonderful ... yes, she was thrilled ... of course it was a triumph for the whole company ... the music was a miracle ... thank you, thank you, thank you. And for goodness sake would you all please go away. But that thought she had to keep to herself.

They were just about to close the door on the last lingering visitor when Oliver appeared.

'Where have you *been*?' Tina demanded indignantly.

'Talking to Ransu. I knew he wouldn't sleep until he knew how we'd made out. I told him it had been a triumph — which it was.'

He took hold of Meg, the dresser, by the shoulders and ushered her firmly to the door.

'Give us five minutes,' he said.

'Make it ten,' Tina said.

Oliver shut the door and leaned his back against it.

'Well, we did it,' he said.

'I told you we would,' Tina said, watching him.

'Together. We could do anything together.'

'But are we going to be together?'

'Of course we are. I've been in love with you for years.'

'Oliver, that's nonsense,' Tina said, really shaken.

'Years and years,' Oliver said firmly. 'Damn it, I'm the one who's suffered, I ought to know. I was only waiting for Annis to go off to Australia ...'

'As long ago as *that*?'

'Truly. It was daft of me to feel inhibited about making up to you while she was still there to watch ...'

'Considering it hadn't stopped you leaping into bed with any number of other girls.'

Oliver waved an impatient hand. 'Unimportant little flings ...'

'I wonder if they thought so? I always knew you were heartless.'

'Only because I'd given my heart to you.'

'That's very pretty,' Tina said admiringly.

'Tina, will you shut up? There I was, all set to sweep you off your feet and what happened? You took up with Jerry Bilchester. I could have killed him and you, too.'

'I knew you were a bit unenthusiastic, but I had no idea it went that deep. Oliver, Ros was here and we're friends again.'

'I'm glad about that, but I wish you'd let me keep to the point.'

'You're being terribly slow about it,' Tina complained.

306

'Ros is pregnant. I envy her that. I'd like a baby, Oliver.'

'What can I say? May I be the lucky father?'

'Only if you marry me first.'

'That's what I had in mind. Tina ...'

'I thought you'd never get round to it,' Tina said as his arms closed round her. 'Yes, Oliver, anything you want, any time ... well, perhaps not right here and now ...'

Her voice stopped as he closed her mouth with his. They clung together, swaying slightly with the force of the emotion that swept through them.

'I shall have to sit down,' Tina whispered at last, freeing herself. 'All my bones have melted.'

'Darling ... you haven't said you love me. Say it, Tina.'

'I love you. And the ridiculous thing is, I've only admitted it to myself in the last few days. How could I have been so blind? All those years wasted.'

'Not wasted. We were growing towards one another. And now, tonight ... what a triumph. Tina, I love you as a woman − as *my* woman − but as an artist I worship you.'

Tina was very still and then she said, 'I can't escape from it. You know that, don't you?'

'Yes, dear. I put it into my opera. Your artistic life has to go on, but we can build a domestic life around it, I'm sure we can.'

'I've got to go to America next year to sing *Tosca*. I'm committed.'

'I'll come with you, of course. As long as I have a piano and a supply of manuscript paper I can get on with my career side by side with yours.'

'Is it possible?' Tina whispered. 'Can I really be so lucky?'

'Why not? We're not children and we know what the life we've chosen demands of us. I have to make music, you have to interpret it. As long as my inspiration lasts and you retain your wonderful voice we're music's slaves, but that doesn't mean we can't build a life for ourselves. A satisfying, wonderful life, Tina.'

On an impulse he turned towards the green leather box and took out the crown of glass.

'You were afraid of this,' he said. 'But you have no need to be. Will you wear it for me? Just for a moment before the world breaks in on us again.'

Tina bowed her head and Oliver set the crown on it. She looked at herself in the brilliantly lit mirror. The crown glittered on her head. It was still heavy and the glass felt cold, but Oliver was right, she had overcome her nervous dread of the burden it symbolised. Tina lifted her chin. She was a queen, acknowledged by her peers to be without rival in her chosen realm. She would wear the crown for as long as she retained a right to it, but she would have a home and a family and a loving companion, too. *Diva* ... wife ... mother ... all difficult roles to sustain. Oliver had said that together they could do anything and that was true. They had proved it that evening. They would go on proving it for the rest of their lives.